TO THE CHUKCHI PENINSULA

AND

TO THE TLINGIT INDIANS 1881/1882:

JOURNALS AND LETTERS BY
AUREL AND ARTHUR KRAUSE

Aurel Krause   *Arthur Krause*

TO THE CHUKCHI PENINSULA

AND

TO THE TLINGIT INDIANS 1881/1882:

JOURNALS AND LETTERS BY
AUREL AND ARTHUR KRAUSE

Translated by
Margot Krause McCaffrey

University of Alaska Press
Fairbanks, 1993

Library of Congress Cataloging-in-Publication Data

Krause, Aurel, 1848-
   [Zur Tschuktschen-Halbinsel und zu den Tlinkit-Indianern,
1881/82. English]
   To the Chukchi Peninsula and to the Tlingit Indians, 1881/1882 :
journals and letters by Aurel and Arthur Krause / translated by
Margot Krause McCaffrey.
      p. cm. -- (The Rasmuson Library historical translation
series, ISSN 0890-7935 ; v. 8)
    ISBN 0-912006-66-8
    1. Tlingit Indians. 2. Krause, Aurel, 1848---Journeys.
3. Krause, Arthur, 1851---Journeys. 4. Alaska--Description and
travel--1867-1896. 5. Chukchi Peninsula (Russia)--Description and
travel. 6. Northwest Coast of North America--Description and
travel. I. Krause, Arthur, 1851- . II. Title. III. Series
E99.T6K9313   1993
915.7'7--dc20   92-47100
[B]   CIP

International Standard Series Number: 0890-7935
International Standard Book Number: 0-912006-66-8
Library of Congress Catalog Card Number: 92-47100

Cartography on pages 38-39 and 203 by Nancy van Veenen.
Publication coordination by Pamela Odom.
Design and production by Jennifer Thompson,
with assistance from Deborah Van Stone.

CONTENTS

EDITOR'S NOTE

These travel journals and letters have been made available through the efforts of interested Krause family members over several generations. The journals were originally kept in an antique shorthand that has long been out of use. Following his death in 1908, Aurel Krause's belongings were placed in storage. Through the efforts of one of his daughters, Ella, his notebooks were saved. She began working with them in 1918 and was able to find someone who could decipher the shorthand in 1926. She then spent decades putting everything in order.

Letters and descriptions written by both brothers were used to complete the story told by the journals. Ella Krause further enhanced the book by adding comments to place narrative in context (italicized in this translation). Gerhard and Ingeborg Krause edited this material for publication in Germany by the Dietrich Reimer Verlag in 1984. The book before you is a translation of an unpublished, revised edition of the German publication, *Zur Tschuktschen-Halbinsel und zu den Tlinkit-Indianern 1881/82, Reisetagebücher und Briefe von Aurel und Arthur Krause.* This translation was made by Aurel's granddaughter, Margot Krause McCaffrey, and is published with the kind permission of the Reimer Verlag. Portions copyrighted by Gerhard Krause relating to the time spent in what is now Haines were prepared by McCaffrey and published by the Haines Centennial Commission in 1981. The original journals themselves are quite fragile and remain under the care of Gerhard Krause.

This is the human side of the expedition made by two trained scientists. The formal ethnography published by Aurel Krause (*Die Tlinket Indianer*, Jena, 1885) quickly became an enduring and classic source for the study of the Tlingit Indians of Alaska. It is best known in North America in a translation by the anthropologist Erna Gunther (*The Tlingit Indians: Results of a Trip to the Northwest Coast of America and the Bering Straits*) published by the University of Washington Press in 1956. It continues to be widely read and the paperback edition of 1970 has been frequently reprinted.

The journey came at a time of activity and change in Southeast Alaska and the Bering Sea. Commercial activity was extensive. The Krause brothers traveled via whaling and other commercial vessels and while in Haines stayed with a merchant. They were a part of a wider international effort, reaching back into the eighteenth century, to collect materials for the study of the natural sciences, ethnography and art.[1]

A. E. Nordenskjöld had just completed one of most spectacular voyages of the day from Europe to the Bering Strait, known as the Northeast Passage. He had spent the winter of 1878-79 on the Chukchi Peninsula.[2] The Krause brothers worked to expand upon Nordenskjöld's work, especially the collection of natural history specimens (plants and lower marine forms). They also corrected ambiguities in existing maps of the contours of the East Cape. This collecting activity continued on their second voyage to Southeast Alaska. A summary of publications related to their travels and collections was published in Aurel's *Tlinkit-Indianer* in 1885 (see Gunter's translation, pp. 7-10).

There are some ambiguities that remain in this translation, especially in documenting details about the original letters and accounts written by the two brothers used to fill gaps in Aurel's journal. We have simply followed the German publication in this, as there is no practical way to verify these details without a painstaking examination of the original, fragile manuscripts in Germany. We have added to the translation, however, two new, redrawn maps that correspond with original cartography to help the reader with current-day place names (pp 38-39 and 203).

INTRODUCTION

In January 1881, the Geographical Society of Bremen in Germany, formerly the Association for Polar Exploration, decided to follow up previous research done by Adolf E. Nordenskjöld—scientist, cartographer, and arctic explorer—and to organize and equip a scientific ethnological expedition to the coastal areas of the Bering Strait and Bering Sea, particularly the Chukchi Peninsula. Later it was decided also to plan explorations in those areas of Alaska of which there was little scientific and ethnological knowledge at that time.

In a letter to the boards of directors of the various German geographical societies in February 1881, the Bremen Society asked for recommendations for qualified scientists to carry out this proposal. It was emphasized "that full physical fitness, general scientific and geographical education, practical experience in geological investigations, collection and conservation of natural science objects, the use of a gun, and finally some ability in English are absolute requirements. Knowledge of the Russian language would be very desirable."

With the recommendation of Professor Von Martens of Berlin University, two Berlin teachers—Drs. Aurel and Arthur Krause—took their application to Dr. Gustav Nachtigal, director of the Berlin Society for Geography. They met the required conditions. On March 13, 1881, during the meeting of the Geographical Society of Bremen, the appointment was awarded to the brothers, who were in attendance.

Aurel Krause was born December 30, 1848, and Arthur January 25, 1851, at the estate Polish Konopath, district of Schwetz, in West Prussia. Both graduated from high school in Bromberg. At first Aurel studied architecture, but when the Franco-Prussian War broke out, he enlisted as a soldier. After the war, at the end of his military service, he studied natural sciences at Berlin University, as did his brother Arthur. Aurel was especially attracted by geology and devoted his doctoral thesis (1877) to Silurian boulder detritus in the North German plains. In the next few years he continued his research and published several treatises on fossil ostracoda (small bivalved crustaceans). Both brothers were employed as teachers of natural sciences at the Luisenstädtische Gewerbeschule, later known as Oberrealschule, and after working the required number of years, each earned the title professor. Aurel's subjects were chemistry, mineralogy, botany, zoology, mathematics, physics, and French (*Vocation*, July 3, 1876). Arthur apparently taught the same subjects.

In addition to their full-time teaching positions, each brother worked in the literary field. Aurel was coeditor of *Meyer's Encyclopedia* for the special "Explorers'" and "Northwest American Indian Tribes" subject areas. He was also a respected author. One reviewer in the *Journal for Ethnology* writes of his book, *The Tlingit Indians*, "[It] is a credit to the newer ethnological literature and will certainly be used as an important authoritative resource for a long time." Arthur Krause was editor of a high school chemistry text published by Rudorff-Lübke.

They both lived in Lichterfelde, a residential suburb of Berlin, but traveled extensively to gain practical experience in their fields of interest. Physically well trained, they used their vacations for hiking and scientific study trips to the mountains in central Germany, the Alps, Italy, Sweden, and in 1880, to northern Norway. They were unmarried at the time and, given their independence, used every opportunity for exploring, gaining knowledge, and collecting objects of scientific and ethnological significance.

After their deaths—Aurel on March 14, 1908, and Arthur on September 29, 1920—their scientific collections were donated to the appropriate institutes. The ethnological objects were given to the museums in Bremen, Hamburg, and Berlin. The Krause brothers' collections were often praised by experts in the field for their excellent condition and variety of objects.

This selection of Aurel's diary, which references reports made by both brothers to the Geographical Society in Bremen and letters to their mother and sisters in Bromberg, is intended to give the reader and the brothers' descendants an insight into the adventurous course of the expedition.

Ella Krause

FOREWORD

Much idealism and philanthropy are connected with this journey. The Krause brothers undertook this research mandate only to serve science, without remuneration. The documents about this journey, now stored in the State Archives in Bremen, state that the director of the Geographical Society at that time, George Albrecht, assured the advance payment of all travel expenses. Mr. Albrecht, who was the owner of the firm Joh. Lange Sohn's Wwe & Co. in Bremen, importer of tobacco and supplier to the Imperial and Royal Austrian-Hungarian Tobacco Monopoly Administration in Vienna, quietly assumed all expenses of this expedition.

Dr. Lindemann asked the board of trustees about the expected amount of expenses. Due to his efforts, the travelers also received addresses and letters of recommendation in New York, Washington, and San Francisco. Preparations beyond San Francisco, however, were impossible; the area of the Bering Strait was too far away and unknown. Through diplomatic channels, however, the Imperial Russian Government was asked for protection for the two explorers, which was granted by virtue of the coincidental deployment of a warship.

When the brothers arrived in San Francisco, the last whaler of the season had left port. This meant a stay of four weeks for the brothers until the sailing of the supply ship, the *Legal Tender*, that was to return with the whalers' first catch. The unfitness of the ship upon its return resulted in an additional delay of four weeks. In spite of all these delays, the brothers succeeded in solving their logistical and scientific problems and increasing the knowledge about this part of the world. Fridjof Nansen visited the two explorers in Berlin before his polar expedition described in his book, *Farthest North*. He was interested in their observations in the Bering Strait, because he expected to come out of the polar ice there. At that time hardly any literature about this area existed.

There were no delays for their work with the Tlingit Indians. On the contrary, the research was aided and accelerated by two fortunate circumstances. The first bit of luck was that during their visit in San Francisco, it was recommended to the brothers to turn to Paul Schulze of Portland, Oregon, about their journey to the Indians. Mr. Schulze was president of the North West Trading Company in Portland and was from Berlin. He offered the two Berlin teachers a room free of charge at the newly established trading station (factory) of his company in southeast Alaska. There the company's agent Dickinson and the missionary and his wife were the only non-Indians. The Indians came into this trading station from near and far. Eager for the desired industrial products of civilization, they brought furs for trade. Furs were highly desired in industrialized countries. So, from the day of their arrival the explorers had a chance to talk to the Indians and make appointments for visits in their huts.

The second bit of luck was Mr. Dickinson's wife, daughter of a neighboring tribe's chief. Also a teacher in the missionary school for Indian children, she took good care of the brothers and taught them the language of the Indians in the course of their daily contact. Grammar and vocabulary of the Tlingit language are an important chapter of the book, *The Tlingit Indians.*

During the long winter evenings, they often could not leave the house because of deep snow and darkness, so they were forced to work at home: arranging collections, writing reports, and stuffing birds they had shot for museums in Germany. Several times the journal mentions: "Mrs. Dickinson tells us about the life of the Indians." She had attentive listeners, anxious to learn. Everything she told was taken down in stenography. This also served as subject and stimulation for conversations in the Indian huts and with the missionary.

After four months of diligent research the ethnological studies could be concluded. Aurel, who had taken over the compiling and editing of the ethnological results, returned home with the notes of both explorers.

Arthur was granted six more months of leave. He used the summer for day-long or longer excursions through the now snow-free mountains to complete the natural science collections.

Dr. Erna Gunther, Professor of Anthropology and Director of the Washington State Museum in Seattle, translated *The Tlingit Indians* in 1956. In 1970 this translation was published in paperback (University of Washington Press, Seattle). When asked why she translated this book seventy years after its original publication, Dr. Gunther answered: "It is the most complete description of the Tlingits' life in existence. Other good books were published, but they only deal with subtopics."

On a trip to Alaska in 1973, Arthur Krause's son Werner met an old Indian woman who remembered exactly that her parents often talked about the Krause brothers. "They have eaten our food, they have visited us in our huts, they have spoken our language—therefore we accepted them!"

In 1978 Margot Krause McCaffrey, with her husband and youngest daughter, vacationed in Alaska following her grandfather Aurel's tracks. She was surprised to find that in all museums and in scientific circles she was welcomed with much attention and joy. The stimulating, friendly conversations motivated her to translate excerpts of the brothers' journals. She sent the manuscript to the Chilkat Valley Historical Society in Haines with the request to add present–day names to the Indian names of geo- graphical places. (The town of Haines was founded in 1881. The trading station where the brothers lived and the mission were the only two non– Indian houses. At that time the Indians called the place *Deshchu*, meaning "End of the Trail.")

The Chilkat Valley Historical Society replied with the request to make the manuscript available to the town. Thus in 1981, in the 100th year of the town, the sixty-nine-page anniversary booklet *Journey to the Tlingits by Aurel and Arthur Krause 1881/82* was published by the Haines Centennial Commission, copyright by Gerhard Aurel Krause, Heidelberg, West Germany. The art work on the cover was designed by an Indian artist. The president of the Chilkat Valley Historical Society and chairman of the Centennial Commission, Karl Ward, wrote to Heidelberg, "It was a wonderful experience for me."

The Hamburg Museum for Ethnology dedicated the catalog *Thunderbird and Killerwhale* of its 1979 anniversary exhibit of Indian Art of the Northwest Coast of North America to the memory of the first director of the museum, C.W. Lüders, and to three explorers, "the men of the first hour": Aurel Krause, Adrian Jacobsen,[1] and Franz Boas.[2]

The attention paid to the journey and its results induced us, Aurel Krause's son and granddaughter, to follow Ella Krause's wish and edit her collection, which originally was intended for family use only. We thank the Dietrich Reimer Verlag for its kind assistance in the editing of this book.

Gerhard Krause
Ingeborg Krause
Heidelberg, August 1983

PART ONE:

TO THE CHUKCHI PENINSULA

CHAPTER ONE

FROM BERLIN/BREMEN TO SAN FRANCISCO

From Berlin via Bremen to Bremerhaven

April 15, 1881

At nine o'clock sharp we left by train from Lehrter Station in Berlin. The day before our departure was taken up by farewell visits and necessary purchases. We had to rush to get all our packing done in time. Finally we counted twelve large pieces of luggage: four containing hunting gear, two larger crates with trapping and preserving equipment for botanical and zoological specimens, two smaller boxes with photographic plates, one large wooden suitcase with scientific instruments, one medium-sized suitcase with books and instruments, and two smaller suitcases with personal items needed for the trip. Furthermore, we had to carry separately the tripod for the large camera, the plant press with several books, and travel blankets; everything else was sent by express the day before. Schacko[1] with his young daughter, as well as our colleagues Nehring with his son Erich, and Gerlach and his wife, met us at the station to say good-bye.

In Bremen we left our luggage at the station and checked into the Hotel Sydenburg where we met Dr. Lindemann. He gave us several letters of introduction and a letter from Nordenskjöld with a manuscript by Nordquist (a Chukchi vocabulary). Then all of us went to see Dr. Wolkenhauer.[2]

In the evening these gentlemen took us to the Ratskeller where we had Kulmbach beer and a jovial time. We did not return to the hotel until 1:00 A.M.

April 16

Last evening showed its consequences. We woke up with a rather bad hangover which we cured with a morning walk through Citizen Park. After our return we visited Mr. Albrecht (President of the Geographical Society) and our colleague Dr. Krüger from Berlin, whom we met when we returned from our hotel. At 2:00 P.M. we had dinner at the hotel with Mr. Albrecht and his father-in-law Baron Knoop. The old Knoop turned out to be a very gracious gentleman who adored Russia and tried to convince us to travel across Siberia.

After dinner we looked after our luggage and found it all together. Then we spent an hour with these same gentlemen and Dr. Krüger in the Rathaus.

Easter Sunday, April 17

At 7:30 A.M. the Lloyd steamer took us and our luggage to Bremerhaven. Dr. Krüger, Dr. Lindemann and his daughter, Dr. Wolkenhauer, and a Mr. Schapier accompanied us on part of the trip on the ship.

Upon our arrival in Bremerhaven we had trouble collecting all our luggage and made the unpleasant discovery that we had left the keys to our luggage and a brush at the hotel. Arthur, accompanied by the very anxious Mr. Schapier, quickly went downtown to get a few keys. Fortunately they could be filed to fit our luggage.

At 12:30 P.M. the steamer *Rhine* departed from Bremerhaven for New York.

Arrival in New York

Saturday, April 30

After a thirteen-day voyage we landed in Hoboken on April 30 at 3:00 P.M. Dr. Schumacher, German Consul General and honorary member of the Geographical Society, was unable to meet us personally but sent an employee to welcome and assist us upon our arrival. We cleared customs quickly without opening our luggage. Then we went to the Hotel Nägely, popular with German travelers. Several other passengers from our ship stayed here, too. After a quick snack the consulate employee accompanied us on our trip to the consul. For three cents we took the ferry across the Hudson to New York. First we bought some maps of the city and then took the elevated train to Eighty-Eighth Street. Suddenly our guide left us. Since we had forgotten to bring along the consul's letter with his private address, we left the train perplexed. Asking questions and consulting a directory were useless, so we had to go back to the office, a fast twenty-five-minute ride. There we found out the private address, went back on the train and reached the consul's apartment at 8:30 P.M. He received us very graciously, inquired whether we had had any difficulties with customs, and offered his further services in shipping all our letters and packages, which was most useful for us. We stayed for about half an hour. Then we returned to our hotel in Hoboken and went to bed rather tired.

The first impression we had of New York was overwhelming. We admired the colossal structures visible upon entering the harbor, particularly the giant piers of the still-uncompleted Brooklyn Bridge,[3] the lively traffic on the Hudson, and the numerous, always crowded, strange-looking ferryboats. The entrance to Stockholm or Kristiania[4] harbors offers a more abundant scenery. Nowhere, however, are such impressions solely produced by human efforts.

From New York to Washington

Monday, May 2

Last evening we boarded the train to Washington. We did not use sleeping cars but stretched out on our seats during the night, which was possible because there were not too many passengers.

About 7:00 A.M. the train crossed the Potomac River and shortly thereafter stopped in Washington. On the banks of the Potomac, surrounded by low wooded hills, Washington with its clean broad asphalt streets can truly be considered the most beautiful city of the United States. The city has been in existence for less than 100 years. Before its founding in 1790, not even a village existed in its place.

The population has a high representation of Negroes. Almost half the inhabitants are blacks, although most of them work in low positions as waiters, barbers, shoeblacks, etc. People here do not seem to have too favorable an opinion about the developmental possibilities of this race. One cannot deny that this race has considerable energy and capability for adaptation. Since the possibility for freer development was granted only in recent years, the question whether this race will play an important role in the future cannot receive a final answer today.

There was insufficient time to consider and absorb these impressions, because the main purpose was to establish connections and to collect information for the journey to the Bering Strait. Therefore, we visited Professor Baird, secretary of the famous Smithsonian Institution. He promised us 20 gallons of alcohol for the conservation of molluscs, copper vessels, dredge nets, and chests with compartments. We had detailed discussions with polar explorer Dr. Emil Bessels.[5] We spent the entire afternoon and also several hours of the following day with Professor Dall, who reported on his trips to Alaska and showed us sketches and photos. In the evening we visited George Kennan, well known for his trips to the Chukchi Peninsula. We were almost constantly on our feet all day. Except for breakfast at the hotel and a small oyster breakfast which Bessel offered us, we had not eaten all day and finally had a plentiful dinner at night. Afterward we took a short walk through the city and returned rather tired. When we were just about ready to go to bed, Baron Schlözer arrived. Arthur had already taken off his boots, and I sat in shirtsleeves without collar and necktie. Schlözer, who had given us a friendly reception in the morning, good advice, and letters from Lindemann, only came to find out what we had accomplished.

Wednesday, May 4

On Wednesday, too, discussions were held with Bessels and Baird. It took several hours to translate Nordquist's vocabularies which were written in Chukchi-Swedish. With the help of an English-Danish dictionary we accomplished this task.

From Washington to San Francisco

Thursday, May 5

After a small breakfast we paid our bill at the hotel and were startled at its high amount. Then we drove to the station where it took us quite a while to straighten out our luggage. For the excess freight we had to pay a considerable sum. Also all untied pieces of luggage had to be secured with a strap. We bought extra tickets for the sleeping car which cost five dollars for the trip to Chicago. In the railway carriage we sat opposite each other on comfortable upholstered seats.

Up to Baltimore the scenery was familiar to us from our trip to Washington. Beyond Baltimore we passed through an area richly divided by rivers and chains of hills. We pass through York and Susquehanna. The view of the opposite bank with forest and decorated with settlements is beautiful. In Harrington there is a longer stop and we have dinner for seventy-five cents. Here a magnificent bridge spans the Susquehanna and we cross it to the opposite bank. For a long time we travel on the right bank of the river. The places we pass look very presentable from the train. They consist mostly of clean, white-painted, one-story wooden houses with a porch. The valley becomes narrower, the river smaller, the banks steeper but still wooded. After Altoona there is a splendid view of a deep valley to the left. In large bends with pretty views we pass the divide between the Susquehanna and Ohio rivers, then the valley drops downward quickly. Here there is more industry and numerous coal mines. Before Pittsburgh we see a prosperous built-up area.

Friday, May 6

During the night we did not sleep well in the sleeping car. In Pittsburgh another traveler joined us. He was assigned the upper berth so that we sat and slept rather uncomfortably. Also it was too warm. The last part of the trip to Chicago passed through a wide, low plain with huge corn fields alternating with swampy, still partly flooded areas. Around ten o'clock we reached Chicago. In an overcrowded bus we took a terribly slow trip through lively, dirty streets to another station. Perhaps we did not pass through the best section of the city. In a rather bleak room we had to wait till noon for the departure of the train. This time we did not take the sleeping car for the continuation of the trip and, at least for the moment, we were lucky to reserve a bench for each of us. With a beautiful view, we travel along Lake Michigan in a large arc. Mostly we travel through flat, very fertile land with large corn fields on both sides of the train. The flora, however, is very poor, as far as we can observe it from the train. At 8:00 P.M. we arrive at the Mississippi River. Large swamps have to be passed before we reach the main river. The west bank, however, ascends steeply directly from the river. During the night we adjusted the seats to face each other so that we could stretch out fairly well.

Saturday, May 7

Repeatedly we are delayed by damage to the railway embankment due to heavy rainstorms. A derailed, completely demolished engine lies on one track. At every stop we jump off to look for strange plants, but find very little right near the stopping places.

Not until noon and with considerable delay do we reach the Transfer House between Council Bluff and Omaha, the starting point of the Northern Pacific Railroad on the east bank of the Missouri. Here the railroad cars are exchanged, luggage has to be checked again, this time to San Francisco. We are unpleasantly surprised by the fact that we now have

7

to pay even more for excess freight because on this stretch the free allowance is considerably lower. The crossing of the Missouri generally resembles the trip across the Mississippi. In both cases there are wide swampy areas on the east side, whereas the west bank ascends steeply. In Omaha, the last large city for a long while, we have a lengthy stop. Beyond Omaha the prairie spreads out. At first several farms surrounded by small trees offer the viewer some diversity. Mostly they are occupied by Germans. On the following day, however, Sunday, May 8, the fourth day of our railroad journey, we see prairie untouched by civilization, treeless and covered with low grasses expanding on both sides of the Platte River. Numerous cadavers of cattle lie on both sides of the train. They are victims of the past severe winter. To judge by the evidence we saw, thousands of cattle must have perished. Here only a few settlers raise cattle in large numbers. Herds of several hundred head are not unusual. Otherwise few animals are living in the prairie. The herds of buffalo which roamed these areas only a few years ago were driven away by the railroad and settlements, and only seldom can one see a few. Herds of a kind of antelope (*Antilocapra americana*) can be seen quite frequently. Once we even saw a herd of twenty-four head. These antelopes, just like deer, cast off their branched antlers annually. The train traverses subterranean towns of the prairie dog that spread out for miles. Occasionally one can see the residents at the entrance of their mound-like dwellings curiously staring at the train rushing past or being frightened and fleeing into their burrows.

Unfortunately we find mostly just ordinary plants at the stops, whereas we had seen many beautiful flowering plants from the rear platform of the moving train. When getting off the train one should not go too far away, because the engine does not give a signal for the departure. Only a few hardly audible bells indicate that the train is leaving. On the other hand, nobody objects when passengers get on while the train is moving.

For a long time we have the Platte River on our left side, then we leave it and slowly go upward through an infertile valley strewn with stones and enclosed by walls of rock. Finally the valley becomes a narrow gorge in some places protected by snowsheds[6] through which the train is winding. But no tree, no bush, no friendly green enlivens these rocky masses. Only a small number of plants can be found on these barren slopes and in the gravel at the bottom of the valley; even these do not display the fresh green and vivid colors of the blossoms of our alpine plants.

Now the terrain becomes very picturesque. During this part of the trip we remain on the platform in spite of the warning sign "Passengers are not allowed to stand on the platform." The scenery turns more and more magnificent. At Sherman we reach the summit, the highest point of the entire railway at an elevation of 8,242 feet (2,473 meters). From here we have a gorgeous view of the snow-covered peaks of the Rocky Mountains, which we had been seeing all day.

Beyond Laramie the train stops for a long time. An overturned engine lies next to the railway. Workers are occupied with the clearing of the track. Meanwhile we botanize and even find a large number of interesting plants.

Monday, May 9

During the night we arranged both benches lengthwise so that we could stretch out rather comfortably on these improvised beds. Upon awakening we found ourselves again in a desolate desert. Bare yellow and reddish vertical sandstone walls enclosed the valley through which a little, dirty-yellow river ran. Only scarce vegetation can be maintained here, a few prickly chenopodia, but mostly an artemesia and the characteristic sage-brush. Patches of snow reach all the way down into the valley. Repeatedly we drive through snowsheds. At the Aspen station we are at an elevation of 2,350 meters, the second highest point of the entire railway, on the lowest pass of the Uinta Mountains. Then it goes downward again and soon a complete change in scenery follows.

Trees reappear, small-leaf aspen first, and after a few more stations beyond Evanston, we see the most luscious vegetation unfolding. We pass through narrow canyons with vertical dark red sandstone walls, cleft and hollowed in the most bizarre way. The names of the stations—Castle Rock, Hanging Rock, Devil's Gate—are suitable expressions of the magnificent nature of this stretch which appears even more effective because it stands in such harsh contrast to the bleakness of the desert which we passed a few hours ago. It is difficult to say which part of these canyons should win the prize. When we approached the narrow gorge of Devil's Gate with the roaring water of the river at the bottom, walls of rock covered with the most luscious green of evergreen bushes and trees and decorated with blossoms in vivid colors, a semicircle of snow-covered peaks of the Uinta Mountains, behind us in the east black clouds, before us a dark blue firmament with the sun beginning to set, that was a picture indelibly impressed into our memories.

We are in the state of the Mormons—Utah—and soon we reach Ogden near the Salt Lake. The city pleasantly occupies a fertile plain surrounded by snow-covered mountains. Ogden is the terminal of the Union Pacific Railroad, the beginning of the Central Pacific. Here the cars are exchanged again. After sunset we continue our trip directly along the Salt Lake with its surface glowing in the evening light and surrounded by the dark crests of mountains. Its banks are covered with salt crystals which look like a crust of snow.

Tuesday, May 10

During the night it hailed heavily. Next morning rain and snow alternate. We climbed again during the night and now we are at an elevation of 1,800 meters. In Elko we stop for breakfast; however, it rains and snows steadily, so we do not dare go outside. The poor weather continues as we pass the Humboldt Palisades. We therefore could only get an incomplete impression of these steep rock walls which can be compared with the Weber Canyon. Around noon the sky clears again. In Argenta, where the train stops for a few minutes, we have the best chance to collect typical prairie plants, also some samples of the peculiar lava, as well as a snout beetle. We had hoped to have lunch in Battle Mountain, but the train stops for a short while only. From one of our fellow travelers we received a primula, which seemed to us to be plentiful while the train was moving, but at the stops we could not reach any. We proceeded quickly to Humboldt, the lunch stop, where we collect a few plants. After Humboldt the desert becomes more and more desolate, until finally in the middle of the Nevada Desert near the Humboldt Lakes we see large areas of salt crystals inhibiting all vegetation. Only two typical desert plants, sagebrush and a thorny goose-foot (chenopodium), can be found at one stop. In Reno we have dinner.

Wednesday, May 11

We awake at the earliest dawn and find ourselves in the midst of tree-covered gorges which stand in sharp contrast to the barren landscape we passed through yesterday. During the night we crossed the Sierra Nevada and now go down its densely wooded western slopes. It is a gorgeous morning. Very early in the morning we stand on the platform. The sun has not yet risen over the mountains in the east, but soon its first rays illuminate the tips of evergreen oaks and tall conifers and between its dark leaves the white clustered blossoms of the California horse chestnut are glowing. A carpet of flowers covers the ground; the closely spaced whitish-blue blossoms of the lupine are its most beautiful decoration. The train quickly hurries through these charming valleys and passes through several larger settlements. Soon we drive across a large wooden bridge at the confluence of the American and Sacramento rivers and arrive in Sacramento, a city situated only 9 meters above sea level in a large plain. We stop for one hour, have a good breakfast, and finally a chance to get some stamps, so we can mail home the letters we had written a long time ago.

At eight o'clock the trip continues through fertile wheat fields, vineyards, and orchards. On this hot day a multitude of insects comes alive. Beautifully colored butterflies flutter in the fully blooming fruit trees. On the fences along the train we repeatedly see burrowing owls watching the passing train with a stern mien. We also observed one rushing toward its burrows accompanied by squirrels.

Arrival and Stay in San Francisco

Finally we reached the Bay of San Francisco. The first sight is not satisfying. The water is a dirty yellow. Yet, there appears to be a varied fauna. Numerous gulls, ospreys, and other birds populate the beach. We often see large fish cast on the bank. The railroad tracks are partly cut into the rocky slopes which are covered with dense, typical vegetation. Especially sagebrush appears again, most beautifully decorated with its clusters of blossoms. We pass a place where entire trains are taken aboard a boat, the *Solano*, to be transported across the Bay. Then beyond Oakland, we go far out on a wooden pier where all passengers and their luggage are transferred to a ferryboat in order to cross over to San Francisco. The city is hidden by fog and smoke and it does not become visible until we are in its immediate vicinity. Within a few minutes we arrive there and thus have completed our journey across the continent. A temporary resting place is reached.

Let us look back on this trip! Without interruption we drove by train from Washington to San Francisco. This tour of about 3000 English miles took six and a half days. Had we continued at the same speed we had during the first leg of the trip from Washington to Chicago (which took twenty-six hours), we could have made the entire distance in considerably shorter time. In fact, the distance from New York to San Francisco has been covered in less than eighty-four hours. In spite of its long duration, we cannot say that this trip was tiring or uninteresting. First of all, the considerable freedom of movement enjoyed in American railroad cars is a

11

Ferryboat. San Francisco, May 1881.

great advantage. During the trip one can walk through several cars. Nobody prohibits the use of the outside platform. Warning signs are posted on the door only to protect the company against liability in case of accidents. As soon as the train stops one can jump off immediately; of course one has to watch out for its sudden unannounced departure. We made ample use of this freedom, enjoyed from the platform the unobscured view of long stretches of interesting scenery, botanized at almost all stops, and many a plant will remind us later of how we had to run after the moving train because of it. Fortunately, the cars were not fully occupied, so most of the time we could easily spread out our small store of plant paper which we had allocated for this trip.

Unfortunately, it was very difficult to find appropriate shipping facilities from San Francisco to the Chukchi Peninsula. Most of the whaling ships left in March. Many people have to be approached, countless negotiations take place, often without results. Even the plan to charter a schooner for the four-month journey failed due to the extremely high demand of $750 per month. After a month of searching we finally booked passage for St. Lawrence Bay[7] on the Chukchi Peninsula for the high sum of $600 on the sailing vessel *Legal Tender*. This small bark was sent to the Arctic Ocean to take supplies to the fleet of whalers.

From May 11 to June 11, in San Francisco, the brothers had to wait for this opportunity. They received advice and assistance from a number of

Germans, some of whom shall be listed here: Dr. Behr, botanist and university lecturer at the local Academy, to whom the brothers had brought letters of recommendation from Bastian, Virchow, and Lindemann. He invited them repeatedly to meetings and lectures at the Academy and on excursions, on which they eagerly botanized.

The German Consul Rosenthal took care of the mail and gave them a letter and keys from Lindemann with an enclosure by Nordenskjöld. Captain von Oterendorp, who lived in Alameda, advised them several times about the continuation of their trip to Alaska. Pastor Mülsteph, who had attended high school in Berlin and later was pastor of the Luisen Kirche, had several mutual acquaintances, for example Director Bandow.[8] *Our travelers also were guests of the families of all these gentlemen, were invited to musical evenings or to play chess, and went on longer excursions by foot or carriage with several of them. They were introduced to friends of these people and got to know the city and its environment. The stories of these families were interesting to the brothers. Some of them had become rich very quickly. Especially the younger members had already adapted to the American lifestyle.*

Difficulties arose about the transportation of the alcohol. Several telegrams had to be sent to secure the necessary permissions. A telegram was also sent to Mr. Paul Schulze, Director of the North West Trading Company, to inquire about the possibilities of exploration in Alaska, whereupon he made the gracious offer that the brothers may spend the winter at one of the company's agencies. Arthur writes about this:

A winter stay at a coastal place in Alaska sounds especially promising, since we cannot conceal the fact that under the prevailing circumstances we may not be able to organize extensive collections in the Bering Strait. Since we will be landing in the Lorenz [St. Lawrence] Bay, at first we will have to live in a tent. Even if we leave part of our luggage here and limit the provisions and barter goods we take along to the bare essentials, the weight will still reach almost 1000 kilograms. Under no circumstances do we give up excursions into the interior. We will have to leave our helper behind to guard the luggage and have to entrust ourselves entirely to the Natives. We have been able to complete the assembly of our equipment satisfactorily with the kind assistance of the gentlemen of the Alaska Company.

A tent and a whaleboat with all accessories were bought for the equipment, furthermore, fishing lines and hooks, woolen blankets and other woolen goods of especially good quality, and less expensive than in Germany.

A letter by Aurel to his mother and sister reporting about impressions of the city and their further travel plans follows in excerpts :

San Francisco, Tuesday, June 7, 1881

We are still in San Francisco, but the day of our departure moves nearer, although that day has the peculiar habit of moving forward at the same rate as we are approaching it. It will be Thursday or Saturday, we are told. Well, we have to grin and bear it. Meanwhile we have an opportunity to take a thorough look at San Francisco. Therefore I will try to describe this city for you.

The first house here was built in 1835. Now the city has three hundred thousand inhabitants. From the above sketch you may gather its approximate location. As all American cities, of course, it is built in an orderly way with streets crossing at right angles. There are, however, as you can tell from the sketch, two different systems in existence. What you cannot see, however, is the hilly and rocky terrain; therefore rightfully San

This map-like sketch of San Francisco is part of a letter to Aurel Krause's mother and sister. June 7, 1881.

Francisco is called the city of a thousand hills. There may not be one thousand, but one could count about one hundred. Some of these hills are about 120 meters high. Often the streets are so steep that walking becomes difficult, driving almost impossible, so the city built "cable cars," i.e. trolleys pulled by a cable which is kept constantly moving by a steam engine under the pavement. Without steam or horses these cars move up and down hill at the same speed. There are also many horse-drawn cars and steam buses on which one can ride long distances for relatively low far. One has to say "relatively low," because in Germany these prices would not be so low. The smallest coin available is five cents. Copper coins exist only in the East, not here. For five cents one can travel the shortest or the longest distance up to five miles. The fare is the same everywhere. For five cents you can have your boots polished, but often, and always on Sundays, it is ten cents, which equals forty-two German pfennig. Boot polishing is usually done in the streets. One sits in a specially built chair, reading a newspaper while a bootjack polishes one's shoes. It is said that many Americans polish their boots themselves; the servants refuse to do it.

All over the city one sees telephone wires, and electric light is frequently used. Interesting are the quarters of the Chinese. Next to attractive houses and wealth we also see many poor people.

Our stay with the Chukchi people will hardly exceed the duration of two months, an extraordinarily short time for such a long trip, after so much has been written about it.

For the winter we have been offered an inexpensive trip and an even less expensive stay in Alaska, north of Sitka. There we could easily spend the mild winter and work in comfort.

Whether we are departing this Saturday is still uncertain, although we are told it is definite. Part of our luggage is already on the ship. We also bought a boat and hired a man as helper and boatsman. Christian Frantzen, from Riga, speaks English, German, and some Russian. He was highly recommended and made a good impression on us. For $50 a month he agreed to accompany us. For some time he served as second mate on the schooner *Leo* hunting seals. Already he is concerned about our boat, found the oars too weak, bought an anchor and a water barrel, and checked the sails.

In the journals and letters we also read that the brothers made several scientific excursions into the vicinity of San Francisco. During one trip to the redwood forests some precious zoological and botanical specimens were found. They climbed Mt. Tamalpais (792 meters), the highest mountain of the vicinity north of Sausalito. This was rather difficult in the extreme dryness and heat. Only small footpaths, almost hidden by oak bushes and rhododendrons, led to the top. A large number of beautiful, strange plants were found along the way. There was an exceptionally beautiful view in all directions from the top, but it was hazy in the distance.

The brothers entered their names in the guest book kept under a rock. On these excursions they had to use the ferryboat across the Golden Gate. It did not run too frequently; sometimes the brothers had to hurry in order not to miss it. Here is the journal of an excursion on Sunday, June 5:

Early in the morning we took the ferry to Sausalito, had an expensive, bad breakfast there, and then walked along the shore as far as possible toward the mouth of the bay. Level stretches of shore are interrupted by serpentine rocks, rising steeply from the ocean. Numerous fishermen have positioned themselves on such rocks. After we had passed the fortification, we had to follow the path more toward the interior. The flora was very scarce and offered little that was new; there was more fauna. Under rocks we found numerous beetles, although most of them the same kind, also a cricket. Then we observed a rattlesnake coiled on the path. We killed it and saved the rattle. Farther on we disturbed a quail with her young chicks; we also saw hummingbirds again. Finally the path went down from the mountains into a valley with a small brook flowing into a lake which was separated from the ocean by a small dam. At the ocean we again find numerous animals. New to us were a kind of lepas, sitting in large numbers on rocks, sea anemones, and starfish. A kind of woodlouse was also found in large numbers on the beach. Wind and surf were strong. We went swimming, but could not go very far out into the ocean because of the surf. We found some beautiful samples of algae and collected a few of them. One isolated rock was completely covered with cormorants. We walked on to Cape Bonitas where the lighthouse keeper gave us a tour. On our way back we left the main road, but finally lost the footpath and now had to take an unpleasant hike uphill and downhill. It was getting late, and when we finally reached the main road, we actually had to run. We reached the ferry just in time, covered with perspiration. A farmer, whose house we passed running down a hill, offered us a glass of fresh milk which we gratefully accepted. Otherwise we had had very little to eat on this day, just a roll and a few oranges which we had taken along. At eight o'clock we arrived home, cleaned up and changed, and went to Pastor Mülsteph, where we had dinner. Since he was not feeling well, we only stayed for a short while.

The following journal entry (dated May 18) is Aurel's detailed description of a carriage trip with Pastor Mülsteph:

At 6:30 A.M., as promised, we arrived at the pastor's house. After breakfast we started out under clear skies. We passed through a pretty residential area. These homes with their beautifully landscaped gardens, their cleanliness, and elegant embellishments can be compared to the villas in the Tiergarten Street in Berlin. Because of the earthquakes, most houses are built of wood. The new coat of paint they get every few years gives them a very friendly look. The trip continued through Golden Gate Park, very extensive, long park grounds in the middle of barren sand deserts. Here, beautiful lawns, stately trees, especially conifers, but also mimosa, and many flowering shrubs please the eye. The paths were very interesting, especially in the first part. First we drove right on the beach. The tracks of the wheels and horse hooves left only a shallow imprint in the sand hardened by the surf. A few golden plovers animated the beach. Otherwise there were not many animals, only a few animal remains were cast ashore. In the early morning the weather was magnificent. In the afternoon wind and dust are supposed to be annoying. On both sides of the park near the shore they try to keep the sand in place with yellow lupines. They grow like dunegrass on little mounds. We arrived at the Cliff House and from the porch we can see the Seal Rocks, steep rock formations close to the shore on which a large number of seals were lying. At first the view was restricted by dense fog, but soon it became clearer. The seals, which are protected there, are the most interesting sight. From our position, with the help of opera glasses, we can observe their awkward movements on the rocks, how they climb out of the water, and how they drop from a height of several feet down into the ocean. The distance is hardly more than 200 to 300 paces. So far we never had a chance to watch such long breakers. The sandy, extremely level beach probably extends way out into the ocean. The formation of a breaker can easily be observed from here: First the rising of a little foam, then a constantly broadening white crest as the breaker rolls toward the beach.

With Pastor Mülsteph they also took a trip to the town of Haywards to the estate of the Zeile family, who had kindly invited them. This is the journal entry of their trip:

At 7:30 A.M. the pastor picked us up. First we went by omnibus to Haywards, a trip of one and a half hours. From there we walked to Mr. Zeile's place. On the way we met Mr. Zeile and two sons who were driving to the reservoir hatchery to buy some trout which Mr. Zeile wanted to put into his brook. At the house, therefore, we met only Mrs. Zeile and her two

17

daughters. Although we arrived unexpectedly, we were welcomed very graciously. We toured the orchards, sampled several kinds of cherries from the trees, looked at the stables, even had ourselves weighed. Arthur weighed 75 kilograms, I only 72 kilograms. Then we had a plentiful lunch. In the orchards they grew in addition to apples and pears, plums, cherries, oranges, apricots, almonds, figs, olives, walnuts, and edible chestnuts. The latter were cultivated only as a small bush. Mr. Zeile also planted a vineyard. The grapevines were in full bloom just then. The soil in the garden was hard as a rock and dry. Melons were planted between the trees. When Mr. Zeile returned with his fish, they had to be put into the brook immediately, since they had become weak during transportation. Then the oldest daughter drove us to the station and gave us some oranges freshly picked in the garden.

On our return trip we left the omnibus in Oakland and visited a friend of the pastor, Mr. Ilse. Then we drove to Alameda, where we had a refreshing swim and then returned home. After supper we went to our hotel to arrange our plant collections, write our journals, and do some bookkeeping. Today is Decoration Day, on which graves of soldiers who died during the war are decorated. It is a legal holiday (May 30).

Once we drove to the university town of Berkeley. First you go by ferry over to Oakland, then by train always along the Bay. Berkeley is situated at the foot of the hills. We walked through the Botanical Garden which still looks rather wild. At the university we first visited Professor Rising to whom we presented a card from Arzeroni. He showed us his chemical laboratory and introduced us to his two assistants, one of them a German. Primarily, we visited the zoological and the paleontological collections of the university. In the zoological collection they even had a live rattlesnake. When incited, it sounded its rattle. This noise might be compared with the sound of a singing cricket or cicada, only lower. The collection of sand snails, freshwater snails, and marine snails was of interest to us; it was quite nice.

Even though all these excursions and tours were quite stimulating, the brothers were troubled by the long wait, but were relieved when finally they could continue their journey on the Legal Tender.

CHAPTER TWO

ON BOARD THE *LEGAL TENDER* FROM
SAN FRANCISCO TO THE CHUKCHI PENINSULA

The following is a letter written by Arthur Krause to Dr. Lindemann. The letter was written while Arthur was aboard the Legal Tender:

June 26, 1881

On Saturday, June 11, at 3:00 P.M., a small tugboat pulled us out of San Francisco Bay through the Golden Gate.

It was not the friendliest weather as we said good-bye to the city which had been our host for a full month. A cold northwest wind blew and a haze prevented a good view. It was typical California weather. In spite of all its advantages, during the summer San Francisco, unfortunately, has frequent fog and cold winds. From the tops of the city's "one thousand hills" one should have a beautiful view of the city, the bay, the surrounding towns, and the distant mountains. Instead, the clear views were often obliterated by haziness. Our enjoyment of the view while leaving the harbor was also considerably diminished. We could, however, watch the coastline of the bay, its abrupt serpentine rocks, and also other areas through which we had hiked.

After passing the lighthouse, the tugboat left us, the sails were hoisted, and we were on our way in a westerly direction. The rough sea and the unaccustomed rolling of the sailing vessel made us feel somewhat uncomfortable, at least the six o'clock dinner did not really taste good. Yet we had not had a bite to eat since 8:00 A.M. because of the last-minute rush of preparations. The next day we were accustomed to life on sea and from then on attended all meals with good appetite, although the menu, without any fresh meat, was not really according to our taste.

We now had time to thoroughly inspect the vessel, which was to be our home for probably one month. The *Legal Tender* is a bark of 207 tons, a rather old vessel, built about forty years ago.

19

This trip was to be her last into the Arctic Sea. The insurance company did not want to accept her until after completion of extensive repairs and payment of a high insurance premium (25 percent). The captain also had to agree not to go beyond Point Barrow and return from Cape Lisburne by September 1 in order to pass the Bering Strait by the fifteenth. Thus those whalers who were not insured had a chance to send home safely at least part of their precious cargo, especially whalebone. In addition, the *Legal Tender* carries mail and brings fresh provisions. She therefore is a welcome guest up north.

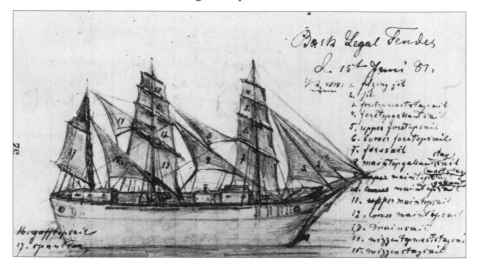

Bark Legal Tender. *All 17 sails are identified and listed by name.*
June 15, 1881.

The *Legal Tender* did not even get a new coat of paint for this trip. The cabin is on deck and is most plainly furnished. We were given the first mate's cabin which contained a second bed. The cabin next to ours with two bunks had to be shared by both mates and the cook. Even the captain had to put up a passenger in his narrow room, a young man going north to assume a vacant officer's position on one of the whalers. There was even less room for the crew. Two sailors on different watches had to share one bunk to make room for our Frantzen.

Under these circumstances the demanded fare of $600 appeared very high, even if one considers the risk of a landing. We, therefore, had hesitated to the very last moment to accept these conditions; however, there was actually no other opportunity available to reach the Chukchi Peninsula this summer.

The *Legal Tender* carries fresh provisions to the whalers who left San Francisco this past spring mostly during the month of March. In return she accepts their load of whale oil and whalebone. The most prominent items among the fresh provisions are potatoes and fresh water, the latter stored in barrels which will be filled with the oil. Thirteen whalers belonging to four different companies will be visited. The captain hopes to meet most of them in Kotzebue Sound, otherwise he has to sail along the Ice Coast to search for them, a dangerous task for his fragile ship.

We are really pleased with our acceptance by the captain and his crew. Captain Fischer is German, born in Neustadt an der Hardt. Although the exceptionally adverse weather depressed him, which he tries to blame on the comet or some other mysterious cause, he and his crew made every effort to support our eagerness to collect and observe. We soon found the voyage on this sailing vessel, although she was not at all outfitted for passengers, much more entertaining than a trip on a steamer. One pays much more attention to every change in weather because of the greater dependence on it. The slower speed allows better observations of oceanic fauna. Unless there are high waves, the vessel's motion is much calmer than that of a steamer which is constantly trembling because of the engine's activity. Even in today's weather when the bark is rolled back and forth in heavy seas so that it takes an effort to stand upright, it is still easier to read or write than it would be under equal circumstances on a steamer.

After the first five days during which we sailed westward in favorable, rather strong wind, other days followed with light winds or sometimes almost absolute calm. The captain was furious, and the entire crew in a bad mood. One day, in order to release his anger, the captain tore off the horseshoe nailed to his

*Californian Goonies. Five goonies are shown in various positions.
June 19, 1881.*

door and threw it overboard! These days gave us a chance to rearrange our luggage in a more practical way and to get our fishing gear to catch some interesting marine life. At times we could even work comfortably with the microscope, although one of the large water barrels on the deck outside our cabin had to serve as a table.

During this entire time we were accompanied by birds, particularly Californian goonies which followed us with greatest persistence, greedily diving for scraps from our meals which were thrown overboard. These impudent birds can easily be caught with fishing tackle. In stormy weather they skillfully soar over the waves; however, on deck they appear helpless since they are unable to lift off due to their extraordinary wingspan. When returned to freedom, they again display no timidity.

Rather frequently we see whales. Since the captain had served on whalers for some time, we can get some information about the different kinds of whales being hunted and the entire whaling business.

For six days we have had strong westerly winds which forced us to change our course considerably to the east. The captain had counted on reaching Unimak[9] in three weeks at the most. Now there is no chance to reach that first goal on time. This vessel is really a rather poor sailer. In strong wind a large number of sails have to be reefed and during the last few days often only five of the seventeen sails were hoisted. We may have to resign ourselves to the fact that we might not reach Lawrence Bay until the end of July, so we shall have barely two months in the Bering Strait. We hope that conditions then will allow us to make full use of our time.

Fortunately it appears that Christian Frantzen turns out to be a man capable of aiding us in all our activities. Already here aboard ship he intelligently and eagerly helped us in many ways. His experiences with Natives and camping while hunting seals and otters will certainly be useful to us.

Journal, Aurel

June 25, 1881

All night a strong wind blew, becoming so violent that all sails except five had to be taken down. Only the foretop mast sail, the lower foretop sail, the foresail, the lower maintop sail, and the mizzen sail remained. This slowed down the speed and caused a severe pitch of the ship. Today eating was no small endeavor, but it went on without any accident. A few dishes broke, in our cabin the glass cylinder of a lamp fell down, also the microscope, however, it sustained no damage. Several waves drenched us more or less.

June 26

There is still a rather strong wind from the southwest, but a few sails are hoisted. The captain does not like our northern direction. In the evening a whale is sighted. At dinner Mr. Norton reports that he had seen a comet last night.

Monday, June 27

The same wind, a few more sails are hoisted, but they have to be pulled down from time to time, when a new squall arrives. The weather is cold and unpleasant. In the afternoon we steer toward south-southwest, but in the evening we resume the old course to north. The captain is in bad spirits and accuses the comet or similar events of causing the poor weather. Today a seal was seen.

Tuesday, June 28

Through the night we again go with only five sails in a northerly direction, sometimes a little toward east. It was especially stormy around midnight; we were tossed back and forth in our bunks. The unfavorable weather continued all day without the slightest sign of quick improvement. We sail north by east toward Sitka.

Friday, July 1

The wind is west-southwest to west. In the morning the same direction as yesterday, north with slight deviation to west, changing later on. The captain told us a few details about the whaling business. He remembers there were 250 ships in the Arctic Sea and half that many in the Sea of Okhotsk. Ten years ago most whalers started out from Honolulu. There is a better harbor and better weather than in San Francisco. In San Francisco the winter storms are so strong that ships cannot tie up to the docks, especially the southern wharf. Now the agents, however, are in a better position to control the business than they used to be. Also, the ships stay out longer. Now the whalers leave San Francisco in spring, mostly the middle of March, and travel to the ice at 54° to 58° latitude. The edge of the ice stretches from south of Petropavlovsk to the Commander Islands and from there to St. Paul. They go along the ice edge until they can pass the Bering Strait at the end of June or beginning of July. This year there are twenty to twenty-one whalers up north, most of them from New Bedford, hunting sperm whale during the summer north of 40° to 50° latitude, during the winter south of these latitudes. A general report about whaling is published by the government, which collects reports about it. Now the whalers also hunt walrus. Consequently one of the most important animals of the Natives' livelihood is being destroyed. The Natives have to venture out 200 miles from the coast to hunt walrus.

Saturday, July 2

The weather is better. In the afternoons mostly clear but cold, air temperature 8.5°C and the same unfavorable wind. We are sailing north far beyond our destination and if the wind does not change we have to tack.

Today huge pieces of an alga, kelp, were floating past us. Frequently we see gray-whitish birds with a large owl-like head. At 8:00 P.M. we are turning south.

Sunday, July 3

At 11:30 last night, Mr. Norton woke us to show us the comet. The sky was covered by a few light clouds, but we could see the comet more and more clearly, its tail pointing to the polar star. Through the night and the following morning the wind remained unchanged. Again we see two finback whales. Agreeing with the captain's statement, Mr. Winchester tells us that sperm whales can stay under water for sixty to seventy-five minutes, especially the larger ones, the smaller ones only twenty to thirty minutes. Finback whales stay submerged only fifteen to twenty minutes. Soon after noon we saw a large finback whale, about 20 yards long, larger than half the ship. When surfacing he very noisily spouted water, then dove. He surfaced a second and third time in the same curved line, first the head, then the back with the fin, last the tail, then he dove. A little later he repeated the same maneuver on the other side of the ship. Three times seems to be normal, sometimes they surface only once or twice, sometimes more than six times. Larger than the finback whale is the sulphur-bottom whale living in the middle latitudes, but it is not hunted by whalers because its baleen is rather small. It looks like the finback whale but has a smaller dorsal fin. When harpooned it rushes away at great speed in a straight line, whereas the finback whale dives down. The California graybacks, according to Frantzen, attack and crush boats when they are wounded or have young.

In the afternoon the wind turned south again. The ship is holding 7 points against the wind. All day the weather was cool, 8° to 9°C, but not unpleasant, partly cloudy. In the evening we steered northward. Just to pass the time I once climbed up into the crow's nest. The pitch of the ship did not bother me, but I was not used to the swaying rope ladder and found it to be strenuous.

Monday, July 4

Today is Independence Day, the most important holiday in the United States, but aboard ship it is not observed. The captain is in the worst mood. At 2:00 A.M. he commands the ship to go "on the other tack," southward, but soon we turned to southeast so that at 8:00 A.M. we again pointed north.

Saturday, July 9

During the night the wind increased again so that the heavy rolling of the ship made it impossible to sleep well. In the morning the wind was still strong and at 8:00 A.M. the sails had to be changed again and a course to northwest was taken. The captain had a bad cold. The first mate also repeated over and over that he was sick, homesick or weathersick. His dog was sick last night, probably because he had eaten some lead. The taller one of the two Negroes aboard was on a ship last year which capsized, filled with water, and lost its masts. On the partly submerged stern he and a few other sailors spent several days without food. When most of them were overpowered by exhaustion and perished, only he and one other sailor were rescued by a passing ship. Captain Fischer reported that a few years ago a captain was killed in Plover Bay. One year earlier during a violent storm this captain did not permit some Natives aboard his ship to go ashore while the storm lasted. They jumped overboard, tried to swim, but they all drowned. Several humpback whales were visible today. Around five o'clock we saw Ukamok once more, until eight o'clock we steered north along its eastern coast. Huge pieces of seaweed floated by; Frantzen even caught a complete sample. The weather improved toward evening, the wind decreased. After tacking, the sails were set against the wind to make it possible to fish, and several codfish weighing three to six pounds were caught. The surface of their bodies was covered by numerous fish lice. The stomach of one cod contained a crab and a young thornback. The liver was infested with threadlike worms.

Sunday, July 10

We have been on the sea for four weeks and are still far away from our destination. We have not seen such a clear beautiful morning in a long time, even Old Jack, the dog, is feeling better again. After being given a dose of salt he threw up pieces of bone which had been stuck in his throat and probably were the cause of his illness.

Monday, July 11

The captain thinks there is a witch aboard. The first mate thinks the loss of the horseshoe, which the captain had thrown overboard, is to be blamed for the steady head winds. The captain never wants to sail this ship again, but possibly return to Germany next summer. He had told his agent that he had taken this ship for the last time, because he preferred to die a natural death.

Continuation of Arthur's letter to Dr. Lindemann:

July 12, 1881

Against all expectations we are still on our vessel and still a very long distance away from our goal. I no longer praise journeys on a sailing vessel, at least not the kind we are on.

Calm days were followed by strong westerly winds with few interruptions. These winds allowed us to continue our course north, but not west. When we arrived in the area of Kodiak, we had no choice but to tack against the wind. According to the helmsman, the vessel was built for good wind only and not for head wind. Consequently, after a twenty-four-hour trip which covered 130 sea miles, we saw the island Ukamok southwest of Kodiak in almost the same place where we had seen it the day before. For about eight days we have been continuously changing our course from north to south and from south to north. Finally today, we have slightly better wind which at least allows us to move ahead in a northwesterly direction.

One of the two black sailors on our ship served on the *Loleta* last year, which was trading, in part illegally, with the Natives along the coast of the Bering Sea. We get some information from him about places visited by the traders, the most wanted barter goods, and the various trade objects. The American government prohibits trade in alcohol, breech-loader guns, and cartridges. Every year one or two revenue cutters are sent there to look for ships with such illegal items aboard. Although this will not suppress the trade, so destructive for the Natives, especially with alcohol, it is at least kept within bounds.

Aurel's Journal:

Wednesday, July 13

During the night the wind was more favorable. In the morning we sail almost in a southwesterly direction. Only seldom the sun breaks through the fog. During the day the course south-southwest becomes unfavorable. The fog persists all the time. With his back turned toward the ocean, the captain again throws an old horseshoe overboard to attract good winds.

Friday, July 15

During the night the wind became unfavorable again. Early in the morning there was a dense fog. Flocks of birds, clumps of seaweed, and green water indicate the vicinity of land. At 7:30 we see the Shumagin Islands. Breakfast is eaten quickly and then after eight o'clock the ship is turned and a line is thrown out for codfish. The water was 55 fathoms deep. Unfortunately, no fish were caught. In rather clear weather we now take a course south. In order to show how slow our journey is, we figured that at a steady rate of one mile per hour in a straight line from San Francisco, we should have covered the same distance. All day we sail in clear weather at considerable speed in high waves in a southerly direction. At eight o'clock the ship turns north again.

Continuation of Arthur's Letter to Dr. Lindemann:

July 19, 1881

I had planned to wait with the continuation of my travel report until we passed through the Strait of Unimak into the Bering Sea. Our crisscrossing voyage during the past weeks has taken us only very slowly toward that goal. A favorable wind might take us there in a day or two; however, after our experiences so far, we shall have to be prepared for sailing around for weeks. We did accept with skepticism the assurance that the entire voyage to Lawrence Bay would take twenty-five to thirty days; however, we never expected it to take double that time. Last year the ship indeed covered the trip in only thirty days, as the captain proved from his log. In former years it took sometimes longer, sometimes shorter. This year is, therefore, especially unfavorable. The captain's insistence that such weather has never happened before as long as the world exists, is quite an exaggeration.

One week after we had seen the first island, Ukamok, we caught sight of the Shumagin Islands. We again saw the islands on the following two days from points only a few nautical miles to the west. We did travel fast, about 120 to 130 nautical miles per day. The fact that this vessel is absolutely incapable of pointing is the only reason for our slow progress. Had we been able to head into the wind by one more point, as is possible on other vessels, we should have passed the Aleutian Chain weeks ago.

Since there is nothing we can do about it, we have tried to use this situation to our advantage. While sailing near land, we often collected floating algae with numerous animal inhabitants. In the limited space in our cabin we had to store this catch in a number of bottles and preserving jars. The preliminary work of selecting had to be done on deck. At an almost constant temperature of 8.5°C of air and ocean, this work is no longer as pleasant as it was at 35° to 40° latitude.

Journal, Aurel:

Wednesday, July 20

In the morning we sail in a northeasterly direction. At six o'clock the ship tacked again, at first to northwest, but half an hour later again to northeast. Again the captain swore the ship was bewitched and not until eight o'clock did he tack to the south. The weather was very rainy, gradually the wind turned north until we finally had partly cloudy sky with rather steady north wind. Frantzen caught the stem of a giant seaweed; we measured its dimensions. The sample was incomplete, rotten at the bottom, therefore, the leaves were missing. Its length was 12 meters. The upper part can be made into giant trumpets. The Natives use the lower part for fishing lines and anchor ropes. They do not last in the air or in fresh water. When we tested its strength, we were rather surprised to find that two strong men could not tear this piece thick as a finger. Not until we put it across the rung of a rope ladder and one man pulled at each end did we succeed in tearing the piece apart. Frantzen caught another piece with only a few leaves covered with pretty bryozoa. We also saw a sleeping sea otter in the same coiled position as snakes with its head in the center. In the afternoon the wind grew stronger, turning into a heavy gale in the evening and increasing in violence during the night, especially from midnight to 2:00 A.M.

Thursday, July 21

In the morning the wind was still quite strong. We had barely a moment of sleep during the night. In the evening we were in quite some danger due to the negligence of one of the black sailors who took his hand off the wheel because one spoke broke. In the log it was recorded that the sailor who held the steering wheel let go of it for fear he might be drenched by a splashing wave. Consequently, the ship was turned into the wind, the sails flapped back, and the spoke of the wheel broke. Through the interference of another sailor, the tall Negro, who turned the wheel back again, considerable damage was prevented. Sometimes during the night only two or three sails were hoisted.

Saturday, July 23

The seventh week begins and we have not yet passed the Aleutian Islands. Around 5:00 A.M. Frantzen called us to view the snow-covered mountains on Unalaska appearing ahead of us. During the morning some of the floating seaweed was collected, and in it we found large numbers of

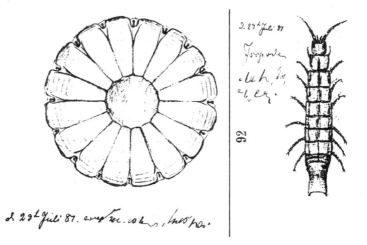

Isopod. A new aquatic crustacean was found among seaweed.
July 23, 1881.

small crabs, but also a new isopod. An albatross had set down forward of the bow of the ship where we could easily observe it. When touching the suspended nets at night, one could see glowing dots. We collected these in gauze.

Letter, Arthur:

July 28, north of Akutan Pass

Last night we passed the Aleutian Chain. When I wrote my last lines nine days ago, I was worried we might have to cruise in front of this island chain for weeks. In spite of our bad experiences so far, I never seriously believed it might take that long. So many adversities as we experienced on this journey have hardly been seen by the much traveled and much tested noble sufferer Odysseus on his return voyage. I will try to give an idea of our zigzag cruise. It took us eleven days to get from the island of Ukamok to the Shumagin Islands. During these days we noted several times that the vessel turned into the opposite direction while tacking. She simply cannot sail windward. The next day, July 20, at 6:00 A.M., our course is north, at 8:00 A.M. again south. During the day the wind becomes more favorable and a strong northern wind lets us sail in the desired southwestern direction at a speed of 7 to 8 knots. During the night the wind velocity increased considerably. We had a small gale during which the vessel was in real danger, the sailor at the helm let go of the wheel when one of the handgrips broke off. On the twenty-first the same gale continued, though not quite so strong. Now we have to change course; we have sailed far enough west. Now we have to turn north toward Unimak Pass, from which we are farther removed than on the day before. On the twenty-second we move away from the Pass; during the last two days we had been as close as 85 nautical miles. The captain decides to take the next one, Akutan Pass. Again we sail northeast.

On the morning of the twenty-third we are near the southeast coast of Unalaska, only half a day's trip from Akutan Pass. In the meantime, however, the wind changed to east. We cannot move ahead, turn, and look for the next pass near Four Mountains.

In very light wind we sail on this day and the next day, the twenty-fourth, southwest until noon, when the southwest end of the island Umnak suddenly appears out of the fog in close proximity. But now we cannot sail ahead. The wind had changed to southwest. After a futile attempt to gain through tacking, we have to give up this pass, too, and sail back northwest to Akutan Pass. On the twenty-fifth and twenty-sixth we had light winds, in part complete calm, so we moved only a few miles. Finally in the afternoon of the twenty-seventh, a light southeast wind took us closer to Akutan Pass. Fortunately, the dense fog lifted. It had covered the land all morning. At 8:00 P.M. we were near the entrance of the pass. A new obstacle arose, a strong tidal current kept us in one position from 9:00 to 10:00 P.M. in spite of a strong southwesterly breeze, which under other circumstances might have given us a speed of 5 to 6 knots. It seems as if the ship moved ahead at great speed, but a look at the rocks at both sides showed that we were standing still in one spot. The situation was critical, since the land threatened to disappear in heavy fog at any moment. Suddenly at 10:00 P.M. the current stopped and soon high tide going in the opposite direction aided us, so that we reached the Bering Sea by midnight.

It was difficult for us to give up the entire month of July in the Bering Strait, especially a great deal of botanical and ornithological research will be lost. The work we did aboard in these days is only a small compensation, although we did have plenty of opportunity for interesting observations.

While the ship stood still on calm days, the crew caught codfish. The most favorable result was near Umnak Pass on the twenty-fifth, when eighty codfish (related to European *Gadus morrhua*, Kabeljau) and three halibut were caught. These good-tasting fish brought a welcome change to the daily monotony of salted meat. The captain, however, was not quite satisfied with the result of this catch. In past years during calm weather in Unimak Pass he had caught several hundred, which not only supplied the crew with fresh fish for ten days, but also were salted and filled several barrels. The largest of the halibut caught weighed 30 pounds, but sometimes specimens of 300 pounds and over are caught. The codfish are usually much larger than our Kabeljau. The weight of a middle-sized codfish after removal of the intestines is about 9 pounds. The best fishing grounds are near the Shumagin Islands. There, thousands of these fish are caught every year. Three companies in San Francisco dispatch small fishing vessels of about 120 tons to this area.

We, too, did not pass up this chance to fish. Of course, we were not prepared for such great depth with our dredging net apparatus, but we managed to pick up something from the bottom with a lighter net. Also the floating net near the surface yielded a rich catch, especially jellyfish. Many interesting specimens attached to pulled-up seaweed were also found. We obtained only incomplete pieces of the giant seaweed which forms marine forests south of the Alaska Peninsula. Some of these seaweeds are extraordinarily strong. Judging from our glimpse of the Aleutian Islands, we are sorry not to be able to get to know them better. Almost everywhere rocks ascend abruptly from the ocean. Only in the interior part of the bays are softer slopes covered with fresh green. Next to beautiful, perfectly regular, cone-shaped mountains, extinct as well as active volcanoes, we see the strangest, most irregular rock formations. Steep, snow-covered mountains, e.g. the Peak of Unimak, which we see gleaming for over 100 miles, remind us of scenes in the Alps. A larger survey of the coastline was rarely possible. Usually by noon everything was shrouded in dense fog. Later light winds dispersed it and between 4:00 and 6:00 P.M. one usually had the best view. Toward evening fog rolled in again and between 10:00 and 11:00 all land disappeared.

The laws of ocean currents in this area apparently have not been studied very well; conditions here seem to be most complicated. According to Dall, the flood-tide going toward the Bering Sea in the passes is especially strong, while the opposite tide is hardly noticeable. In accordance with this, the captain also tells us that he was able to sail through Unimak Pass against a strong north wind with the aid of the current. The ebb-tide current can be just as strong, as we experienced in Akutan Pass. As usual, the boundary of the current was distinctly marked. Previously smooth water suddenly seemed to be boiling. Last year we had observed a similar condition at Saltenfjord in Norway. At the same time the surface temperature of the water sank from 8.5° to 6°C.

July 31

On our first day in the Bering Sea, the ocean was filled with numerous killer whales whose giant dorsal fins, called "gaff

33

topsail" by whalers, surfaced everywhere. Their appearance apparently excited the also numerous seals. The favorable wind did not last long. For the last two days we had almost no wind, finally today we move ahead again in light wind with moderate speed. We can hardly count on reaching [St.] Lawrence Bay before August 10, a month later than planned at the beginning of the trip.

Journal, Aurel:

Sunday, July 31

Again a Sunday aboard ship, our eighth! I hear Mr. Norton sigh, "I wished my room was empty." It is hoped his wish will be fulfilled soon. During the day the wind grows stronger and the waves are higher. Our average speed is 5 knots in a northwesterly direction. A few whales as well as seals are visible again.

These two snails were collected from the bottom of the Bering Sea. August 1, 1881.

Monday, August 1

The wind diminished and is less favorable; we are going too far west. Early in the morning Frantzen catches a large number of pretty little jellyfish. When there was no wind and the ship sat almost motionless in the afternoon, Frantzen again lowered his nets. The first time he raised up a quantity of mud with numerous large foraminifera, a few clams and snails, especially turban, as well as numerous crabs, some of these a kind we had not found before. The second netful brought just a few small snails. In the evening black clouds gathered in the west, but they moved and the expected wind never came.

Tuesday, August 2

All day long we had favorable wind, so that we could move north a good distance. In the morning the sea was rather calm; now the waves are higher, but they do not get very long in this shallow water (25 fathoms).

Wednesday, August 3

All night long the favorable wind kept up and around noon we had covered 170 miles in twenty-four hours, by far the best speed the ship has made during this journey. When the captain asked us to pack our things, we started immediately. In the afternoon the wind became weaker and our direction was less favorable. We are heading directly toward the west point of St. Lawrence Island. All day the weather is cloudy, partly rainy.

From a Letter by Aurel while aboard Legal Tender:

August 4, 1881

Finally, finally! Asia in sight! We can still see toward the southeast the 200-foot-high rocks at the northwest end of St. Lawrence Island and to the left ahead the high mountains of Cape Chukotskiy appear out of the fog. Before dusk we hope to reach Indian Point (this is what is usually called Chaplin Point here). Tomorrow we may be able to land at [St.] Lawrence Bay, if the wind remains favorable; if not, well, then we just have to wait one or two days longer. We have become patient. The long voyage and the disappointed hopes have taught us this: "Aequam rebus in arduis servare mentem."[10] I do not want to fall into the mood of old wives who might have added in our case: "Who knows what it is good for?" More important and more comforting seems to us the observation that there is still a lot of snow on the island as well as on the mainland in the lower valleys and gorges, in some places all the way down to the water level. Even Nordenskjöld found [St.] Lawrence Bay on July 20 and Konyam

Bay on the thirtieth full of ice, so we can at least hope that our yield of plants will not be too incomplete. It will be different with our ornithological collections. The best time for these is probably over; we really had hoped for interesting results in this area.

Although the voyage was extremely long and the impatience to reach the desired goal was great, I must say, time went fast. Regular work, constantly interrupted by fresh opportunities for observations, seemed to make the eight weeks much shorter than the four weeks in San Francisco.

As we approach our destination, more and more the captain and mate want to scare us. Descriptions of importunate, drunken Natives, lack of food and hunger pain, stormy seas and dangerous boat trips in ever changing variations are used as scare tactics. They probably mean well, but fortunately they use so many contradictions that the effect is lost. The only result was that the captain sold us a sack full of hard bread, a can of syrup, and two sides of bacon, the latter to fry our fish which we shall have to catch, the two former to treat the Natives upon our arrival. We are told that they are used to such handouts from traders and whalers.

Journal, Aurel:

Friday, August 5

We definitely had expected to land in [St.] Lawrence Bay today. Indeed, we had passed Indian Point last night and were sailing north favored by strong southerly winds. Heavy fog, however, covered the horizon and although the fog eater[11] appeared in beautiful rainbow colors, the fog closed in so that in the afternoon visibility was hardly 200 paces. Around noon we had to sail south, since in all probability we already had arrived near [St.] Lawrence Bay. Also, Frantzen claimed to have seen land.

Our course was changed several times during the day. Already in the morning the captain got out the fog horn, but its sound barely reached beyond the length of the vessel. In the afternoon the wind increased steadily, turning into a heavy breeze in the evening, causing a strong roll of the ship.

Saturday, August 6

When we woke up this morning, land was already in sight, yet the captain and mate were unsure whether it really was [St.] Lawrence Bay. Again a heavy fog rolled in, but around 11:00 A.M. the horizon cleared and suddenly we saw land close ahead of us. We were very close to the northern tip of Lawrence Bay. A good wind arose so that we could sail slowly into the bay. At two o'clock the anchor fell at Lütke's Harbor.

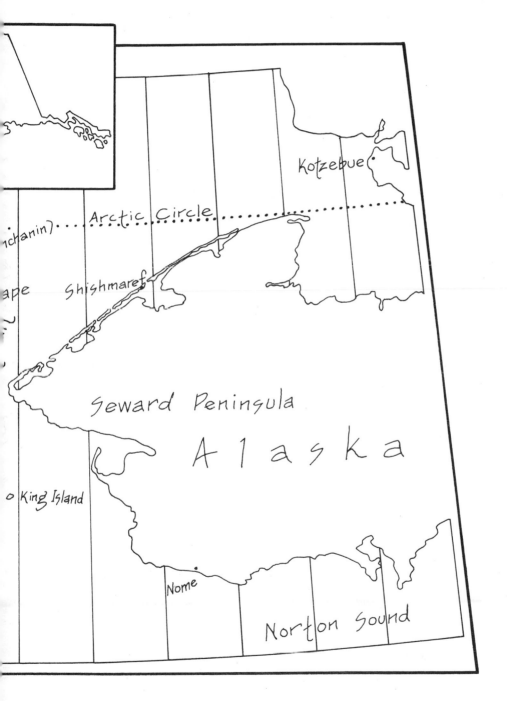

Kotzebue

Arctic Circle

ıchanin)

ape

Shishmaref

Seward Peninsula

A l a s k a

o King Island

Nome

Norton Sound

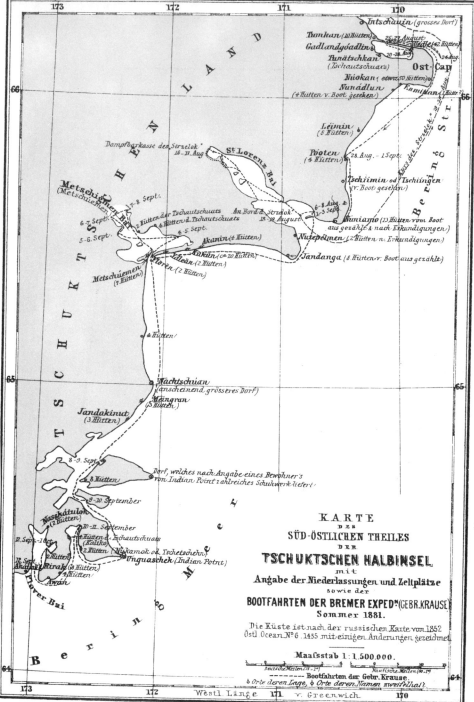

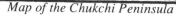

Map of the Chukchi Peninsula

40

CHAPTER THREE

CAMPING AND BOAT TRIPS ALONG THE COASTS OF THE CHUKCHI PENINSULA[12]

Lütke's Harbor, St. Lawrence Bay

Saturday, August 6, 1881

Foggy and rainy was the day on which we stepped on firm land after our two-month-long voyage. No wonder the desolate shore with its extremely sparse flora and the few patches of snow reaching down to the ocean gave us an impression of the most infertile soil.

For the first time we saw the Natives in their peculiar fur clothing tastefully made of seal and reindeer skin. Over this they often wore the typical overgarment of all polar people made of seal gut, the *okonchek*.

Soon we saw them—men, women, and children—gathered around a pile of hard bread and a dish of syrup consuming their *kaukau*[13] with great enjoyment. How much they enjoyed this food was obvious in their effort to finish it to the last drop by licking every trace of the sweet nectar off their fingers.

After their meal they brought out some goods for trading, especially seal boots with matching leather stockings and gloves. As sly traders they did not show their entire stock at once but piece by piece in order to drive up prices as high as possible. The Natives' footwear is most practical, as we found out later. It is extraordinarily light, keeps the foot warm and dry in wet and cold weather, and when taken good care of, it is quite durable. On the sharp-edged rocks on mountain slopes, however, our leather boots are more serviceable. Often it was most painful for us to climb down steep rocky slopes in Native boots. Every unevenness was felt through the thin soles and every bump into a rock was very painful. Of course, we had neglected to stuff dry grass and heather between leather stocking and boot, as the Natives did. This keeps the foot considerably warmer and protects it better against pressure and bumps.

The people who had come aboard the *Legal Tender* lived in Nuniamo, a poor fishing village on the north side of [St.] Lawrence Bay close to its mouth. At once they willingly helped us offload our luggage and four of them rowed us ashore.

Upon the recommendation of the captain of the *Legal Tender*, we had chosen the southern corner of Lütke's Harbor as our landing and camping site. There a sand point formed a little inlet, where our boat was protected from strong surf. Later on this place proved to be most suitable again. At first we had hoped to bring our boat into a little lagoon inside the sand point, but the entrance was not deep enough. All freshwater brooks nearby were dried up, so we had to get our drinking water from quite a distance. These were the only disadvantages. On the whole, this site was as well protected as might be possible on a bare coast.

Campsite in Lütke's Harbor (Lawrence Bay).
This tent is pitched next to large whale bones. In Lawrence Bay the
schooner O.S. Fowler *(Capt. Nye) is anchored. August 12, 1881.*

At this place there had been three huts; we could only see traces of them. Later we learned that the inhabitants had moved to the opposite bank. A number of whale bones were scattered all over the place; during the last few years whalers repeatedly landed here to render oil and wash whalebone. A few Natives helped us pitch our tent next to two colossal whale skulls. Meanwhile another Native fished for salmon trout with set-nets which he pushed from the shore into the water with long poles.

Rather late we completed the establishment of our campsite. Now we had to take a look at our research area as far as fog and rain allowed. Immediately behind the gravel beach where we had pitched our tent, there was a stretch of marshy soil; at the moment it was dry and covered with rushes and grasses. We were overjoyed when we found a rich flora at its edge. Several faded blossoms of plants reminded us that we had to pay immediate attention to the short-lived flora of the arctic summer. Thanks to the reminder, we started our collection of flowering plants on the first day.

After a long sea voyage one rarely spends a quiet night; one misses the accustomed rolling. After the first part of the night we were awakened by Frantzen's cry. He had dreamed one of the Natives had crawled into the tent. Half awake, he thought the bread sack with a hat on top next to the tent entrance was a Chukchi and he was afraid of it. Next morning we all laughed about this story. It was also rather cold that night. Frantzen, who suffered most from the cold because he had not covered himself sufficiently, got up at 2:00 A.M. to make some tea. We, too, rose about 3:00 A.M. because we were quite cold. Later on we could sleep well at much lower temperatures, partly because we made better use of our blankets, but also because we became acclimatized to local conditions.

Sunday, August 7

Our fire soon attracted a number of Natives. They had fished all night long and now curiously watched our activities. Now we, too, had more leisure to observe them more closely. There were men, women, and children, all of them dirty to the highest degree. All the women are tattooed with blue lines produced by scratching soot into the skin with needles. Two lines go from the forehead to the tip of the nose, several double lines are at the chin, and more complicated drawings with straight and circular lines are scratched into the cheeks and lower arms. Later we saw the same tattoos all along the coast from the East Cape to Plover Bay, just once in a while some small variations. The operation takes place when a girl is about nine or ten years old, but occasionally we saw even younger girls with tattoos. The men usually are not tattooed; a few of them have a small drawing on their cheeks, arm, or chin. Both sexes also wear different hairdos. The women have long black hair with one part almost reaching the forehead, two loosely braided pigtails in front of their ears, and a tuft of hair hanging over their forehead. The latter is reminiscent of the fashion which recently disfigured so many faces in Europe. The men wear their hair closely cropped. They only leave a wreath of $1^1/_2$- to 2-inch-long hair hanging straight down. Sometimes one or several beads are braided into it right in the middle of the forehead.

The clothing was identical in all places we visited. The man's overcoat is a sacklike jacket made of reindeer or sealskin, which reaches down to the

On the right is a frontal view portrait of a woman of the Trooshin family with facial tattoos. On the left is a sketch of the tattoos on her lower right arm. The description gives the Chukchi names of the tattoos: tattoo of the arm, meniokadlgit; *tattoo of the nose,* inkadlgit; *tattoo of the cheek,* elpukadlgit; *tattoo of the chin,* uelkalkadlgit. *Lawrence Bay, Lütke's Harbor, August 10, 1881.*

knees. It is worn with the fur on the outside and pulled over the head. Under this only the wealthy men wear a kind of leather shirt or, in cold weather, a second fur coat with the fur to the inside. Collar and sleeves are often trimmed with long-hair dog fur. The tightly fitting pants, usually made of sealskin for the coastal population, are tied above the ankle. The boots are pulled over the pants and tied tightly below the knee. The result is an almost watertight cover for the entire leg. A leather belt from which a tobacco pouch and a knife sheath are suspended, and hoodlike hat complete the men's outfit. The women's clothes are different. Their wide, baggy pants and jacket are one piece. In wet weather both sexes wear the well-known overgarment with hood made of seal gut, a raincoat which can compete in watertightness with the best Mackintosh and is far superior to it because of its light weight. The use of ornaments is not very common among men; the women, however, generally wear strings of beads around their necks and arms and various kinds of earrings.

During the night we had to leave a large part of our belongings unguarded outside our tent. To our great satisfaction we found everything in its place the next morning. We were somewhat worried, since we had been warned aboard ship about the Natives' tendency to steal. Even later we rarely had to complain about the people's lack of honesty. A few small items were stolen in St. Lawrence Bay, among them, strangely enough, a bar of soap which we had left lying around under the assumption that the Chukchi had no use for it.

Here, and in other places, we were more annoyed by their begging for kaukau and tobacco, as well as by their importunate curiosity. Generally, the people did not mind when we did not allow anybody to enter our tent except heads of families. It is the custom of many captains of whalers and trading vessels to invite the chiefs of the "Indians," as all Natives on either side of the Bering Strait are called, into their cabins for a meal.

Communication with the inhabitants was not difficult for us. Because of their steady contact with Americans, many of these people know the English language quite well. Every season many Natives from various places—particularly Plover Bay, Indian Point, [St.] Lawrence Bay, and East Cape—were used on American whalers. Some of the expressions of whaling jargon have been adopted into their language. Along the coast the corrupt Spanish phrases *mi savi* and *mi no savi* for "I know" and "I don't know" are used, as well as the above-mentioned kaukau. Also used is the word *pau*, the equivalent of the Chukchi word *uinga*, meaning "nothing" or "there is nothing." Right from the beginning we were convinced about the usefulness and reliability of Nordquist's Chukchi dictionary, which Nordenskjöld had graciously sent us at the last moment. Very often, of course, the international sign language had to be used.

45

On the second day of our stay at [St.] Lawrence Bay we made a not unimportant discovery. Fifteen minutes from our camping site toward Nuniamo we found directly at the ocean deposits up to 30 meters high of clearly layered dark grey clay marl containing calcium concretions with numerous fossils. Later we also found mammoth bones in these clay cliffs. Such young sedimentations have been found on the American coast, especially at Kotzebue Sound, some time ago. It was quite interesting for us to find them also on the Asiatic side, because this confirms a considerable rise of the coast since diluvian times. As far as a quick superficial examination of the calcium concretions revealed, there was not much difference between the fossil fauna and the one existing at the bay now. By the way, we did not find other such deposits along the entire coast from East Cape to Plover Bay in spite of specific attention. Only once did we find some indistinct remnants of fossils in some gravel at Markus Bay, probably dating from the Paleozoic Era.

A Chukchi woman sitting on pebbles on the beach and sleeping through the night. Lütke's Harbor, Lawrence Bay, August 8, 1881.

Although the nearest Chukchi villages were about one German mile away, hardly a day went by when we did not receive guests. Most frequently, fishermen from Nuniamo came sometimes over land, sometimes by sea. Also from the opposite side, called "South Head" by the Americans, several boats crossed over. The people then usually stayed longer near our tent and spent the night under their turned-over boats or on the beach without any special protection in a sitting, bent-over position.

When they had put out their nets, which was quickly done, *dolce far niente* (in sweet idleness) they curiously watched our activities, always hungrily begging for kaukau. They rejected nothing edible. Bread and sugar in any form were their favorites. Often they asked for flour. They had learned to prepare from it together with seal blubber a porridgelike dish. In coffee and tea they seemed to taste only the sugar. They were no friends of pepper and salt, but they did not mind small amounts in their food. Often we saw especially women and children eat pieces of seaweed that was thrown by the ocean onto the beach. On the East Cape and at Indian Point they also collected ascidians, and various roots and leaves of *Polygonum bistortum* (pink plumes), *Oxyria reniformis* (sourgrass), and *Saxifraga rotundifolia*. They ate these either raw or prepared as a spinachlike vegetable. When we bought fish from them, they usually asked for the heads, which they ate raw on the spot without further preparation.

We always got along well with the people from Nuniamo, but were somewhat annoyed by their curiosity. Visits by the people from the south coast were less pleasant. Especially a family named Trooshin was notorious along the entire coast. Its chief, recognizable by a bullet wound in his cheek inflicted by an inhabitant from the Diomede Islands, made us fear violence. He was a young, strong man with a surly expression, who tried to provoke a wrestling match with me. He threw me by tripping me up and made such a wild face that for a long time we were in doubt about the true nature of his intentions. Arthur already thought of getting the pistols. This fellow lifted me high up, but after he held me up in the air for quite a while, he finally got tired and let me go again. Gradually he calmed down and shook hands with me. I thought it best to consider this matter as a joke. We afterwards incited the people to participate in some footraces, stone throws, and jumps. They exhibited unusual skill. The young man who had wrestled with me showed particular strength and agility.

Next to all Native settlements and also the deserted tent sites in our vicinity, we found a grassy place designated for athletic exercises. Especially strange is a kind of footrace on a well-trodden circular track, called *hash kumil,* where endurance and speed count. The winner is the one who stays on the track last.

Often the Natives were quite helpful. Arthur trained a fisherman to catch beetles for us. Several times he actually brought a cartridge shell filled with beetles and was very satisfied to receive small pieces of tobacco. He also carried water for us. The Natives were amazed at our way of blowing our noses with a handkerchief. They immediately demonstrated how they do it, naturally with their hand, the same way it is done by some people at home. In the afternoon of the second day a larger group of fishermen arrived, some of whom spent the entire night in our vicinity. The children were overjoyed when Frantzen allowed them to lie in our boat.

Monday, August 8

Our human contact was not limited to Natives for very long. On the third day after our arrival, a small trading schooner sailed into the harbor, Captain Ney's [Nye] *O.S. Fowler*. Even before they landed they shot their gun to salute us. We replied with two rifle shots. It was a small trading schooner of 35 tons. She left San Francisco on April 8 and sailed up the American coast trading all the way to Kotzebue Sound and was now on her return. During the night they had seen the *Legal Tender* near the entrance to the harbor. The captain and his second mate visited us in a boat and graciously offered to carry any mail or packages to San Francisco. He reported that the Arctic Sea was unusually free of ice this year, that the whalers had made a good catch, and that one of them already had returned with a full load. Captain Ney also had had good trading opportunities with the Natives, especially on the American side. He only regretted that his little vessel did not have more storage space for a larger supply of goods. Because of the small amount of snow during the winter, the Indians did not hunt as many fur animals as in previous years.

He received, however, a full load of walrus teeth and whalebone. Tobacco, flour, gunpowder, and lead were his main trading goods. We were highly interested in his news that he could sell goods and products from one coast to people on the other coast. He could make more profit selling sea otter and beaver skins cut into small strips on the Asiatic coast than in San Francisco, while he could find a good market in Alaska for boots made by Chukchi and American Eskimos. He also carried two kayaks from King Island which he planned to sell on the Aleutian Islands. He did not show much consideration for women, who frequently went aboard visiting ships, and for Natives in general, but they put up with it. He wanted to stay a few days to clean the whalebone and get fresh water. He of course asked us to visit him soon aboard ship.

After the captain left us, the Natives stayed for a while, but now we no longer let their presence disturb us. Soon they left, too, to go aboard the schooner.

All these visits had delayed our noon meal. Since we were not quite sure about the exact time of the day, we set up a sun dial. After lunch we went on a hike; I carried the gun, Arthur a folder for plants and a butterfly net. We climbed up the mountain in an easterly direction, but soon lost sight of each other and went our separate ways. Upon our return we put our collection in order. Among beetles we had mainly collected tiger beetles

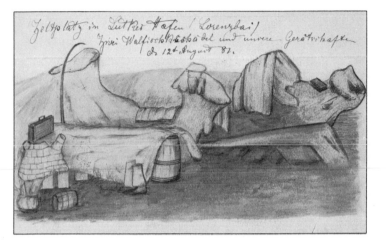

Campsite in Lütke's Harbor (Lawrence Bay).
This sketch shows two whale skulls and some of the authors'
belongings. August 12, 1881.

which can be found under rocks. A snail, *Succinea*, is very common on and under moss. Arthur returned with a number of very beautiful plants.

A few Natives, among them a lame man from Nuniamo, again were fishing nearby. They watched our work, but did not disturb us in any way. They gratefully accepted the remainder of our supper, cooked fish, tea, and bread. The evening is rather cool.

Tuesday, August 9

We rise at 4:30 A.M. Almost all the Natives had left during the night. Our breakfast consists of erbswurst (dried pea soup shaped like a sausage), hard bread, and coffee and tastes very good. Again it is rather cool early in the morning, but calm. At 7:30 A.M. the second mate from the schooner, a

German, arrives by boat on the beach to wash whalebone. He invites us to have lunch aboard ship.

Excerpt from a Letter by Aurel:

Lütke's Harbor, St. Lawrence Bay,
August 10 and 11, 1881

Dear Mother and Sisters,

We have been at this place for six days now. Today, Thursday, is cloudy and rainy, but we already had a few very nice days when it was a real pleasure to go for walks in the countryside. We do not have to worry about any danger. When not going hunting, we leave all weapons, even the pistol, in the tent and we hike wherever we please to go. The Natives are entirely good natured, although sometimes a little irritating because of their constant begging for kaukau. Wild animals, like bears, etc., do not exist here.

Unfortunately, there are not many animals here. Only one kind of marmot is everywhere. The flora, however, is abundant. Plenty of beautiful and interesting plants are found here, many more than we had expected. Many of them have faded already.

Much of our time is taken up by the contact with the Natives. Of course, they are curious to the highest degree and we had several visits, some of them very formal. We did not yet visit Nuniamo, the nearest larger village, but several people from there came here to fish. Some visitors canoe from great distances, because a trading schooner, that will transport our letters, is anchored in the harbor.

We have settled down quite comfortably. Frantzen takes care of the kitchen; we don't have to worry about it. In every other respect he assists us very well, whether we go hunting, preserve birds' skins, dredge[14] with the boat, or do anything else. Now as ever, we can only say that we could not have found a better helper.

One crate full of erbswurst which we had lugged along from Bremen and which often had been a nuisance during the trip, has provided us with many tasty meals. The day before yesterday the captain of the schooner invited us for lunch, which we gratefully accepted. The roasted wild duck he served tasted very delicious.

Either by boat or by land, we plan to go from here to the East Cape, and from there south to Plover Bay, where we expect to meet whalers who can take us back to San Francisco.

From the Natives we heard that two schooners were stranded near the East Cape; possibly the *Legal Tender* is one of them, which would not surprise me because of her poor seaworthiness. The crew would probably be unharmed, but our luggage might be damaged. By the way, we left on the ship a crate with various objects and collections gathered during the journey.

Journal by Aurel:

Wednesday, August 10

Late in the evening another boat with Natives arrived. They slept at night under their turned-over boat and were amazed at our activities the next morning. We first examined yesterday's catch in our dredging net. Then we asked a woman to sew a bag for us from a sealskin we had traded yesterday. Another woman allowed me to draw a sketch of her beautiful face and the tattoos on her arm. When the people's frequent begging for kaukau became annoying, we closed the tent and started pressing the plants. The Natives did not mind, but we missed our pliers, which apparently were stolen. The leader of these Natives, called Sonny, showed us a letter from a captain which stated that the lad was content as long as he was given kaukau. He demanded a similar written statement from us which we gladly gave to him.

Thursday, August 11

At five o'clock in the morning we get up and drink our coffee. A boy sells us some fish. Then the mate from the schooner arrives to wash whalebone. We invite him for breakfast, which he accepts with gratitude. We have fish soup, fish, coffee, and jelly. We write letters and take care of some birds and animals. In the afternoon Arthur and Frantzen take the boat to dredge near the island, while I stay here to complete work on the collections, which we want to send with the schooner.

Friday, August 12

The mate from the schooner arrives in the morning. We have coffee together and take a picture of the tent with the mate and a man from Nuniamo. Then the mate took along our letters and a crate with our completed collections.

Our old friends from Nuniamo brought us carved animals, which we bought for five needles each.

Then we again explored the vicinity. Our goal was a mountain north of here. From its summit we took bearings of several points in all directions. Not until 5:00 P.M. did we return to our tent, where Frantzen received us with soup ready to eat and coffee prepared for cooking.

Later we went to the clay cliffs, but lost each other. A thick fog rolled in. My glasses were covered with condensation. I could not see very well, so I soon returned. A little while later Arthur came back with some beautiful mammoth teeth.

On this day we again brought in a beautiful collection of plants. In this moist weather it is becoming more and more difficult to dry and store them properly. The old fisherman from Nuniamo spent the night under our tent using our boat cover. Instead of thanking us he probably stole the bacon which we had bought on the *Legal Tender*.

The fauna of this land was poor compared to the flora. When we walked through the meadow there was complete silence around us. Now and then one can hear the whistle of the pika who stands up on his hind feet in front of the entrance to his rocky cave and turns around to stare curiously at the strange intruder. Only this motion makes it possible to distinguish him from the rocks of identical color. Lower down on the grassy slopes and in the meadows is the home of the Siberian marmot. A loud "cheerch" makes us notice this rabbit-sized animal, which stands up as straight as an arrow. With every call he beats his short little tail on the ground, but disappears as fast as lightning into his subterranean burrow as soon as he perceives a suspicious movement.

Larger animals like foxes, bears, wolves, wild reindeer, or mountain sheep were never visible to us on our repeated hunting trips. Now and then they are found in these coastal areas, according to reports by Natives.

Even insects were not abundant, at least during this season. A few large and small butterflies animated the flowery slopes. A bumblebee could be found in any place full of blossoms; however, we were glad to miss the huge swarms of mosquitoes, the general pest of arctic lands. We remembered them only too well from our trip across the snowfields of Norwegian fjelds last year.

Although many plants reminded us of our excursions over Stormdalsfjeld and Dovrefjeld, we found an essential difference in the character of the scenery of the two northern mountain lands. Here we see the same rocky coasts descending vertically to the ocean with deeply cut gorges. Here, too, the interior is an undulating high plateau interrupted by wide valleys, but the smooth rock walls are missing, the rocks are broken up, sharp-edged boulders cover the mountain slopes everywhere. Although this high plateau shows a variety of lichen and mosses, it cannot be compared to the abundance of vegetation on Norwegian fjelds. One has to search for the few phanerogams or other vegetation growing here in the gaps between loose rocky gravel. The surface of the coastal rocks covered with dark stone lichen tires the eye with its uniform grey color. The "stony tundra" has the same appearance all along the coast from the East Cape to Plover Bay. Different kinds of rocks do not change the appearance. Perhaps in July there might be a friendlier view when the white, yellow, and red flowers of various plants offer some variety in at least a few places.

In deep and moist places we found the "moss tundra" which is quite different in character yet equally monotonous. It mostly consists of cushions of moss, sedge, and cottongrass. In between and on top of these, salmonberries and bog blueberries and, in dry places, crowberries grow abundantly. In late summer the fruit of these supply an important source of nourishment for the Native population. Here are also the proper soil conditions for dwarf birches and weedlike willows, less than a foot high, almost the only representatives of the tree and bush vegetation. A long walk across this tundra is as troublesome as a hike across the loose rocks. In both cases one has to pay close attention to the ground, otherwise one's foot might get stuck in a crack between rocks or in the deep holes between the cushions of sedge.

In addition, we have to consider a third kind of vegetation when we want to describe a true impression of the character of the scenery. It is the flora of the slopes, gorges, springs, and brooks. Here we find the abundance which delighted Chamisso when he visited [St.] Lawrence Bay. There the traits of the stony or lichen tundra are combined with those of the moss tundra, but many new plants are added, and the result is a colorful carpet of flowers which reminds us of our Alps. In well-protected valleys, often only a few feet from large patches of snow remaining there all summer, one meets such lush flora as is not expected in this land. We did not forget to note that we saw willow bushes about 1 meter high; we had not seen any bush or tree of such height in this land.

The marine flora was not as poor as the land flora, although it is characterized not by variety, but by massive existence of individual species. Almost entirely undeveloped is the beach fauna. Here we found almost no life except numerous gammarids whose voracity we used to our advantage for cleaning skeletons.

A more abundant animal life existed only at a depth of over 4 fathoms. From a depth of 8 to 15 fathoms our dredge nets usually brought up the best yield, particularly amphipods. Their strange form and coloration were so similar to that of their surroundings that they offered an excellent example of mimicry. In the lower depth of 20 to 25 fathoms we found a more uniform fauna, different at each level, of course.

Birds were not too numerous in the vicinity of our camp site in Lütke's Harbor. There were more on the low Lütke's Island, where we found large numbers of different kinds of ducks, a few golden plovers, but mostly the extraordinarily tame sandpipers and phalaropes. Flocks of dainty sea swallows and several larger and smaller gulls were constantly fishing nearby. Occasionally their fish were snatched away from them by a parasitic jaeger. Along the bank on the green meadows we met snow buntings and water wagtails, while at higher elevations the merry wheatear animated the bleak stone desert where pikas were the only other inhabitants. Next to our tent we rarely saw ravens; they are found in large numbers near the Chukchi villages. On the rocky shore of the bay cormorants and puffins lived. In the bay we saw, among the larger mammals, a whale now and then, seals more frequently.

Monday, August 15

We get up at 4:00 A.M. The wind of the previous day diminished, the rain stopped. It is a beautiful, though cold, morning. We immediately take part of our things out to dry.

Arthur and Frantzen go by boat to Nuniamo to visit the Natives in their own *yarangas,* [or dwellings]. Unfortunately, it was impossible to land because of the extremely strong surf. They could only tell from the boat that the village had thirteen, which are built on a grassy area steeply sloping down to the ocean. According to our information, the population may be sixty to eighty souls.

Since there were no Natives near our tent, I could preserve some of the collected specimens in alcohol. Most carefully we had to keep our alcohol supply from the Natives' eyes and noses. The adulteration with tartar emetic would not prevent them from drinking it. This precaution was justified, as proven by repeated requests for rum. Fortunately, this year they apparently did not receive as much rum as previously. Reports unanimously agree that the ruinous effects of alcohol consumption by Natives is unimaginable. For a few gulps of brandy they give away anything. They will give away their good furs, on which they are so dependent for protection during the extreme cold of the winter. While drunk they are so irresponsible that the women take away their husbands' knives in order to prevent great tragedies. Quite a few murders during the last several years along this coast were caused by alcohol. In those cases where white people were the victims, the whites mostly were at fault. In some places alcoholism resulted in insufficient provision of an adequate food supply. Both the American and Russian governments strictly prohibit all trade in alcohol. In spite of this, brandy of the worst quality was supplied by the barrel in former years, especially by traders from Honolulu.

Indirectly, the brandy contributed to a decrease in population. Another reason for this reduction is the hunting of whales and walrus along this coast. While a few years ago the entire Bering Strait and parts of the Arctic Ocean were full of walrus, now only a few are found there. The Natives, therefore, rarely succeed in catching whales or walruses. They more and more depend on the whalers, often going with them to the northern Arctic Ocean. At the end of the season, mostly September, they are dropped off at [St.] Lawrence Bay or Plover Bay.

The Russian clipper, sailing here this year, is also supposed to prevent the trade of alcohol. In any case, these efforts for the protection of the Natives are to be recommended. Of course, the most effective means would be the restriction and regulation of whale and walrus fishing to return the former abundance of the animals to these coasts.

When I finished my work in the tent, I walked to the beach to collect some specimens thrown up by the storm. There I spotted a steamship steering into [St.] Lawrence Bay. It was a Russian warship, the *Strelok*. Shortly thereafter I watched through the field glass that our sailboat returned and stopped at the steamer. We learned that the *Strelok* wanted to wait here in order to deliver livestock it transported for the *Rodgers*. Then both ships wanted to sail to the Arctic together, but planned to return by the end of this month. Captain de Livron, who was informed about our planned journey by his government (through gracious intervention of the Imperial Foreign Office in Berlin), offered us all possible assistance in our activities. On the same day he visited us in our tent and invited us aboard ship for the evening. Not until 1:00 A.M. did we return ashore, accompanied by a number of officers. We conversed in German and English with the officers; most of the crew spoke Russian only. For the following day, in case of good weather, a trip by steam-powered small boat to the interior of the bay was planned, and we were kindly invited to participate. Lt. Beklemishoff [Beklemishov], who was in charge of it, had done a detailed survey of Plover Bay a few days ago. There he had found that the interior was unusually deep, with up to 80 fathoms and more measured in some places.

Tuesday, August 16

When we woke up at 5:00 A.M., the Chukchi who had stayed in our vicinity with two boats again approached our tent. We had to resist their importunities energetically. As agreed upon, the *Strelok* also hoisted the German flag. Around 7:00 A.M. the little steamboat picked us up. We left our tent and all our belongings under the care of our trusted sailor Frantzen.

Under a clear sky we now went to the interior of the bay. Constant soundings showed comparatively shallow depths, decreasing toward the interior; only in a few places did the depth reach 30 fathoms. The surface temperature of the water was 5°C at 8:00 A.M.; the temperature of the air was the same.

First we landed at a sandy point on the northern bank. While Lt. Beklemishoff took some bearings, we examined the flora, which here, too, was extremely sparse. Numerous shells were evidence that Natives had eaten shellfish.

The second time we landed on one of the two little rocky islands in the interior of the bay. Here we found in a comparatively small space a most lush and varied flora. Animals were also more abundant here than in any other place of the bay. All this, together with the beautiful weather and the splendid view of the magnificent mountain scenery south and west with its partly regular, partly wildly broken up mountains and the wide green valleys in the foreground, made this part of the trip one of the most enjoyable.

During the continuation of our trip the weather worsened; it became windy and rainy. After passing a sandbar, we went into the last inlet of the bay, but went aground in 2 to 3 feet of water, where older maps had indicated a depth of 4 to 5 fathoms. All attempts at getting the boat afloat were in vain. Several times the sailors stepped into the cold water, where the surface temperature was still 9°C. When finally the tide went out and the water level was even lower, we had to resign ourselves to spending a rainy night in uncomfortable positions in the boat, instead of pitching a tent on land as we had hoped to do. Crouched together, we slept under a canvas roof. One officer, dressed in his fur, spent the entire night on deck, unsuccessfully trying to get us afloat even at high tide.

Wednesday, August 17

The next morning we were still in the same place, but wind and rain had lessened, and a beautiful day seemed to be ahead of us. Strengthened by tea and breakfast, we decided to wade ashore during low tide. After tying our rubber boots above our thighs and taking bag and gun, we went into the water, which was deep in only a few places. With a bamboo pole we sounded the bottom. Right at the beginning we passed through a greater depth, the result of the boat screw. For long stretches we could walk on exposed land. In all, this hike took about half an hour and our feet became completely wet. On shore a rich flora compensated us for our efforts. Several kinds of willows formed real bushes. Protected by them, larkspur, primula, and wintergreen (pyrola) dared raise their leaves higher than usual. The steep rocky slopes were almost entirely covered by the unusually large leaves of the ivylike netvein dwarf willow. We walked around the outermost corner of the bay and reached a river with plenty of water. We waded up to our knees through the many arms at its mouth. The water was extremely clear, but showed not the slightest sign of animal life.

After hiking for several hours along the southern shore, we were picked up around noon by the boat, which was afloat again, and returned to Lütke's Harbor. Here we found everything in good order. Two Chukchi boys had tried to steal lead, but Frantzen had energetically interfered, supported by the presence of the Russian warship. They returned everything and were also punished by the older Natives.

Thursday, August 18

In the morning the *Rodgers* arrived in the harbor. It is a ship sent by the American government to search for the missing *Jeanette,* which had gone out on an expedition. Soon thereafter the captain of the *Strelok* and his first mate arrived in a boat. They brought us a can of butter and a Russian flag, which was to protect our tent. At the same time we were invited to go aboard the *Strelok* that afternoon. We had previously gratefully accepted Captain de Livron's offer to take us to the East Cape.[15] We quickly packed our luggage and boarded the Russian ship in the evening. The captain immediately invited us to have supper in his cabin. Then we went to the officers' lounge where we also met Captain Berry of the *Rodgers* and several of his officers. Here, we again could enjoy the long-missed luxury of a friendly social gathering.

Friday, August 19

We did not get up until 8:00 A.M. and had morning coffee. Since departure was prevented by thick fog, we used the time to write a few letters and had an officer give us a tour of the ship and her equipment.

At twelve o'clock breakfast was served, and the main meal at 6:00 P.M. Then we took a boat to visit the *Rodgers*, until an officer of the Russian ship came to take us back. The captain wanted to leave at 9:30 P.M. because the fog had lifted. Captain Berry also decided to leave immediately, so both ships lifted anchor at about 9:00 P.M. and sailed out of the bay, the *Strelok* under steam, the *Rodgers* under sail. We soon went to sleep.

Our stay at [St.] Lawrence Bay had lasted almost two weeks. In spite of the advanced season, we gained a fairly complete picture of the coastal flora. We were less satisfied with the results of our zoological collections. The number of settlers on [St.] Lawrence Bay was very small. The decrease in population, compared to former reports, was visible everywhere. Remnants of former settlements, ovals built of large rocks as the foundations of yarangas, remnants of graves, antlers and bones of reindeer were found by us in various places, also close to our camp site. The interior of the bay was almost entirely unsettled.

We found a considerable number of old graves on the stony tundra. The type of funeral is very simple. The body is placed on the stony ground and surrounded by an oval of large rocks. The men are given spears, bows, and arrows, and the women get kitchen tools. Ravens and dogs, perhaps also foxes and wolves, devour the earthly remains to such an extent that even in younger graves only a few scattered bones and more or less damaged skulls can be found. Only a few of the tools still were to be found.

The weather during our stay at [St.] Lawrence Bay was not as unfavorable as we had expected, although we had only two beautiful clear days during the entire time. Frequently there was fog, almost every morning and evening. On six days it rained, but only on August 14 did it rain the entire day with a strong easterly wind and a very low barometer. Mostly we had light southerly winds. The temperature of the air was rather constant; during the day it generally ranged between 6°and 8°C. The observed extremes were 9.8°C on August 7 at 8:00 A.M. and 5°C on August 16 at 8:00 A.M.

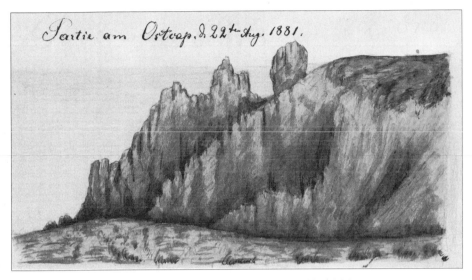

Scenery on the East Cape. August 22, 1881.

Saturday, August 20

Early in the morning we were awakened with the news that the East Cape was in sight. Like walls of a fortress, the towering rocks of the eastern end of the Old World rise up steeply from the ocean. It was a beautiful clear day, but a biting wind blew against us and caused strong waves on the northerly current. The *Rodgers* had stayed back quite a way, since she was slowed down by the head winds.

It took quite a long time before our boat could be lowered. In the meantime, we had breakfast and chatted. As soon as we had passed the East Cape and steered a westerly course, the wind and current diminished. Around noon we left the ship where we had received such friendly hospitality. Upon our departure, the commander handed us a Russian flag as a symbol of the protection he wanted to bestow on our endeavors.

Soon the *Strelok* and the following *Rodgers* disappeared from sight, while we turned our boat toward shore about 8 miles away. In most beautiful weather and a light wind we sailed toward the place where the northern rocky bluffs of the East Cape change over into flat land, and the map indicates the settlement of Uedle. Here, we also hoped to find a suitable landing site. At that time, neither American nor Russian maps showed us a clear picture of the situation; their drawings were inaccurate and not conforming. Our assumption proved correct when, after a long trip, we distinguished huts on the beach resembling molehills.

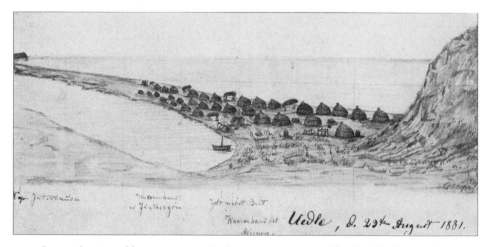

Several rows of huts are stretched out on a tongue of land with the wooden warehouse of Jinkérgin on the left and that of Akenen on the right. In the center are the authors' tent and boat.
On the extreme left is Cape Intschauin [Inchoun].
Uedle, August 23, 1881.

Soon thereafter, we saw two boats approaching us. In the meantime, the wind had died down and we had to use our oars. We, therefore, accepted the people's assistance to row us to the shore still quite some distance away, which they gladly did for a few pieces of tobacco.

The boats, however, had not come out to sea because of us. Two whales surfacing in our vicinity from time to time had attracted the Natives, and we had a chance to observe the hunt. With our consent, the people left us to participate in the hunt. From several sides they paddled as quickly as possible to the place where the whale last surfaced. Every time it came up, they immediately stopped to avoid any kind of noise. The harpooner stands in the bow of the boat. His weapon seems somewhat unsuited for hunting such a giant animal, especially when compared with the heavy iron harpoon of white whalers. The Native, however, would not think of tying his boat to the whale. When his throw succeeds, only the point, made of iron and ivory, which detaches from the wooden shaft, stays in the skin. Tied to it with a long rope of cut up walrus skin are one or several air-filled seal sacks. These make it difficult for the hit animal to submerge, and show the pursuers the way until they have a chance for a second and third throw and finally the death blow.

This time the hunt was unsuccessful, since the whales swam farther and farther away. Now the boats came back to us. After the usual questions of "Where from?" and "Where to?" were answered as well as possible, an understanding was quickly reached with the magic word *chalupa* (tobacco). Five young people climbed into our boat and now a race began to the still distant shore. Our crew, gayly cheering each other, proved that they could handle the heavy oars of a whaling boat as skillfully as the short paddles of their light leather boats.

During hunting season, almost all of them had been aboard a whaler, as they proudly told us, naming captain and ship.

Soon we were close to the village and saw on the beach a group of men, women, and children, who waited for our landing. A strong surf, however, made this a risk which could easily lead to the loss of our heavily laden boat. Upon the Natives' suggestion, we tried to take ashore the largest part of our luggage in their light leather canoes. In order not to lose sight of our belongings, we each climbed into one of these. The landing of these boats turned into a most interesting episode for us. The boat rises and sinks with the heavy swell like a feather. The roar of the surf and the noise of the rocks rolling forward and backward drown the loud calls of the men. Then, just as one especially high wave almost tossed the boat on the beach, a man in the bow throws a blown-up seal sack tied to a long rope into the breaker, which takes it far up onto the flat shore. At the same time the crew paddles with all its might backward to withdraw the boat from the dangerously close beach. The stranded sack is quickly grabbed by the people who waited there, and pulled higher up. Young and old, about fifteen to twenty people, grasp the rope and during the next favorable breaker, at a given

61

signal in cooperation with the paddlers, they pull the boat ashore. At the same moment the crew jumps out and carries the boat higher up away from the next breaker. Not every landing is that perfect.

We, too, were caught by a second unexpected breaker which did not seriously harm us. It just soaked our luggage and filled one of my boots with water.

So, we finally landed safely, but our boat with Frantzen and part of our belongings was still out on the water. Based on the experience we had just had, we decided not to land our boat in the same way. The thin wooden hull would hardly stand up against the powerful surf as the flexible leather hulls of the *atcuats* did. We had learned that there was a lagoon behind the village with its entrance farther west, so we signaled Frantzen to take that way and persuaded some people, not without difficulty, to take the trip with him.

Not without apprehension did we watch our boat leave. We learned that it might not arrive until night. From several utterances by the Natives, we concluded that the entrance to the lagoon was not without danger. On the other hand, the Natives' behavior seemed to reassure us about our situation. Rather unabashedly they rummaged through our things, and several of the young men looked at and examined our guns and rifles, but everything was carefully replaced. The eagerness with which young and old Natives helped carry our luggage was certainly not caused by the prospect of reward alone.

An old, toothless man, called Akenen, was pointed out to us as the chief of the village. To him and one of his relatives, named Atelen, who spoke English quite well, we explained our intention to spend a few days with them. Thereupon, Akenen assured us that none of our things would be stolen, and that we could find shelter in his house, an offer gladly accepted by us under the existing circumstances.

From the ocean we had earlier noticed among all the huts one wooden house built in European style. Akenen now led us to the other side of the beach wall to two similar houses, solidly constructed from beams and boards with lockable doors. After they made room for us in the larger one, they carried all our things into this house, apparently a warehouse. Now we tried as well as possible to get some work done with all the people here. That was not easy. Everybody who could do so squeezed into the room, so that we were prevented from any free movement. Outside there was an equally large crowd, curiously watching our activities and longingly waiting for a chance to get close to us. Convinced that the patience of these

This portrait is a frontal view of Atelen whose American
name is Shark. Uedle, August 22, 1881.

good people would not tire too soon, we finally took up our hunting bag and rifle. After Akenen drove out all visitors and locked the house, we hiked to the nearest hills, accompanied only by Atelen and a few boys, to orient ourselves about the position of Uedle. The weather was splendid. We did not catch any of the numerous ducks, since they were extremely timid. The villagers killed several with their slings, after they irritated a flock flying from the lagoon with whistling and screaming so that some of them flew very low. Upon our return we built a wood fire and cooked some pea soup. Then the people prepared a good soft bed for us with reindeer skins on which we soon enjoyed a healthy sleep after the last spectators, who had again crowded in, left.

Frantzen did not arrive with the boat until after midnight. On the entire stretch the people had to row strenuously. The entrance to the lagoon had caused especially great effort because of the existing strong current. During the trip he had become very cold; now he lay down and soon got warm.

Sunday, August 21

We slept well the remainder of the night. Not until seven o'clock, when the Natives started to move about, did we get up. Not far from the wooden house we now pitched our tent and carried all our things into it. Since

Frantzen could manage unpacking everything himself, we made use of the good weather and, accompanied by a young man and a boy from Uedle, we hiked toward the bluffs, perhaps to reach the East Cape. At first we went along the beach, until bluffs rising directly from the ocean stopped us. Now we climbed up a narrow ravine to the high plateau to continue our hike there. The flora here was the same as at [St.] Lawrence Bay, only scarcer and a little more advanced. In vain we looked for strange species which we had hoped to find here, where the Old and the New World are separated by only a narrow arm of the ocean. We collected mostly lichen and mosses.

Scenery with rocks on East Cape. August 22, 1881.

The bulk of the rock was a light syenite, while the steep rocks on the shore were formed by beautifully banded and often magnificently folded siliceous slate. Three lemmings were shot, one of them by our Chukchi companion to whom I had loaned my rifle while I sketched some rocks.

When the weather turned windy and rainy, we decided to discontinue our hike since we no longer had a clear overview. We climbed one more elevation and then returned across the gravel-covered slope. The view from the high plateau gave us a better understanding of the situation than what we had learned from all maps. The rocky massif of the East Cape almost forms an island. Only very flat land, cut up everywhere by lagoons, connects the Cape with the mainland. One can almost see one continuous stretch of water from the Bering Sea to the Polar Sea. A long narrow tongue of land stretches from the East Cape almost to Cape Intschauin [Inchoun].

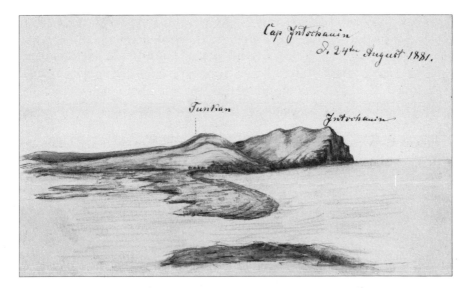

The view from East Cape toward northwest shows the settlement of Tunkan in the center and Cape Intschauin on the right. August 24, 1881.

On it are the two villages, Uedle on its eastern end and Tunkan on its western end. The wide lagoon, which is separated from the ocean by this narrow tongue of land, is connected with the Polar Sea at only one small cut through the tongue of land.

During our descent on the gravel, we passed a grave site very similar to the one described at [St.] Lawrence Bay. This one seemed to be still in use; many bones and newer skulls were seen here. Our companion told us that many people died of starvation last winter; he, too, had lost a child. Again we saw kitchen tools next to women's graves, mostly clay pots and wooden dishes, but also a few cans that had been converted to cooking pots. Next to the men's graves were, in addition to spears, bows, and arrows, also sleds. The Natives did not display any special awe of the grave sites, but they were afraid to touch the bones and skulls. When Frantzen once brought two carved wooden figures he had found near the graves, they declared that "not good," so that we thought it prudent to have him return them to the same place.

Upon our return, we found the tent full of people from Uedle, Frantzen in their midst. He had not been able to keep them off. When we told them that there was not enough space, only the younger ones left. During our three-day stay in Uedle we had to get used to the fact that we were constantly surrounded by large crowds. On the one hand this had the advantage that we could collect all kinds of valuable information (language studies, local geography, etc.), but on the other hand these crowds greatly impeded our work. During the entire time we could not touch our supply of alcohol and we were unable to use our instruments with such large crowds present.

Finally the weather became very unpleasant with strong wind and rain. With the Natives' assistance Frantzen pushed the boat into the water and anchored it, but the wind drove it onto the land and it had to be anchored again, this time more securely. For their efforts the adults received some tobacco, the boys some sugar. Then we went to bed early, after we had politely removed all people from the tent.

Monday, August 22

We did not get up until seven o'clock. Through the entire night it had been quite stormy, and rain and wind continued during the morning, so we limited our activities to studies of the village and its people. Led by Atelen, who served as our interpreter, we visited the individual yarangas, distributing tobacco to the men and sugar and needles to the women and children. In twenty-eight huts we asked for the number of inhabitants and their sex. There were seventy-nine male and eighty-seven female individuals, 166 persons altogether. Most men, however, were away hunting seals. Then we counted another fourteen yarangas with a population given as eighty-three, which we did not visit because we had run out of sugar and needles. In general, the women and children were quite pleased with our visit, also a few men, but they were somewhat worried about our written notes. Our companion explained to us that some of the men were afraid Russian warships might come and kill them.

The construction of the huts was the same everywhere; they differed only in size. In all huts the entrance was toward the west. Most of them were almost in a straight row, immediately behind the stone wall on top of the tongue of land, and the others were scattered on the meadows toward the lagoon. Large boulders, whale bones, and driftwood formed a kind of foundation for each hut. Up to a height of about $1^1/_3$ meters the walls rise vertically from the ground. There the oblique, cone-shaped roof begins, its ridge positioned toward the first third near the entrance. When one has passed through the narrow entrance in bent-over position, one enters first

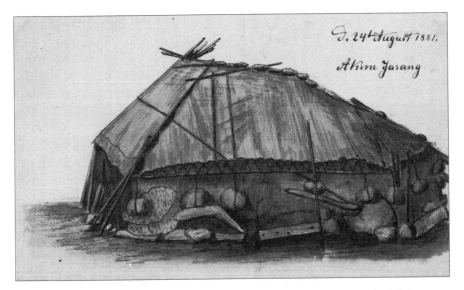

Akenen's yaranga. The vertical base wall of skins is reinforced with large boulders, whale bones, and driftwood. The ridge of the oblique cone-shaped roof rises toward the entrance of the hut. August 24, 1881 .

the larger room, the living area of the family. Here a fire is built, and the people spend most of their time sitting on animal skins.

The main support of the building is a strong wooden pole, from arm to thigh thickness, or a whale rib reaching from the middle of the living room to the ridge of the roof. Five to six weaker poles, placed around the rib obliquely against the roof, serve as additional support. A complicated system of wooden poles and whale bones completes the skeleton of the roof and walls. It is covered by tightly stretched walrus skins, held in place by leather straps or heavy stones. In winter another tent of reindeer skins is pitched inside, serving then as living room.

In the center of the back room is a square enclosure about 1¹/₂ meters high, the family bedroom, the walls of which are thickly hung with reindeer skins. Under a large fur, faces of old women, children, or sick people peep out. The women's upper bodies were half nude.

In severe cold the people do not put their arms into their sleeves. A conversation in Plover Bay illustrated how the Chukchi are used to the cold climate. A Chukchi lived there who had been taken to New York by the captain of a whaler. He resolutely declined an invitation to go back there with the remark that he never again wanted to live in such a hot summer which made people sick.

In general, the men in Uedle are of medium size, but strong and well built. Protruding cheek bones, slightly narrow slit eyes, and a broad, flat nose were characteristic features here, too. In hairdo, tattoos, and clothing, we did not see any significant difference from that which we observed at [St.] Lawrence Bay.

The two most influential people were Akenen and Jinkérgin. Both owned large wooden houses and well-furnished yarangas. They lived in the

Both men are shown in frontal view portraits. Akenen on the left
wears a visor (kittelschukuk). Jinkérgin is on the right.
Uedle, August 22, 1881.

latter, whereas the houses were used as warehouses. Unfortunately, we could not get any definite information about their construction, but assumed their origin is due to an American trading company. In these warehouses we saw, in addition to fox furs, walrus teeth, and whalebone for trade with white men, raw walrus and seal skins for their own use, as well as a large number of Native products like fish and seal nets; sleds and dog harnesses; whips, bows and arrows; harpoons, and snowshoes. But there also were the products of foreigners: boxes with tobacco; barrels of flour; muskets, powder and lead, cloth, axes, saws, and other tools. As far as we could see, all these things were made in America.

Less wealthy was Atelen, whose services as guide and interpreter we had used several times. In his house the captain of a stranded whaler, whose name was Barker, spent the winter of 1870.

The authority which these above-mentioned men obviously exercise is probably due to their larger property. The "chief" in every community is the richest man, a "big man," as he is called by the Americans and the English-speaking Natives.

Nowhere did we find traces of a political community; only the head of the family exercises power over its members. Old traditional customs, however, without definite norms, rule the activities of the village population. We could trust the chiefs in the distribution of our gifts as reward for services rendered to us. Each single one received his share according to merit and dignity. Of course, they kept the lion's share for themselves. No opposition was heard; we actually never observed any fight or quarrel. According to our observation, they also conscientiously respect each other's property. The use of lockable warehouses and cabinets, as we have seen often, however, does not speak of too much trust and honesty among the Natives.

One question of special interest to us was the relationship of Coastal Chukchi to the Reindeer Chukchi. Atelen, whom we invited into our tent to take some notes, said, "Every reindeer man mi savi, Diomede man and [St.] Lawrence Island man non savi." Later investigations also yielded the identical result. Coastal and Reindeer Chukchis speak the same language; in all probability only different customs separate the two. The older references about a fishing tribe entirely different from the Chukchis are correct, since there is indeed a strange tribe of people on the Diomede Islands and in a settlement opposite from these on the East Cape, called Nuokan, which probably has an American origin. Furthermore, a not too numerous fishing tribe with entirely different language is settled on the southern coast from Cape Chaplin (Indian Point) toward the west in the midst of the Chukchi settlements.

Differences between Reindeer and Coastal Chukchis relate to their clothing and tools, which, of course, depend on their differing life styles. These differences, however, are not evident within families. A few have a brother among the Reindeer Chukchi. Jinkergin, who owns a yaranga and a big warehouse in Uedle, has a sizeable reindeer herd on the southwestern side of the lagoon. Later we met him during our stay in Tunkan, as leader of a canoe going out to hunt walrus at Cape Inchanin.

69

From Cape Serdtse in the northwest to Indian Point in the south, the coast was more or less known to individual people from Uedle. Seldom do they take such long trips in their boats in the summertime; they rarely go south beyond [St.] Lawrence Bay. Longer journeys are taken by reindeer sled or dog sled during the winter, sometimes to the Russians at the Kolyma. They told us that the Russians live in wooden houses. The trip there is said to take three months.

The inhabitants of Uedle were not aware of being part of Russia, while in [St.] Lawrence Bay and later also in Plover Bay the people who considered us Russian often introduced themselves as Russians. Atelen showed us Russian instructions, printed in the English language, telling Americans that the hunting of whales and walruses near the coast is prohibited. Not without bitterness, he also said that the captains to whom he had shown this letter had laughed at him. Only international agreements might perhaps prevent the complete extermination of the walrus and whale.

It was already mentioned that the Chukchi frequently go with the American whalers to the Polar Sea in the spring. They are useful and cheap labor, for the Chukchi does not value his physical services, as long as he gets enough to eat. In his joy over his scarce wages in the form of tobacco, knives, and other things, he forgets that he has lost the entire summer during which time he should have provided for the coming winter.

On the other hand, contact with the Americans makes it easy for the coastal Natives to trade their whalebone, their walrus teeth, and their furs for better weapons, hunting gear, and tools. Unfortunately, they often lose this advantage when the unscrupulous trader offers illegal rum.

Still today, the main food of the population is the meat of whale, walrus, and seal. Fish (salmon and cod) are plentiful only in a few places. Among birds there are mostly flocks of ducks, the small sandpipers, and grey geese. Young and old people most zealously hunt ducks. In Uedle almost everyone carries a duck sling. It consists of five to seven pieces of bone connected by narrow leather cords. When not in use, the sling is wound around the head so that the large balls dangle in the center of the forehead and the cords are covered by hair. We observed this fashion only on the East Cape.

In addition to the duck sling, every boy and man carries a stone-sling on his belt, which is identical to those used by our German boys. Only the throw is completely different, because it and also the duck sling are swung horizontally, not vertically.

Although the use of guns is becoming more common everywhere, in Uedle bows and arrows are still very much in use for the hunt of smaller animals. The arrowheads, mostly made of bone and ivory, are shaped differently according to their purpose. Remarkable are the multipointed duck arrows, which are tied to a long cord made of fish bone. When bending the bow, the arrow is held not between thumb and index finger, but between index and middle fingers. When the weather permitted, we saw the women and children go to the nearby mountain meadows to collect leaves and roots of various plants, partly for immediate needs, partly as provisions for the winter. They are eaten raw with seal oil or cooked in water to a spinachlike consistency. We tried it ourselves and found this dish not bad at all.

Only the head of a Uedle man identified as Poiogidlan is visible, as he looks through the door into the interior of the tent. The Chukchi name of his cap is kaidlin. *Uedle, August 23, 1881.*

Tuesday, August 23

At nine o'clock in the morning the barometer reads 739.8 millimeters of mercury, the temperature 12°C. The gale is even stronger than yesterday. Last night our tent partly collapsed. That, however, was mostly due to the curiosity of the people who had pushed against the entrance. The walls of the tent had several holes from beating against the wooden boxes and the poles repeatedly had to be hammered down. The Natives came very late and only a few entered our tent to trade a few things. Toward evening when the rain subsided somewhat and we dared go out for a walk, the force of the wind was so strong that it took all our strength to fight against it. Only the bluffs along the ocean offered some protection. Numerous sandpipers had fled to here and from this shelter we could leisurely watch the spectacular drama of the turbulent sea.

Wednesday, August 24

During the night the storm ceased entirely. Around 4:30 A.M. we got up, had coffee, and prepared for our departure. A longer stay in Uedle might have been important for better acquaintance with the people, but we had to consider the advanced season and the many tasks still to be accomplished in addition to a long boat journey; therefore, we could no longer postpone our return. We bought several Native tools and passed out gifts to those who eagerly helped us load our luggage. Then the anchor was weighed and the course was set first toward the west and the narrow passage to the ocean.

We had wanted to take Atelen along to [St.] Lawrence Bay, and yesterday he was willing to accompany us. At the last moment he changed his mind and nobody else could be found, so that we had to go alone. Perhaps the people were held back by the uncertain weather or perhaps by the fact that whalers were just returning with a good catch. The four approaching whalers sailing quickly with a favorable wind offered a picturesque sight. Each one carried two sails neatly sewn together with blue and white calico, a smaller one in the shape of a rectangle above the larger, more square-shaped mainsail. The latter was held in this position by two poles slanted forward from the gunwales of the ship.

So, we departed alone. We had to tack against the adverse wind in the lagoon and, therefore, reached the passage after a lengthy trip. In order to orient ourselves about tide conditions we had to land. We found a strong current coming toward us, obviously too powerful for our strength. We had no choice but to wait for the tide to go out.

In the meantime a boat had arrived from the other side of the lagoon. The people in it were willing to row us through the now much weaker current for a few pieces of tobacco. The people were friendly and offered us a few small things in exchange for tobacco. Now we had to cross only two high waves and reached the open sea safely, although these people, who are accustomed to small paddles, did not quite know how to handle the big oars. In a light southwest breeze and beautiful clear weather we continued our journey, following the coast in an easterly direction. At four o'clock in the afternoon the temperature of the air was 6°C, the surface of the water was around 4.5°C. As soon as we had passed Uedle again and had the steep rocky coast of the East Cape to our right, the wind disappeared entirely so that by rowing we made only little progress. The sun had already set when we saw a boat approach us from the coast. They were people from Nuokan who had gone out hunting walrus. They were easily persuaded to row us to their village, but after a short while they suddenly left us with the promise, as far as we understood, to return with a larger boat and more crew. Because we were not familiar with the coastal water, and the existing maps were entirely useless, we considered it advisable not to continue our journey in the dark. We therefore dropped anchor near the shore and tried to rest a little as well as possible under the dropped sail. The perceptible cold of the starlit night, however, kept us awake.

Thursday, August 25

Before dawn Frantzen, also frozen, made some coffee. We tried to tack against a fresh southeasterly wind, at first successfully. But as the wind grew stronger and the high tide going north in the Bering Strait prevented us from any gain, and the boat took in water several times, we, unfortunately, had to return. There was no safe landing site nearby, neither at the steep bluffs, nor at the adjacent narrow tongue of land. We therefore had to continue our forced return into the lagoon. Now, of course, with the strong wind we could quickly cover the 10 to 12 nautical miles to the entrance and reached it around eleven o'clock. Quite a long time was required to pass the entrance. The current was now going out to sea and was so strong that we could hardly hope to overcome it, but an attempt was made. We rowed close to the beach, where we convinced ourselves that with rowing alone we could not force our way any farther. After we had dropped the anchor, Frantzen jumped out of the boat onto land with a rope to pull the boat. His strength, however, was insufficient, so I also jumped out, and with tremendous combined effort and strength we succeeded to get through while Arthur steered. Of course, our things were completely soaked and my high rubber boots filled with water.

It was two o'clock in the afternoon when we finally pitched our tent on the pebbly beach and were soon again comfortably established. Our wet clothes and collections had to be dried and we cooked something warm to eat. In the meantime, the people of Tunkan had arrived. They helped us and were friendly, but annoyed us with too much begging for tobacco. In the evening we went on a short hunting trip, talked with the people, and went to bed early.

Friday, August 26

In order to make our boat more seaworthy, Frantzen reduced the sail and shortened the boom. Soon we had more visitors from Tunkan. For our kitchen we were able to trade some fish and reindeer meat, also a few duck slings and raw carved ivory for our ethnological collection, but the people seemed to be very poor. For small presents they carried drinking water and large amounts of driftwood, which was plentiful here. Then we started a mighty fire near our tent, where we dried our boots, socks, pressed plant folder, etc. A young man from Uedle named Hidlako wished to accompany us in exchange for his services. He had rowed our boat with Frantzen into the lagoon on the day of our arrival. Since he seemed to be reliable and spoke fair English, we gladly accepted his offer. He helped a little with cooking and got his portion, but was rather lazy.

Around noon Arthur took a hike to Tunkan, about 2 to 3 miles away, accompanied by most of the people who had come from there. The village is much less important than Uedle; it has forty to fifty people in ten huts. Women and children were occupied all day with the gathering of driftwood. In vain we were looking for characteristic signs which could have given us some information about the origin of the wood. During the course of the day, the weather had improved remarkably. For a short while there was some fog in the afternoon, but then we had a beautiful evening. We took Hidlako into our tent.

Saturday, August 27

In the morning we again started our voyage in a light southerly wind. This time the exit from the lagoon to the open sea succeeded without difficulty. The current was hardly noticeable. When we passed Uedle, Hidlako went ashore for a moment to get a few things for the voyage in a round bag. We had asked him to persuade one of his countrymen to come along on the voyage, but he returned alone. Apparently he was unwilling to share the expected reward with someone else.

The continuation of our trip along the steep coast gave us the best opportunity to get a correct picture of the East Cape. Again it was a beautiful, warm day. In complete calm we rowed close to the shore next to

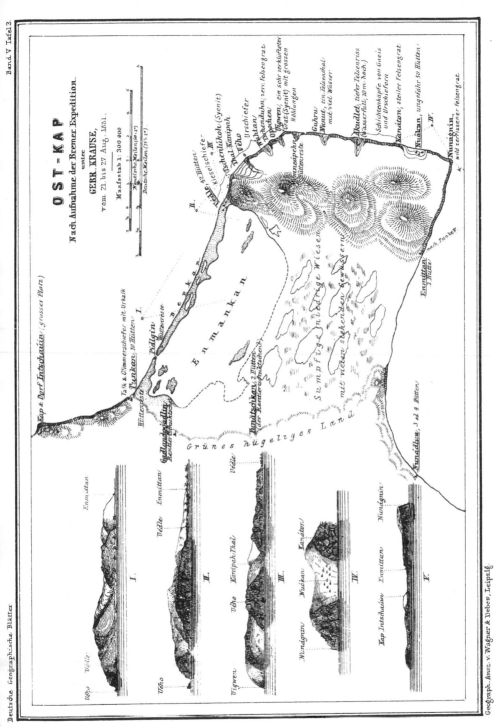

Map of the East Cape

the foaming surf. A rich variety of animals exists on this coast. Every rocky ridge was occupied by numerous sea gulls, auks, and cormorants, and from the waves here and there the mighty head of a walrus or the wide back of a whale surfaced. This coast was well known to Hidlako, for here the people of Uedle and Nuokan go to hunt walrus. He had a special name for each mountain peak, each deep-cut valley, and each single rock.

In order to produce the map of the East Cape, we had already taken bearings from land (Pidlgin and Uedle) with the diopter compass. While traveling by boat in perfectly clear weather, the direction of the coast from Tschenlukoh to Nunagnin was determined by taking bearings from the boat and these specifications were complemented by profiles I through V on the map of the East Cape. The distance given for individual points is based on the estimate of the boat's speed in measured time intervals.

Jagged ridges, bare slopes of crumbled syenite, steep walls with variously shaped and banded siliceous slate, in between here a green valley with a tumbling brook full of water, there a deep gorge with a thundering waterfall, these were the individual pictures in the manifold panorama unfolding before us. With its broad front running almost from north to south, the Cape is facing east. Three mighty mountain masses divided by green valleys form the front. In the most southerly valley is the village Nuokan, the most important of all the settlements on the Chukchi Peninsula known to us. We counted about fifty huts very similar in their construction to those of Uedle, though they are located not so close to the beach but about 20 to 30 meters above sea level. A large number of leather boats with their keels turned up lay on the flat beach on racks made for that purpose. We saw the population busy cutting up a whale and because this occupation involved them so intensely, they did not pay any attention to our boat. We would have liked to land here for a short while, in order to examine with our own observations the statements about the differences between the population of this place and that of the rest of the coast. This place, however, did not offer the slightest protection for our boat and a light wind rising up just now made it advisable to continue our voyage to a safer harbor. Soon we reached the southeastern tip of the East Cape from where we set our course toward a bay marked on the maps near Cape Lütke.

During this passage along the East Cape, we met a rather strong current going from south to north. Among seamen the opinion prevails that in the summer an uninterrupted current, a continuation of the Kuroshio (Japan Current) flows along the Asiatic coast north into the Polar Sea, while during the fall and into winter an opposite current can be observed.

It was already late in the afternoon when we sailed around the East Cape, and now we could view the entire coast. Toward the west the high bluffs soon changed into low land which, as mentioned above, gives the entire East Cape the appearance of an island. The inhabitants of Uedle portage their boats across this depression in early summer when there is still ice in the north and in the strait, in order to trade, hunt, and fish in the Bering Sea.

Only for a short while could we use our sails. Soon the wind stopped and we had to handle our oars again. After the sun set, we still had to go a long distance. Only unclear outlines of the coast were visible. A large spot of snow indicated the approximate direction we had to steer. Not until midnight did we reach the desired bay in complete darkness, hardly able to find a proper landing site. Here, Hidlako knew his way. Quickly our tent was pitched and beds made, where we soon enjoyed a restful sleep after this strenuous day's work (we had rowed almost 40 nautical miles).

Sunday, August 28 to Wednesday, the thirty-first

The following morning shortly after five o'clock we were roused from deep sleep by some Natives. With amazed faces they looked into our tent. They were people from Póoten, a small fishing village consisting of four huts at the entrance of the bay, then also a few people from Tschingin, a place farther south along the coast. The leader of this latter group was a malicious man, who pulled a knife without any provocation several times. Later we learned that a whaler had taken a man from Tschingin aboard and never returned him. Consequently the population intended to kill every white person who fell into their hands. Possibly this was the reason for the Tschingin leader's animosity toward us, which was entirely inexplicable to us at first.

With Tange, the chief of the fishermen from Póoten, we soon were able to communicate. During the four days we spent in Póoten, he and his sons provided us with plenty of tasty fish. They were quite glad to have a chance to trade it for tobacco, knives, and calico.

We had planned to spend one day of rest in Póoten. The unfavorable weather, however, forced us to spend four entire days here. These were again days similar to those in Uedle, only this time the wind blew from the north, not from the south. Again the location of our tent was unprotected against this wind. Also, the loose sandy soil was a poor base, since it did not hold on to our tent pegs. During our arrival at night we naturally did not look very long for a suitable site, and now a change was not possible. On

77

the first two days the air was dry and the cold north wind (the temperature did not go above about 6°C) stirred up the fine beach sand and blew it through all the cracks into our tent.

During the night through August 30 a heavy rain fell which penetrated our dried-out tent walls, so that we had to make every effort to protect our herbaria, papers, and books from complete destruction. The weather remained rainy and foggy on this and the following day. Therefore, our activities were very limited.

At first we tried to orient ourselves about the position of our camping site. The bay is closed by a narrow land tongue of dune sand, 2000 paces long, and only a small entrance is left open at its southern end. Our tent stood opposite the huts of Póoten at the extreme end of this land tongue. A clear brook with plenty of water ran into this bay. The character of the surrounding mountains corresponded to those of [St.] Lawrence Bay.

On the first day we hiked up along this brook, since here we were somewhat protected from the strong winds. The green slopes of the valley yielded a rich variety of plants that we had not yet seen. At the bottom of the gorge, the flowing brook had hollowed out the snow patches, forming a spacious cave 200 paces long, 160 paces wide, and 12 to 15 meters high, the walls of which were covered by an ice crust. Through a wide opening one could enter this snow grotto, which continued farther inward through low passages.

Again on the following day, the northwest wind blew with unabated vehemence. A few fishermen from Póoten came again and offered us some fish. Also our friend from Tschingin appeared again, but was noisy and left soon. In the afternoon, Arthur and Frantzen took the boat trying to explore the bay. Because of the stormy weather, they had to return soon.

On Tuesday we visited the four huts in Póoten. The furnishings were similar to those in Uedle, only everything was much smaller and poorer here, i.e. the entrance was so low that one could pass only in a stooped position. We would have liked to buy a few Native utensils, but not much was available. The people did not even want to trade an oil lamp carved of stone (the fuel is seal oil, the wick is peat moss, sphagnum). Even less willing were they to give us a seal skull, since they believe that the person who gives away the skull of an animal he killed must die. After we had distributed some tobacco and sugar to the some twenty-five souls in the four huts situated close to the beach, we climbed up the green slopes, accompanied by some children, and found remnants of deserted yarangas

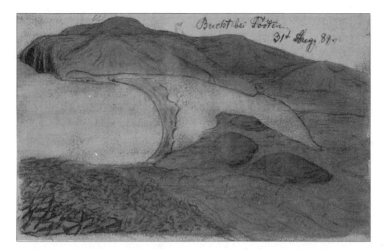

*Bay near Póoten. The bay is almost closed by a long curved land
tongue of dune sand. August 31, 1881.*

and a graveyard. Again there were many animal skulls here, also some very
fresh skulls of polar bears, who frequently come here in the winter.

Hidlako stayed with us the entire time. Actually, we could very well get
along without his services (as with all his countrymen, he had to be spurred
on to activity occasionally with chocolate). In this bad weather we did not
want him to walk back home and we also could get some important
information from him.

Often we heard Hidlako hum to himself a monotonous melody, the
words of which were equally monotonous. He started this way: *uadlutloingen
tipaiinerkin kra, kra, kra*, and continued, *jajagan tipaiinerkin*, which
means "the raven sings kra, kra, kra," and then "the sea gull sings," and so
on, a mere imitation of animal sounds. Hidlako explained that his village
lets everything sing, including ducks, foxes, lemming, etc. He told us that
there lives a magician in Uedle, as also in all other places, who can make
good and bad weather. Once in a while he pulls out his eye and eats it, but
it soon heals. Sometimes he stabs a knife into his chest or has someone
shoot a bullet through his head, but all this does not hurt him. Hidlako also
said, "During a thunderstorm, meat of reindeer and walrus is thrown to
Thunder as a sacrifice, otherwise he will kill a man." He had a satisfactory
explanation for the storm in Póoten: "During these days a boy from the
village had died, and when a person dies, there is always much wind." We

could not ascertain very much about his religious ideas or his superstitious imagining, since he did not entirely understand our questions about them.

He answered negatively our question whether senile people were killed by their relatives, but later we learned that this custom is still in use, though not as frequent as it was in former times. The gifts for the dead in the graveyards seem to speak for a kind of life after death.

Thursday, September 1

During the night the weather took a favorable turn, so we got up early at 4:00 A.M. to be able to reach Metschigmen [Mechigmen] Bay. Rain and fog again held us back a few hours until finally around nine o'clock the sky cleared and nothing prevented our departure. Now we took leave of Hidlako and presented more gifts to him than he had expected. His people had told him that he would not receive very much from us since we had a small boat. Now he could convince them that they were wrong. Not the least of the presents which we gave Hidlako for loyal services was a paper. It was a large letter with the seal of a twenty-dollar piece. In spite of his joy about the presents, he still asked for a few small things, also a little hatchet which he happened to see in our hands, because it would enable him to cut larger pieces of whale meat than with a knife. (When a whale is caught, each villager has the right to cut as much meat as he can.) Hidlako then helped us with our departure, tied his bundle, and started to walk home.

At first when we started, the wind was so weak that again we had to row. But soon a pretty good breeze came up. It finally became so strong that we rushed along the mostly fog-covered coast at a speed of 8 knots. In one valley we discovered a few huts, perhaps belonging to the village of Tschingin. We had been warned not to visit it. Near the entrance to [St.] Lawrence Bay the wind became so violent, that Frantzen did not dare to continue the voyage to Metschigmen Bay. We therefore entered [St.] Lawrence Bay and arrived in Lütke's Harbor around 3:00 P.M., where we pitched our tent in almost the same place where it had stood two weeks ago.

But the area offered an entirely different view. Only a few patches of snow remained in the gorges. Water no longer was scarce; numerous brooks flowed close by from the meadows into the ocean. Even the beach was different. The strong southerly winds of the last few weeks had produced remarkable changes. Not much was left of the rich flora. In this overcast, rainy weather it was easier than before to shoot ducks, so that we could add variety to our food with some fresh meat.

Friday, September 2

This time we spent only one day in [St.] Lawrence Bay. The Natives did not visit us, although the people of Nuniamo had seen us sail into the bay. The poor weather might have kept them home.

Saturday, September 3

Although the morning was overcast again, we decided to get on our way, since the wind was favorable. For a long time the land was completely hidden by fog, but compass and soundings did not let us get off course. Only after we had passed the southern tip of [St.] Lawrence Bay did we again catch sight of the coast. In the afternoon the wind abated and finally stopped entirely. Since there was no appropriate landing site and the oncoming darkness made it impossible to find the entrance to Metschigmen Bay, we had to drop the anchor and again spend a night aboard on the open sea. We tried to shorten the night hours by cooking coffee, tea, and pea soup. We rested for a while under an improvised tent, but did not get warm.

Sunday, September 4

At daybreak the sails were hoisted, and we noticed that we were in front of the narrow land tongue which separates Metschigmen Bay from the ocean. We sailed alongside this tongue but had to tack constantly in a strong head wind. Not until noon did we see the entrance to Metschigmen Bay, when we arrived right in front of it. Until then it had been hidden by the second point protruding from the south. Only a weak countercurrent was noticeable. We therefore entered the bay without difficulties and sailed into its eastern cove to pitch our tent there.

In the few remaining hours of daylight we convinced ourselves that Metschigmen Bay would offer an interesting field for our observations. Nowhere did we find the moss tundra as typically developed as here. The geological formations and the types of rocks showed a greater variety than in [St.] Lawrence Bay and on East Cape. Younger igneous formations which we had not met so far were predominant here.

Monday, September 5

On a beautiful, rather clear, morning we got up around six o'clock. We sailed farther into the interior of the bay. From the huts on the opposite side, a boat with ten to twelve people approached us. We learned that only Tschautschuats live in the interior of the bay and we traded a duck and pretty little boat rack for some tobacco. Then we took leave of the people, who returned to their village. From the boat we saw a herd of reindeer grazing on the tundra and saw a few tents of the Tschautschuats farther inland.

Then we sailed to the other side and dredged several times, yielding some beautiful results. Around four o'clock we arrived at a protected inlet, closed toward the interior by steep mountains. At the foot of these mountains, densely covered with crowberries, we pitched our tent near a merrily running brook. We enjoyed a magnificent view of the mountain scenery on the other side. Late at night when returning to our tent from a successful hunt of grey geese in mild and calm air, and viewing the scenery in the light of the full moon, we had to admit that this barren land did have some beautiful aspects.

Tuesday, September 6

The following morning was beautiful and clear; we had not seen such a morning in a long time. We hiked along the coast to the cliffs of a nearby trachyte dome. The climb was steep and difficult. Upon reaching the top, a strong eastern wind arose which we feared would damage our boat, thus we hurried back. The descent took three-quarters of an hour. Aurel lost his pistol which he had taken out to shoot a raven and then laid aside while picking berries. Unfortunately, we could not find it in spite of intensive searching.

When we arrived at the tent, Frantzen had been waiting for us impatiently. He had everything prepared for the departure. We quickly ate something and soon after three o'clock sailed off in favorable wind. Repeated sounding yielded a depth of only 3 to 4 meters and a few places were so shallow that we could not land. We had to set up our tent at the foot of the mountains which were very close to the bay here. This place offered attractive scenery, similar to that which we enjoyed yesterday. A dense carpet of crowberries covered the ground. High willow bushes were found in the gorges mixed with a spirea and an unusually large umbellifera. On the nearby tundra, densely covered with dwarf birches, numerous salmonberries grew luxuriously; their fruits provided some welcome refreshment for us. The salmonberry (*Rubus chamaemorus*), widespread in Norway and a rarity in some German moors, is by far the best tasting berry in this country, yet, as often as we encountered this plant, we found fruits only at Metschigmen Bay.

Although the entrance to Metschigmen Bay is only 500 paces wide, we found a great deal of driftwood inside the bay. At our campsite we had no trouble maintaining a large wood fire, while we made coffee on our petroleum stove.

Wednesday, September 7

In the afternoon we sailed to the opposite bank. The water showed low salinity and the fauna was definitely brackish water fauna. When we saw a steep, rocky projection on the other bank, we hoped for a good harbor. We found a deeply cut bay there, deep enough to take our boat close to shore. There also was a suitable place for our tent on a carpet of *Empetrum* (crowberry). The bay was closed by a low basalt ridge connected with the mainland only by a narrow tongue of land. The basalt was fissured. The walls at the cape rose vertically from the water about 9 to 10 meters high.

Thursday, September 8

For this day we had planned to take a longer hike to the huts of the Tschautschuats we had seen on the first day, especially since we knew our boat was in a safe harbor. But Frantzen woke us shortly after four o'clock with the news that the wind was favorable for the continuation of our voyage. We therefore got ready and weighed anchor at 6:30 A.M. The weather was beautiful and the wind, moderate and from the northwest, let us sail through the bay at a medium speed of 5 to 6 knots. Once we dredged inside the bay near an island at the entrance. Around 9:30 A.M. we had reached the exit to the ocean. The wind remained favorable and the weather clear so that we could enjoy the best view and had a chance to look around. We used all sails and jibs on three sides so that the boat ride was rather steady. On the entire stretch from Metschigmen to the northwestern part of the island Arakamtschetschene [Arakamchechen] or Kaiyne, where we stopped at Ratmanoff Harbor, we noticed only four or five settlements consisting of a few huts.

After landing in Ratmanoff Harbor we quickly took a walk around the bay to collect some rock specimens. The rocks of the island seem to be of varied nature. We noticed trachyte, typical syenites, dark slate, and crystalline calcium which formed steep cliffs. The flora already had a distinct autumnal character. This observation was a warning to us not to delay the continuation of our journey, although the present beautiful weather and the magnificent scenery invited us to a longer stay.

Friday, September 9

The next day we continued our trip southward, again favored by the most beautiful weather. A gorgeous scenery unfolded in front of our eyes, picturesque mountains, ranging from yellow-grey to black in color, green valleys, and deeply cut gorges.

When we were between the islands of Arakamtschetschene and Yttigrane [Ittygran], some Natives rowed their boat toward us. Since they called us, we sailed toward them. There were only two men, the others were children and women. Some of the younger ones showed rather pretty faces hidden under a thick crust of dirt, the others were horribly ugly with their upper bodies half nude. The people came from a nearby little island where they (i.e. only the women, the men are idle on such occasions) gathered crowberries for the winter. We, of course, distributed some tobacco, which the women enjoy just as much as the men, asked for a few names, and answered their questions about the whalers as well as we could. Then we continued our voyage.

Almost at the narrowest part of the strait between the mainland and the island of Yttigrane, we landed on the island after a trip of several hours. Late in the afternoon we climbed a mountain and during sunset enjoyed a magnificent overview of the marvellous, ragged mountainous landscape.

Saturday, September 10[16]

On the next day we planned to sail around the most southern tip of the Chukchi Peninsula, Point Chaplin or Indian Point, as it is generally called. Since this was again a long stretch without harbors, we had to leave early. The wind was also favorable today. In a short time we had passed the Seniavin Strait and reached the open sea. We continued in a southerly course, following the outline of the coast which gradually flattened from a high declivitous bank to a very low sand spit, the extreme end of which is known as Indian Point. The village situated here bears the same name. The villagers are just as enterprising as those of Nuokan, going on extensive trips along the coast north as far as the East Cape and west to the Anadyr during the summer. From here each summer the whalers take a number of people to the Arctic Ocean. As we sailed around the point, a curious crowd mostly made up of women and children gathered on the beach and with lively gesticulations seemed to ask us to land there.

From now on our course was westward. On the southern side, too, the flat sand spit soon changes into high land with two larger bays, Markus Bay and Plover Bay, deeply carved out. Since the wind abated and it was not feasible to reach Plover Bay before dark, we decided to steer toward the first of these bays. At the entrance we soon saw a boat approaching us from the left bank. Again there was one man sitting at the rudder and one at the bow, while eight to ten women eagerly handled the short, shovel-like paddles. They had been picking berries. On the right bank were their huts, where they paddled after satisfying their curiosity and receiving a few small gifts.

The maps gave us a very inaccurate picture of Markus Bay. We searched in vain for the small inlet near the entrance, which we had picked as a landing site. When we passed two huts on the right bank, the inhabitants soon pushed a boat into the water and begged for some tobacco. They were Reindeer Chukchis, distinctive by the peculiar fashion of wearing a little pigtail braided with beads in the middle of their foreheads.

Not until late in the evening did we find a suitable landing site in the extreme northeastern part of the bay. By direct line it was perhaps 4 miles from yesterday's camp site, but we had traveled 40 nautical miles.

Because of the variety of mountain shapes and types of rocks, as far as we could learn during our fleeting visit, Markus Bay is more interesting than the neighboring Plover Bay. Here, for the first time, we also found Paleozoic sediments with fossils, in addition to younger igneous rocks.

At dusk we climbed one of the nearby mountains, but when we saw a boat approaching our tent, we hastily returned. Again they were Reindeer Chukchis from the other bank who only wanted to visit us at this rather unusual hour (it was around 9:00 P.M. and almost entirely dark).

After some lengthy conversations and the obligatory gifts of tobacco, we told them that we were tired and wanted to rest. They finally left and their doing so did not cause any dissatisfaction. It was a gorgeous starlit evening.

Sunday, September 11

The next morning, when we hurried to the nearby waterholes to wash ourselves, we found a thin cover of ice on them, a warning of the approaching winter. A comparatively short stretch still separated us from Plover Bay and when we started our trip there in the morning, we thought we could reach the final destination of our journey well before dusk. In a calm sea or very light wind we progressed only very slowly. For one sounding near the back part of the bay we did not get bottom at 54 meters.

Again we had visitors from ashore. They came from the two huts on the left bank. Since the people had learned the day before that we desired neither walrus teeth nor whalebone, they now brought us reindeer meat and ivory carvings, the kind they used as children's toys. When we asked them, they were also willing to row us out of the bay. A few strong young men climbed into our boat and after taking off all clothes to the waist, they handled the oars with the greatest effort, while merrily joking and yelling "pull, pull ahead." They paused more and more often. Perhaps they tired quickly, or they did not really want to accompany us any farther. Finally, we preferred to dismiss them and cruise alone out of the bay in light wind.

During the continuation of our trip we met two more fully occupied canoes on their return from Plover Bay to Indian Point. Again we were asked the same questions by the amazed Natives—were we shipwrecked; are the whalers coming soon; did any of their people die aboard ship; were many whales caught—which we answered to our best knowledge. Here, as in other places along the coast, we had the impression that the population considers the arrival and visit of a ship a most enjoyable event.

Using oar and sail alternately, we reached the most southern mountains of the Chukchi Peninsula, a steep, broad cliff, by late evening. During the day the trip had been pleasant in spite of its long duration, because in mild air and clear sky we enjoyed the pretty view of the attractive scenery along the shore. At night, however, it turned quite cold, so that after the exertion of rowing we preferred to sit quietly by the fire.

Monday, September 12, to October 3

Not until two o'clock did we arrive in the harbor, formed by a protruding tongue of land, not far from the village of Rirak, called Plover Bay by the Americans. In the quickly pitched tent we soon sank into deep sleep from which we were awakened, long after sunrise, by the steps and voices of approaching Natives. When we heard from them that a white man was staying at Plover Bay, we naturally visited him soon. Mr. MacDonald (that was his name) had accompanied an expedition by the American government to Point Barrow as ice pilot. The captain, however, had left him here to trade walrus teeth, whalebone, and furs until the ship returned. In the meantime, he had made an advantageous deal with the Natives and now was expecting the return of the schooner any day.

For a longer stay we had selected Emma Harbor farther north in Plover Bay. The bleak barren land surrounding the village of Plover Bay convinced us to hold to our plan, so we left and landed at Emma Harbor after a few hours. With greater care than at other times, we selected our camp site and pitched our tent.

This concluded our boat trips, during which we had pitched our tent at twelve different places. Due to unfavorable weather, we repeatedly were forced to stay longer than originally intended. On the other hand, we had to forego a more thorough exploration of a few especially interesting areas, such as Metschigmen Bay and Markus Bay, because time was running out. Usually in September the incessant northern winds begin, haunting the Bering Sea throughout autumn. Soon after our landing at Emma Harbor, we had the opportunity to become acquainted with the violence of these gales. Even more than the consideration of the weather, the condition of our collections required an end to our boat trips soon. It had been impossible to keep everything dry, and even though decay and the development of mildew occur less quickly in arctic areas, several items, especially bird skins, were ruined.

Now our first concern was to dry all our collections thoroughly and to salvage them, if possible. It turned out to be a frustrating task, like that of the Danaides, because the very next day brought more rain. Several times we experienced that one day's gain was spoiled the next.

The location of our camp site was rather pretty. Here a sandy, flat stretch of beach interrupted the rocky bank, and a bountiful flora covered the gently rising slopes behind it. Toward the south our gaze was drawn to the isolated massive rock of Baldhead; toward the west we could see the huts of Plover Bay and beyond them the open sea. East of here was the wide valley of Lake Moore and in all other directions, the high mountains, their peaks covered with snow on the day of our arrival, formed the background.

Emma Harbor is not occupied this year, although traces of deserted settlements existed near our tent. The nearest hut was so far away that only rarely did we receive visitors.

A trip to Plover Bay, as well as a second one to the huts of the Tschautschuats in Snug Harbor, convinced us of the correctness of our hypothesis that here lives a fishing population that differs in descent and

Plover Bay (Rirak). Several yarangas and one wooden house are located near the beach. October 3, 1881.

language from the Chukchi people. There were no noticeable differences in lifestyle, in clothing, and the building of yarangas, but the language was completely different. Active trade and frequent intermarriages seem to have wiped away the differences among these people here. Accordingly, the physiognomies of the inhabitants of Plover Bay and Indian Point reveal a less uniform character. We noticed smaller statures and broader facial features, as we had previously observed among the people of Nuokan.

A comparison of a few words may show how their language basically differs from that of the Chukchis:

During this advanced season, the flora of Plover Bay offered us little

English	Language of the Tschautschuats	Language of the Southern Population
one	ennen	ataschek
two	nirak	mudlguk
three	nrok	pingajit
wind	jojo	anuka
we	muri	edlpuk
boot	plakidl	kamuk

chance to enrich our botanical collections. Only a few plants of late summer were still in flower. We were particularly interested in the observation of a second blooming period for some spring plants. Never had we seen such a beautifully blooming carpet of *Diapensia lapponica* as here on September 10. Often we also found a white anemone in second bloom.

The vegetation displayed fall colors now. Yellow and brown hues were evident everywhere, except on the plateaus and the steeper slopes, where the uniform grey of the lichen-covered rocks was dominant. The dark green carpet of the crowberry (*Empetrum nigrum*) carried an abundance of black berries, their taste definitely improved by the first frost. In addition to salmonberries, we also found bog blueberries (*Vaccinium uliginosum*), partridgeberry (*Vaccinium vitis idaea*), and alpine bearberries. Of all the indigenous berries, the crowberry is by far the most important one for the Natives because of its abundance. Large supplies are collected in autumn and often long boat trips are made to especially profitable sites. On the twenty-second, a boat had come from Plover Bay to the hills opposite our tent site. While the women picked berries all day, the two men who had taken them there came over to us to talk and to receive some small gifts. In almost every hut we later saw a seal sack filled with crowberries. Covered with fish oil, they are stored for the winter.

With the exception of numerous kinds of ducks, very few animals existed here. A few sandpipers, phalaropes, and golden plovers on the beach, as well as snow buntings on the slopes, and a flock of ravens living unabashedly near our tent, were almost the only birds we saw. Among larger mammals, only seals existed in larger numbers. A few white whales (beluga) visited us several times in Emma Harbor. These large animals, up to 20 feet long, are a strange sight when they raise their white backs out of the water all in a row, one after the other. Although we went on repeated longer excursions, we never met mountain sheep, wild reindeer, or bears. According to the Natives, these are found occasionally on the neighboring hills.

During our stay in Emma Harbor from September 12 to October 1, the temperature did not rise above 10°C. Between 8:00 A.M. and 8:00 P.M. the temperature usually ranged between 4° and 6°C. Not until after September 25 did the days become cooler, on the twenty-seventh snow fell on the nearby hills and did not melt all day. During the night of the twenty-seventh to the twenty-eighth, water runoff was covered with a thin crust of ice and after a clear night with northern lights visible, we were quite amazed the following morning to see the entire Emma Harbor covered with such a thick layer of ice that it was hardly possible to cut through it with a boat. At eight o'clock in the morning the thermometer still showed minus 5°C. The violence of the strong gales, especially from September 15 to the nineteenth and twenty-fifth to the twenty-seventh, prompted us to build a protective stone wall on the northern side of our tent, for which the sharp-edged rocks of the nearby slopes supplied the perfect building material.

On September 28 we saw a schooner enter the harbor. Naturally, we immediately went out there. The ship was the long-awaited schooner *Golden Fleece*. Captain Jacobson, a Dane, intended to stay a few days at Plover Bay, but then wanted to visit various points along the coast to collect walrus teeth and whalebone from the Natives. Indian Point and [St.] Lawrence Bay, perhaps even the East Cape and the American coast opposite it, were to be visited. The prospect of seeing this way a few places on the peninsula hitherto unknown to us, made us decide to go aboard the *Golden Fleece* on the morning of October 1.

Since Captain Jacobson could not leave Plover Bay until October 3 because of adverse weather, we still had a chance to explore the village and its vicinity. The yarangas of Plover Bay are built for summer only. Now only the supports, usually whale ribs, of the winter huts can be seen. Later they will be covered with reindeer skins. The Natives do not establish their winter yarangas until after the ground is solidly frozen, perhaps to prevent snow water from entering them.

By the way, some of the summer huts at Plover Bay were occupied by people from Indian Point who planned to return there before the beginning of winter. A change of residence, a complete move with all possessions, apparently takes place quite often. We met a family in Markus Bay in the process of such a move by boat with tent and all belongings. Also we met people from Rirak in a little hut at Plover Bay, who had moved there to gather berries and hunt for reindeer. This easy temporary change of residence makes all data about the population remain correct for only a short time. Sometimes we could not find a trace of entire villages that were marked on maps, whereas new settlements were founded at other locations.

Nowhere did the coastal population have such intimate contact with Americans as at Plover Bay. The repeated winterings of ships and long stays of traders has introduced the English language to almost general use. Here, and at Indian Point, even young boys can communicate in English.

Return Trip Aboard the Golden Fleece *and Stay in San Francisco:*

October 3

We left Plover Bay, completing this or that little trade with the Natives to the last minute. We noticed a large supply of boots and fur clothing, sewn according to Native patterns, in some of the yarangas, but the owners could not be persuaded to sell us some of these. They were waiting for the whalers from whom they expected a gun in exchange for a complete fur outfit including boots. Our first stop was at [St.] Lawrence Island.

October 4

In the morning we sighted [St.] Lawrence Island. Soon four boats approached our ship. They came from the village of Schiwukak [modern Gambell] at the northwest corner of [St.] Lawrence Island. The twenty to thirty huts of the settlement are at the foot of a mountain several hundred feet high which, just like the East Cape in the Old World, is separated from the main part of the island by flat land. The men and women coming aboard turned out to be eager but cunning and careful traders, who knew the value of their whalebone and ivory and their neatly made fur and leather clothing. For the first time we saw them wear clothing made of skins of various sea birds (ducks and divers). They also wore more jewelry. This was the only place where they asked for beads. Otherwise, these people are the same as those of Rirak (Plover Bay), Awan, and Indian Point, whose language they also speak.

We bought four furs made of bird skins, a cloak, gloves, boots, and socks, as well as a belt with a knife. One woman who came aboard felt flattered when I sketched her tattoos. When the people left us, I unfortunately missed my journal. After a long unsuccessful search I have to assume that they took it. Some tattoos could also be found on men. One man had three double lines on his chin, another one had a circle on each side of his chin.

During the entire summer the people of [St.] Lawrence Island maintain active contact with the southeastern coast of the Chukchi Peninsula, only 34 nautical miles away. They receive reindeer skins from the Chukchis in exchange for wooden utensils, like sleds and boat frames, which they make from driftwood. This comes from the American mainland and accumulates on their shores in large quantities. The people of the nearby mainland find hardly any driftwood on their beaches.

It was not possible to go ashore and visit the huts, because adverse weather conditions forced the captain to weigh anchor after a short while and steer across toward Indian Point. The next morning, October 5, we again saw the well-known mountains of Plover Bay and Markus Bay lying ahead of us, this time covered with a white coat of snow. Only the low land and the flat sand spit of Indian Point were still free from snow. Although the incessant poor weather forced the schooner to change her anchorage and cruise back and forth several times, we did have an opportunity to get in touch with the Natives. A longer visit ashore as well as a trip in one of their leather boats to hunt for the ducks which are extraordinarily numerous here gave us a chance for entirely new observations and acquisitions.

We noticed that the people of Indian Point more than anywhere else try to get a higher price for their goods through long bartering. As soon as they get the desired trading goods, they believe they asked for too little and start demanding more and more. If you give them the demanded hatchet or knife, they want some tobacco in addition to it and after that perhaps some lead, or a few percussion caps, then a few needles, thread, etc. If you insist on the first agreement, they often cancel the entire deal or they postpone it with an indifferent "by and by," *ad calendas Graecas.*

They do not like to trade a larger supply of goods at one time, almost always they keep back a few items, hoping to find a chance for an even better trade. Strangely enough, they think they can get a more advantageous deal with a larger ship than with a small one. Aboard the *Golden Fleece* we received more offers than in our small boat, but even Captain Jacobson was annoyed to learn that the Natives were not sufficiently impressed by his schooner and hoped to receive more from the three-masted whalers.

Here, too, tobacco was the most popular barter item. The people of Indian Point and other coastal villages frequently visited by American ships trade large quantities of tobacco and use it in the winter on their journeys by sled to distant places in exchange for whalebone, walrus teeth, furs, or leather boots, fur stockings and fur clothing. The importance of this trade may be seen in the large yaranga of Quorrys, the richest man in Indian Point, where a large supply of goods is stacked, worth over $5000 according to a conservative estimate. Quorrys had made arrangements with Captain Jacobson for a trade of part of these supplies. In the evening, however, when the whalebone was to be loaded aboard, he declared the sea was too rough. On the following day he sent a message through an agent that he did not want to trade at all because his son was sick.

When we became victims of a few small thefts at St. Lawrence Island and Indian Point, we did not have much trust in the reliability of the inhabitants of these places. Captain Jacobson also found several iron cask-hoops mixed into a bundle of whalebone, which he had traded there, to increase its weight. Of course, often the Natives had been cheated by American traders, although most of them see their advantage in an honest deal.

A second visit to [St.] Lawrence Island was thwarted by the poor weather.

Friday, October 7

We sailed all night. In the morning we are facing the small rocky island between Yttigrane and Arakamtschan. We cruised with a southerly wind and fairly cold weather toward Indian Point and reach it at noon. After we dropped anchor, again Natives came aboard. We trade a lance, two nets, three rings made of whalebone with a sling for duck hunting, a whistle, and small and large boots. The captain also trades some whalebone. Today these people use the same tactics. They seem to accept the offer, but then always demand a little more in exchange. Since I was not willing to give more for the whistle than what was agreed upon, I had a long conversation with the men. When we finally explained their tactics to them, they laughed about it and even seemed to be slightly ashamed.

Between [St.] Lawrence Island and Indian Point we met a bark returning from whale hunting in the Arctic Sea. From her captain we heard that this year the ocean was unusually free from ice. For the whalers it was a most profitable season. The eighteen whalers caught a total of 194 whales.

Saturday, October 8

Before sunrise, soon after 5:00 A.M., we got up. We had gone to sleep early and now had been awake for some time. It is full moon, the sky is clear except for a few clouds on the southern horizon. There is a beautiful sunrise. In light southerly wind we sail toward [St.] Lawrence Island. Later on it becomes foggy, and the wind turns to northeast. In the afternoon a great deal of rain falls. We are mainly occupied with the writing of our journals. It seems the captain now intends to go directly to San Francisco.

Sunday, October 9

At midnight the wind turned to southeast, so now we have adverse winds with high seas. All day long the weather was stormy and rainy, and the violent motions of the ship made our work very difficult. Today the captain speaks about landing on the Matthew Islands and hunting bears there, but I do not think it will come to that.

Wednesday, October 12

The rainy weather, lasting all day, forces us to work in the cabin. We sort dried plants and put yesterday's catch from dredging into alcohol.

Friday, October 14

Again we rise quite early. There is almost no wind, a little fog, but warm weather. Frantzen dredges, starting while it is still dark. He brings up a lot of mud, but it contains only a few animals. Then we try fishing for cod. Altogether twenty-seven are caught, fourteen of them by Frantzen. From Mr. MacDonald we hear that the huts in Plover Bay are summer dwellings only. When the ground freezes, the Natives move into their winter quarters. Now these are frames of large whale bones, which they cover with reindeer skins in winter. Formerly, they also used subterranean houses, but apparently they now no longer move into those.

Monday, October 17

During the night our sleep is interrupted often. The captain is awake most of the time. Before dawn, Frantzen throws out the dredge net six times in a row and gains a rich catch. In the morning we are very close to the Walrus Islands.

Tuesday, October 18

Toward morning, again the wind became stronger, so a few sails had to be reefed. It is a beautiful, starry sky, Jupiter and Venus shine brilliantly, the air is very warm. During a walk with MacDonald I again hear some details about the Natives. No formalities of any kind exist at weddings. In some places they even sell their wives. All wear amulets in a leather pouch which is hung around children's necks right after birth. Occasionally, old people are killed by their children, apparently with their consent, with a knife or through mere exposure. This is done now less frequently than in former times.

During the hard winter of 1879/80 everyone feared for his life. One woman had her little girl set out in the mountains. She was rescued and brought up by two white people. These two white people, who spent the winter there, distributed some flour every day. They fortified their house like a fortress. The walls had peep holes all over, and everything was well locked. Hamlo is the name of the present occupant of that wooden house. MacDonald did not trust him too much. The Natives also stole from each other. Fights were rare, even among children. Formerly he heard them cry, recently he heard it only a few times. Cornelius had already killed two people. Sometimes they escape vendetta by buying themselves off. Old people's teeth are remarkable. The front teeth are bent forward and backward like a saw, perhaps due to the food they eat. To my question, whether the Natives believe in a life after death, MacDonald replied that this must be the case, because they believe that ghosts of their dead sometimes appear to them.

Thursday, October 20

In the morning we are in the Seventy-Two Pass, the islands on our left are visible. The weather keeps changing all day. Mostly high seas from various directions, but no longer the short waves of the Bering Sea. Again we had long conversations with the captain about weather, barometer, and ghosts.

Tuesday, October 25

Throughout the night we did not sleep well, the ship rolled too much. The sea is very high and often waves splash on deck.

Wednesday, October 26

The weather is favorable and the roll of the ship less strong. We work almost all day in the cabin. Today the captain presented to us an ivory knife which he had carved himself.

Thursday, October 27

Mr. MacDonald knows that the Chukchi women do not get any assistance during birth. Afterwards they immediately resume their work and the babies are not cleaned at all.

Friday, October 28

MacDonald does not think the Chukchis have a history. The Tschautschuats' contact with the coastal population is very active. This year, two boats returned from Holy Cross Bay, where they had spent ten years. One boat returned to Indian Point, the other one to Plover Bay. Also Ato from Uatl spent a long time in Eastland. They call each other Cousins (....)[17] when a friend visits someone, he sleeps with that man's wife. Unfortunately, we did not bring back an important house tool, the louse swatter, used to beat lice out of furs and kill them. In winter the furs are taken outdoors, the lice quickly emerge and are killed with the swatter. The same tool is also used to brush snow off clothes.

Saturday, October 29

The weather is beautiful, the wind is good, but every half hour there is a rain or hail shower. The sea is turbulent, so that the ship rolls heavily. The petroleum is almost used up. The remainder is now being mixed with sperm oil. Consequently, the lamps burn very poorly, and in the evening we can neither read nor write.

Monday, October 31

The Natives of Plover Bay call the people on the American side *nakúrrek* meaning "good." They had a fight with them a few years ago, but now they call them *nakúrrek* when they meet them.

Friday, November 4

Beautiful weather, good wind. We hope to arrive in San Francisco tomorrow morning.

Saturday, November 5

When we woke up in the morning, we noticed the ship was lying still. When the wind stopped, the ship had dropped anchors on the Bank of San Francisco. At the beginning of high tide the anchors are weighed. The tide drives us forward quickly. Numerous ships come in with us. Since the tide takes us directly to the Cormorant Rock, the anchor had to be dropped again. Around noon a favorable wind comes up, and we sail into the harbor. In a boat, Mr. Brown approaches the ship to hear the Captain's report. We go ashore with Mr. Brown. Arthur immediately goes to the consul to receive letters, then to a clothing store where I wait for him. After heavy purchases, we go to Kruse. There we say good-bye to Frantzen, who had served us well to the end, and pay him $220. In the Occidental Hotel we get our old room. In the evening the young Kruse visits us in order to learn some names for the *Chronicle.*

Sunday, November 6

In the morning we work on the maps, then we visit the consul, but we do not learn anything about Mr. Schulze, except that he must be very busy. Soon after we returned, the reporter from the *Chronicle* visits us, to whom we give some of our latest news. The afternoon was filled with various visits. Even after 9 P.M., two members of the California Academy came to ask us about our travel experiences.

On Monday, November 7, we asked Wright about the continuation of our journey. There, we met Captain Adrian Jacobsen. At two o'clock we delivered our report to the post office. We received a few more visitors and went to the academy in the evening. There, we were again officially welcomed. After the meeting we had some wine, schnapps, and beer with several gentlemen, particularly with some Russians.

Tuesday, November 8, to Saturday, the twenty-sixth

The main task of the next few days was devoted to the collections. Many things are damp, some even moldy, such as the beetles and mosses, so we have to dry and organize them to get everything salvageable ready for shipment. The collection is also to be shown to interested circles here in San Francisco, so the ethnological objects, the various pressed plants, animals of land and sea, stuffed birds, snails, beetles, etc., as well as rocks and fossils have to be carefully cleaned and then set up.

On November 16, everything is ready to be shown. The exhibit lasted for several days and photographs were taken of each individual section. It was visited by various members of the academy, by the consul and his family, and by many friends.

Several interesting animals and plants from California and Arizona, such as a turtle, several spiders and millipedes, which we had received from some members of the academy, were added to the collections from the Chukchi Peninsula.

During the next few days all these objects were carefully packed into wooden crates, and some of them into tin containers, which a plumber closed by soldering.[18]

After several futile attempts we finally sold the whaleboat for $100.

Although this was the end of the first journey, we simultaneously worked on the preparations for the second journey. Again, some purchases had to be made, such as a sextant, a compass, and a watch.

Upon his mother's request, Aurel had his picture taken at the same photographer who had taken Frederick Schwatka's[19] picture. Arthur had his picture taken shortly after his return to Berlin.

The brothers again attended several meetings at the academy, as they had done during their first stay in San Francisco. They also visited social and musical events with their old friends. Several botanical excursions into the vicinity offered some welcome diversity.

The last few days in San Francisco were filled with continued packing and many visits to say good-bye. On November 27, the journey to Alaska was begun.

POSTSCRIPT TO PART I

The seafarers of the few ships sailing to these northern waters seemed to have little confidence in the success of the brothers' plan to row and sail an open boat along the polar coast and around the rocky area of the East Cape, then south through the Bering Strait. For weeks, even months, they had no opportunity to send home letters, therefore, fears and rumors arose which finally resulted in the following false report in the local section of the Berlin daily paper *Die Post* of January 4, 1882:

> Two Berlin teachers, the brothers Drs. Aurel and Arthur Krause, were granted leave of absence from their school district a year ago, to go on a polar expedition especially to the Chukchi land. According to the *Schwäbischer Merkur* in Philadelphia, the two explorers went from San Francisco to the Arctic Ocean by whaler. There they bought an old whale boat, hired a few sailors, and then continued their trip on their own. The steamship *Corwin*, sent to the Arctic Ocean by the American government,

now heard about them and tried to find and return the young men. However, all they learned about the Krause brothers was that the whalers who had last seen them had the greatest fears. The brothers were poorly equipped, and since they have not been heard from, one must assume that they are lost.

When this false report reached Berlin, the brothers had already returned to San Francisco safe and sound two months previously, and at that time had been with the Tlingit Indians for four weeks.

PART TWO:

TO THE TLINGIT INDIANS

CHAPTER FOUR

FROM SAN FRANCISCO TO ALASKA

Sunday, November 27, 1881

We got up early to go to our workroom to get everything ready, hire a carriage, pay our bill, and drive to the wharf. The coachman first drove us to the wrong wharf, so that we arrived rather late at the right place. Several gentlemen had gathered there to say good-bye to us.

Our luggage was quickly taken care of. On the *Columbia* we get a cabin on deck. Unfortunately, we have to share it with a third passenger. The ship is very comfortably furnished. Soon after ten o'clock she gets under way. Aboard is a German, Theodor Kirchhoff, whom we had met before and who is going to Portland. All day long the weather is beautiful. The ship stays close to shore, which farther north is rather wooded. Rising smoke columns in various places indicate forest fires. We went to bed early, since we were very tired after the strenuous and hurried work and travel preparations of the last few days.

Monday, November 28

At 6:30 A.M. coffee is served in the cabin. At 8:00 A.M. breakfast is served. At lunchtime around noon we pass Cape Blanco. We sail between the coast and several offshore reefs. In the morning we had a strong north wind, but it diminished later on.

Tuesday, November 29

Early in the morning we arrive at the mouth of the Columbia River. A feared sand bar is surrounded by strong surf. Four wrecks of stranded ships are obvious indications of the danger involved. The scenery is rather pretty. Near the mouth is a small fortified military camp, Fort Stephens. We go up river and soon arrive at the city of Astoria. After a two-hour stop, we continue our trip up river. The low mountains on the banks of the Columbia and Willamette, a left tributary of the Columbia, are entirely covered with forests. Once in a while we see clearings with one or more farms, more often salmon canneries with all their buildings. Some of these are occupied only during the summer when salmon are caught, others have become permanent settlements. Even during the winter the people are profitably occupied cutting lumber and hunting the abundant waterfowl and grouse. There is more traffic on the Columbia River than on shore. Several steamships pass us.

In order to get to Portland, we have to leave our steamer at the mouth of the Willamette and transfer to a smaller river boat, because the Willamette is too shallow for the big ship. Portland is about 30 miles from the mouth of the Willamette. At 7:00 P.M. we arrive there, visit with Kirchhoff, and then retire to our hotel. Here in Portland we want to visit the president of the North West Trading Company, Mr. Paul Schulze. He had offered us free transportation to one of the trading posts of his company, the one at Chilkoot at the northern end of Lynn Canal. He had also offered to provide lodging for us free of charge for the winter. We had gratefully accepted this offer and now we want to discuss details with him.

In the morning of November 30, we learn that Mr. Schulze had tried to visit us right after we had left. After a short walk through the city we go to see him in his office. He is about our age, graduated from the Berlin Kloster and studied law for one year. According to Kirchhoff, he is still a Berlin boy. Now he is on his way to becoming a multimillionaire. We also met his friend and agent in Sitka, Mr. Spohn, a cheerful German from the Rhineland.

Mr. Schulze's North West Trading Company was founded just recently, in the spring of 1880. Its purpose is the development of the natural resources of southeastern Alaska to Cook's Inlet and provide transportation to California, Oregon, Washington Territory, and Alaska. So far it has established five trading posts at different points along the coast. One is in Sitka, and the northernmost one at the Chilkat River is our destination.

At Mr. Schulze's office we looked at the ethnological objects he plans to ship. Then we have lunch with him, are introduced to the library, and have dinner at his house.

Thursday, December 1

The beautiful weather entices us to a walk to the nearby hills, from where we enjoy a magnificent view of the city and its surroundings. Imposing are the two snow mountains, Mount St. Helens (2,948 meters) in the north and Mount Hood (3,420 meters) in the east. The forest is frequently cut and burned, after removal of the larger cedar trunks. We assist Mr. Schulze in labeling some ethnological objects, and in the afternoon take another hike into the hills. This time we find two helical-type snails and flowering strawberries!

Friday, December 2

We make a few more purchases, and analyze some black sand for Schulze. However, it does not contain any gold. Then we spend some time at the library and go in the evening for dinner at Schulze's house. Spohn joins us there later. Around 10:00 P.M. we go aboard the ship *Eureka* for our journey to Sitka.

Saturday, December 3

At dawn we leave Portland. With a clear view of Mount St. Helens we sail down the Willamette, then down the Columbia.

The few passengers who are aboard with us mostly want to go to Port Townsend or Victoria.

Excerpts from a letter to their mother Emilie Waetzmann Krause, and one to the Geographical Society in Bremen:

Aboard the steamship *California*, now renamed *Eureka*, I am writing these lines in the midst of the most beautiful surroundings. One really has to look at the calendar to believe that today is already December 3. During our entire stay in San Francisco as well as during our trip to Portland, we continuously had excellent, mild weather. Now we are a few miles from Astoria, and I am writing these lines on an open deck.

The steep peak of Mt. Hood is no longer visible, but the snow-covered dome of Mount St. Helens towers all the more beautifully above the dark coniferous forest. From Portland, both mountains appeared to be giants compared to the not insignificant mountains of the area. Especially during the glow of the afternoon sun, they are a surprisingly beautiful sight.

As I mentioned before, we arrived in Portland on the evening of November 29. Portland is a flourishing city. A few years ago it hardly existed, now it has twenty thousand inhabitants and hopes to have fifty thousand in three to five years. The city does not have any sights worth seeing, and some things make a very primitive impression, but the site is very beautiful. From our hotel window we could view both snowy mountains, Mt. St. Helens and Mt. Hood, in the beautiful, clear weather during the last three days. We had an even better view from the nearby hills west of the city, which we honored with our visit and from where the enclosed samples [perhaps sketches of pressed plants] originated.

Perhaps because of memories of the barren hills of the Chukchi lands or the beautiful, clear weather here, we rarely enjoyed the spicy fragrance of the conifers with such inner satisfaction as now. The forest looks rather wild. The old trunks often measuring 7 feet and more at the base are lying crisscross, while the dense, fast-growing timber is striving to replace the fallen giants. Just as in Germany, they mainly grow one kind of conifer in lots, and rarely other conifers, among them the fragrant *Thuja* or deciduous trees. Only on the very low islands in the river are there oaks and willows in larger numbers.

The local area is really magnificent. But according to photographs we saw in Portland of the Chilkat River and environment, our next place of residence with its magnificent glaciers, mountains, forests, lakes, rivers, and fjords must surpass everything else and at least be comparable to the beautiful mountainous areas of Norway.

I asked Dr. Lindemann to request an extension of my leave until fall. It is imperative for our work that one of us stays in Alaska during the summer.

Toward evening on December 3 we land in Astoria. Since our ship stops here until the next morning, we wander through the city.

Sunday, December 4

In the early morning we leave Astoria, where we had to wait for more favorable tidal conditions. The sand bar at the mouth of the Columbia again poses no difficulties. In calm seas and favorable winds we sail along the sometimes low, sometimes fairly high, densely wooded coast. Around 10:00 P.M. we safely pass the ill-famed Cape Flattery.

Near this cape there is an Indian reservation. A young merchant aboard our ship runs the only government-approved trading post there. He tells us that these tribes, as perhaps many others living farther north, are not destined to become victims of civilization. They live in wooden houses and wear the same clothes as white people. From spring till the end of June, the men find rewarding employment catching fur seals (*Calliorhynchus ursinus*). The Indians and their wooden canoes carved out of one trunk are taken out by small schooners to suitable fishing sites. Summer is the time to catch halibut and other sea fish, mostly for their own use. During harvest time, they work on farms where their services as diligent and strong workers are well paid for in money, no longer in goods. They are active and eager to learn.

A young Indian whom the above-mentioned merchant had taken to San Francisco had looked with great interest at the wonders of civilization, like railroads, factories, printing presses, etc.

Monday, December 5

During the night we pass through the Strait of Juan de Fuca and before dawn we land at its eastern end in Port Townsend. One part of the town is built on a plateau that is 30 meters high, the other part on a low-lying sand bar in front of it. Now the town is still very small, counting barely five thousand inhabitants. With its excellent harbor, it probably has a prosperous future. Port Townsend is connected with Portland by two steamship lines and a railroad. The abundance of lumber in its forests, the nearby bituminous coal mines, and trade in agricultural products attract numerous ships to its harbor.

Our steamer takes on a large number of passengers, among them Mrs. Morris, wife of the customs official in Sitka, to whom we have letters of introduction. At noon we depart for Vancouver Island, where we arrive two hours later in Victoria. The small rocky islands covered with firs, the deep fjords of the bay, and the clean wooden houses remind us of Swedish harbor towns.

Across from our mooring place are some Indian houses. The Indians, small squat figures, are coming across in their nutshell-like canoes to offer fish for sale. Here, too, the Indians are relatively well-to-do and mostly well dressed. Especially the Creoles love to dress up.

We visit the town, which actually has just one respectable street. While shopping, we find one bookstore with a fairly large selection of books. All

The city of Victoria as seen from the harbor.

Departure Bay

prices are given in dollars. In Portland all businesses were in the hands of Jews; here one sees none.

The vicinity of Victoria is mostly flat, in the distance some higher elevations can be seen. Within the city several flat granite rocks are exposed, showing clear evidence of glacial scratches in a north-south direction.

Tuesday, December 6

In the morning we again visit the town. At noon our ship leaves the harbor of Victoria and in the evening we dock at Nanaimo.

Wednesday, December 7

While our ship leaves Nanaimo for the nine-mile trip to Departure Bay to take coal aboard, we take advantage of the good weather and walk there. A good road, completely dry after last night's light frost, leads us through dense evergreen forests. These almost remind us of our German mountain forests; however, the existence of California madrone trees (*Arbutus menziesii*) proved the mild winter weather was no exception on Vancouver Island. There is no great abundance of animals here. A few times we saw coots (*Fulica atra*) and a small squirrel. At noon we catch up with our ship and in the afternoon we take a second hike along the beach.

Thursday, December 8

Since the ship is not to depart before noon, we have enough time for an excursion to the lakes where the coal mines are. The weather is just as beautiful as yesterday. We do not find anything to hunt. A yellow violet is still in bloom. Around 1:00 P.M. the ship continues sailing through some narrow passages. In the evening the weather turns cloudy and cold.

Friday, December 9

We also pass through very narrow channels and past countless islands east and north of Vancouver Island. These islands remind us of a trip through the rocky promontories in Sweden, except those here are more densely wooded. Around noon we reach the north end of Vancouver Island. For 30 miles we are on the open ocean. It is relatively calm, but nevertheless, the ladies and some gold miners are missing at dinner time. In Victoria the number of passengers increased. A woman missionary from Fort Wrangell, a few officers who are going to the warship temporarily stationed there, and also a few gold miners came aboard. Among the lower deck passengers are sixteen sailors hired in San Francisco; however, four of them already deserted in Victoria.

Saturday, December 10

In the morning we again are in a very narrow channel. It has turned colder. A light blanket of snow covers the hills all the way down. A few very pretty valleys with views of large snowfields are passed. During the day it gets colder and colder. We pass the Indian village Metlakatla, a missionary station reportedly doing effective educational work. In the evening we reach the boundary between British Columbia and Alaska. Here begins the territory of the Tlingit Indians, our new field of activity.

CHAPTER FIVE

IN TLINGIT INDIAN TERRITORY
AND THE TRIP TO SITKA

Sunday, December 11, 1881

At first we get acquainted with the home of the Tlingits from our ship. It is a beautiful clear morning, but fairly cold. The temperature is 8°C. We pass through many narrow channels. Farther north, the mountains are getting higher, and several bare, snow-covered peaks are towering above the dark evergreen forest. Just before Fort Wrangell, which we reach at 11:00 A.M., a truly alpine scenery is displayed.

Wrangell is a miserable place. Only a few larger houses stand out among the irregularly scattered log cabins of miners and traders. The missionary building is noteworthy. There, thirty Indian girls receive room, board, and lessons. The Indian village is adjacent, farther south. Here in Wrangell we get our first close look at Tlingit Indians; unfortunately we have only a short time. The Indian houses are built with strong beams, and have doors and glass windows. Their clothing is the same as that of white people. On the other hand, the extraordinarily carved wooden columns decorating some of the houses are reminders of the past. These are called totems. Mostly these are animal figures; bear, eagle, raven, and a kind of tooth-whale found in the local waters have served as models most frequently. They are carved in a very baroque style.

Wrangell is an important starting point for the traffic up the Stikine River to the gold mines of Cassiar in British Columbia. The flourishing business of smuggling brandy is favored by the natural conditions of the land and the closeness of the British border. The prevention of this illegal trade is one of the main goals of the local tax collector.

Around 2:00 P.M. our steamer departs. We enjoy the beautiful views of the snow mountains north of Wrangell. In the darkness we sail through some very narrow passages and are on our way to Sitka.

Monday, December 12 to Wednesday, the fourteenth

The morning of the twelfth we arrive in Sitka. While we are entering the harbor, a snowstorm starts which lasts nearly all day. It seems strange to us when local people tell us that they have never had such bad weather in Sitka. The next two days are more favorable, so that we can appreciate the beautiful location of Sitka.

Soon after we land, we take a walk through the town, then pay a few visits. In the store of Vanderbildt and Withorst we see many Indian tools and objects for sale. Most interesting is our visit to the signal officer who has an apartment in the old Russian Castle, now a meteorological station. From this elevated post one has a gorgeous view of steep mountains up to 900 meters high on one side and numerous smaller and larger wooded islands in the harbor on the other side. In the distance we see the truncated pyramid of Mount Edgecumbe, an extinct volcano on Kruzof Island. In its crater is said to be a lake.

The present Sitka is no longer what it was under the Russians. Everywhere one sees signs of deterioration. The governor's house and the picturesque Greek church are in urgent need of repairs. There also is little left of the pallisade fence with its strong wooden watch towers which once separated the town from the Indian village.

The Indian village consists of about fifty houses with a population of about one thousand. After dusk the Indians have to leave the other town, except for those who are servants of white people and have special permission to stay. Furthermore, a few reliable Indians are maintaining order as members of the police. Captain Glass, commander of the warship presently stationed in local waters, has made the Indians number their houses and keep them and their vicinity clean and dry.

The Indians supply the city with plenty of lumber, fish, and game. A small type of deer is abundant on Baranof Island. The Natives easily earn more than they need for themselves with wood carvings and basket weaving as well as through services at the dock and in stores. We saw beautiful, large Indian boats lying on the beach. Carved doorposts as in Wrangell could not be observed here. Behind the village is the cemetery.

With Captain George, the pilot, we also visit the young Russian priest who arrived here six years ago. He comes from Moscow. He is quite content here, but does not want to stay. The Russian government annually pays a certain sum for the support of the Greek Church in Alaska. The Russian priest told us that he baptized about seventy Indians during the past year and that these attend his services regularly. The ceremonies of the Greek Church definitely make a stronger impression on their minds than the sober Protestant sermon. The Creoles, descendants of Russians and Aleuts, also join the Greek-Catholic religion. Now only a few Russian families are living in the city.

Next we go to the former Russian hospital, now the seat of the Sitka Mission. The missionary gave us a tour of the building. About thirty Indian boys get room, board, and lessons here; about 120 are day students. Apparently the missionaries are very successful. Unfortunately, we could not observe any lessons. While a ship is in the harbor, everyone is so busy reading and writing letters and taking care of received goods that everything else has to be postponed. With our ship came lumber to build a church as well as Christmas presents.

One officer, with a detachment of marine soldiers, is stationed in Sitka to maintain order among the Indians; however, trouble is not expected.

On Wednesday, December 14, we again visited the signal officer and have the same beautiful view from his apartment as last time.

Now the brothers turned their attention to the continuation of their journey. Aurel writes about it in a letter to his mother and sisters:

> Tomorrow we shall be in Harrisburg. There we shall meet an American warship. Should the commandant not transport us by steam bark to Chilkoot, we shall have to charter a canoe. I hope there will be no difficulties on this last leg of the journey. Until now everything has gone smoothly and everywhere we get the best support. In Chilkoot we shall meet three or four whites among the Indians. The missionary and his young wife have been described to us as educated, friendly people.

CHAPTER SIX

FROM SITKA TO CHILKOOT

On December 14 about 10:00 A.M. we leave Sitka. Our trip through the narrow Olga, Nevski, and Peril straits offers gorgeous scenery in clear, frosty weather. Snow-covered mountains with densely wooded slopes, more beautiful than Norway! Numerous islands everywhere. We pass several strong rapids.

In the morning of the fifteenth we land in Harrisburg, a gold-mining town just founded last year. The day before yesterday it was decided that from now on it will bear the proud name Juneau City. The town is on the mainland north of Admiralty and Douglas islands. Our ship docks alongside an American warship for which we had brought coal and provisions. The warship's commander, Captain Glass, had fired the heavy guns to prove their usefulness to the doubting Indians. This had made a great impression on the Natives, who therefore respect him more than the government in Washington. Consequently, it is most valuable for us to receive letters of recommendation from him to the chiefs of the Chilkats and Chilkoots[1] and to the missionary in Chilkoot. In these letters the purpose of our trip is explained, and they are asked not to hinder our efforts. Unfortunately, he cannot take us by small steamboat to Chilkoot, as Mr. Schulze had hoped. So we shall have to wait for favorable weather— yesterday we had a snowstorm—and then take a canoe to Chilkoot, which we hope to reach in four to five days.

We visit Juneau City, in which already eighty gold miners have settled in forty log cabins. We meet several miners. For many years gold has been found in this area, but not until last year were the mines started. The mines are near Taku Bay about 6 miles from the coast, high in the mountains rising steeply from the ocean. Although the daily average yield in gold is only $5 to $6, they are hoping for larger amounts next year. Just a few days ago work had to be interrupted because of the heavy snowfall.

The Indians here do not withdraw from white people; they rather actively seek contact with them. The English language, however, has not been accepted by them. Traders and miners speak the language of the

Natives more or less. It is easier for them to learn Indian because many of them live with Indian women whom they purchase according to local custom. Fifty dollars is the usual price. Miners also employ Indians as earth diggers or wood cutters, whereby the Indians earn $1 to $2 per day. Such a good possibility of earning a living led about 200 Indians from all parts of their territory to build their huts in Juneau City near the miners. We visit this Indian village and step inside some of the huts. There we find the inhabitants, mostly women and children, squatting around the open fire. During the winter the fire is usually kept going all day in the center of the hearth area. They burn dry wood. The radiant heat and the thick smoke filling the entire room do not bother the Tlingit. While we keep as far away as possible from the fire, he moves right next to it. It is the task of men and boys to gather firewood. Every day they go into the woods to get dry wood. The example of white people has not yet induced the Tlingit to store a supply of fresh wood for the winter and let it dry. He only provides enough firewood for his daily needs.

But now let us go back to the white population. Juneau City has a post office and regular monthly connection with San Francisco. Also, one of the factories of the North West Trading Company is located here. When we leave our ship at noon on December 16, we take up lodgings at the trading post. It is quite crowded and we have to hang around the store when we are not outside.

Saturday, December 17

Bear and sheep skins are spread on the floor of the attic for us, and we sleep somewhat comfortably on them during the night. After our ship has left the harbor, at 4:00 A.M., we unfortunately discover that our large canvas suitcase has been left aboard. Captain Glass visits us and brings us the promised letters of introduction.

We had intended to take the trip to Chilkoot in a canoe with Indians. When they demand $50, we prefer to accept the offer of a miner, Mr. Barrents, to transport us by sailboat with the help of two Indians for $35. This way we avoid the risk of Indians going on strike to demand higher wages and thus delaying the trip.

Sunday, December 18

Today we depart, all together six people, since the miner takes along his Indian wife. Around 10:00 A.M. we leave Juneau City. Due to the Indians' tardiness, we lose some precious time for which we had to pay dearly. When we get to a sand bar 6 miles from Juneau City which is passable only at high tide, we go aground near a small island. We are forced to camp here.

Since we originally had not planned on a longer boat trip, we do not have a tent and camping equipment. An outspread sail barely protects us against the wetness and dampness from above and below. Here, plenty of firewood is available everywhere, so we can enjoy a good camp fire which we missed in the land of the Chukchis. Upon our return from a duck hunting trip, we find a large fire prepared by the Indians on which we can cook our food. Covered with our blankets, we sleep fairly well, since the night is not too cold.

Monday, December 19

The next morning the boat is still stuck. The weather is stormy. High tide rises so quickly that it is impossible to reach the boat. When we finally get there it is too late. The Indians apparently are unwilling to travel in this weather. One of the Indians asks for tobacco. When he does not get it, he packs his belongings and starts to go home. After a short time, however, he returns without saying a word.

Tuesday, December 20

In the morning the weather is clear. It takes till ten o'clock to get the boat afloat. At first we move only slowly, but later we have a strong favorable wind. We pass two beautiful snow-covered glaciers.[2] Through a labyrinth of islands we get to Lynn Canal. The wind is growing stronger and it is quite cold in the boat, so we are glad when the arrival of dusk and a broken sailing boom force us to land. We find a beautiful bay protected by some rocky islands and camp at the edge of the forest. We are wet and cold, but considerable time and effort have to be spent to remove several feet of snow before we can enjoy the warmth of the camp fire. This night we are pitching three tents with our sails.

On Wednesday, the twenty-first, we start in beautiful weather, but soon a strong head wind forces us to look for a new camp site. We land at Berners Bay. It is still early, so we have time to take a look at the beautiful forest. Different kinds of mosses cover trees and rocks.

117

Thursday, December 22

The wind is more favorable but at times so strong that we have to wait in a sheltered place. This night we land at the mouth of a small brook, and after removal of the snow, we set up camp under a protruding rock. This way we are sheltered from above, but during the night the melting snow on the ground made us soaking wet.

Friday, December 23

The light wind soon increases so violently that our sails have to be reefed. When our rudder breaks we are in real danger for quite some time. At times the sea is very rough and splashes into the boat. At high speed we cover a long distance.

The clear day allows us the most beautiful view of the magnificent mountain scenery through which Lynn Canal cuts. In almost every ravine we see masses of ice, sometimes high on the slopes, sometimes descending to sea level. Also, in the fjords near the valleys we frequently see glaciers. The varied shapes of glaciers are due to the nature of the valley and the condition of the rocky banks. One glacier tumbles down in several ice cascades, while another one flows in a meandering stream. At this time they are all covered with snow. In summer some glaciers show a glittering bluish surface, while others are densely covered with rocks. They look black from the distance and resemble a mud avalanche. One glacier shows at its lower end a single large opening through which a considerable river flows. The ice masses of another glacier are shaped like a fan at its mouth, and at its periphery, several strong brooks have their source. Snow-covered mountains project sometimes with rugged, sometimes with smooth cone-shaped or rounded peaks. Dense evergreen forests cover the slopes. Once in a while a snow avalanche has produced a clearing.

CHAPTER SEVEN

EXPERIENCES IN CHILKAT TERRITORY
WINTER 1881/1882

On December 23, in the evening of the sixth day of our boat trip, we arrive in Chilkoot,[3] where we really surprise the population. The trader for the North West Trading Company, Mr. Dickinson, immediately puts an adequate room in the warehouse at our disposal. The trader and missionary couple are the only white people here. The trader's wife is a Tsimshian Indian.[4] She was educated in a mission school about 20 kilometers south of Fort Simpson, where, in addition to religious instruction, the Indians learned several crafts as well as strict cleanliness. In 1880 she had started a school in Chilkoot and apparently directed it with more skill and understanding of children than the missionary, Willard, who is now responsible for its direction. The children learn to read English; they learn the small catechism in English and their Native language and they learn some songs.

Saturday, December 24, 1881

Christmas among the Indians! We are busy unpacking and drying our luggage. In the evening we attend the Christmas celebration in the missionary's house. About sixty children—boys and girls—are assembled. A number of adults, among them Chief Don-e-wak, are also present. The celebration itself is very simple. Mrs. Dickinson asks the children a few questions and translates the missionary's questions. The children sing a few hymns with rough voices but in fairly good harmony. From their answers and the way they are singing, it is evident that they attend to it with little comprehension. With more joy they later sing their Native rowing song, joined loudly by their elders. Mrs. Willard attends the celebration lying on a bed; she looks very ill. Among the children are some with very intelligent faces; their abilities are reportedly remarkable.

The following excerpt is included to clarify the journals of the next few months:

The map pictured here has been laboriously drawn by Arthur Krause, based on his own measurements. Lynn Canal is 60 nautical miles (111

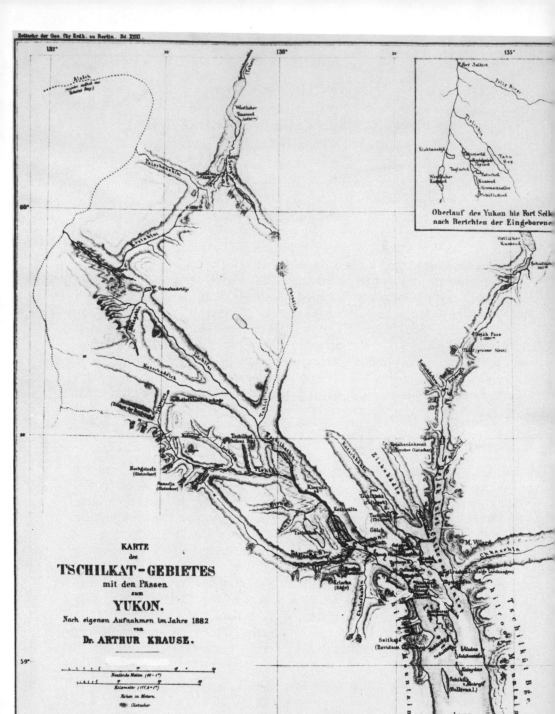

Oberlauf des Yukon bis Fort Selkirk
nach Berichten der Eingeborene

KARTE
des
TSCHILKAT-GEBIETES
mit den Pässen
zum
YUKON.

Nach eigenen Aufnahmen im Jahre 1882
von
Dr. ARTHUR KRAUSE.

Nautische Meilen (60 = 1°)
Kilometer (111,3 = 1°)
Höhen in Metern.
Gletscher.

137° westl. Länge von Greenwich.

Autogr. v. W. Droysen

Berlin, Dietrich Reimer, 1883.

Druck v. H. S. Hermann, Be

120

At left, map of the Chilkat Territory[5]

kilometers) long and an average of 5 miles (9 kilometers) wide. At its northern end, a long narrow peninsula divides it into two arms. The western one is known as Chilkat Bay or Chilkat Inlet, the eastern arm is called Chilkoot Bay or Chilkoot Inlet. The peninsula[6] separating these inlets stretches for about 13 miles (24 kilometers) in a southeasterly direction. It has a few hills about 100 meters high and is densely wooded. Into Chilkat Inlet flows the important Chilkat River, which gave its name to the area through which it flows and to its population, a tribe of the Tlingit Indians. On this river are three larger villages of the Chilkat Indians (Klokwan, Katkwaltu, and Jendestake). On the Chilkoot side there is the less important Chilkoot village, situated on a lake which is connected with the ocean by a short outlet. Traffic between Chilkoot and Chilkat mainly takes place on a well-trodden footpath, the "Trail,"[7] which crosses the narrow peninsula at the place where the peninsula becomes the mainland. Here, on the Chilkoot side, on Portage Bay, is the trading post of the North West Trading Company and the station of the Presbyterian Home Mission. The Natives call this place "Deshu."[8] Furthermore, several temporary Native huts were built here.

Mountains with an elevation of 1,000 to 2,000 meters surround both inlets as well as the valleys of the Chilkat area. In its gorges are numerous large glaciers. The fjords have a considerable depth, averaging 50 fathoms (approximately 90 meters). The banks are very steep, so that it is often impossible to walk along the shore even at low tide. At the mouths of the rivers are extensive sand bars. During low tide (the difference between low and high tide is 6 to 7 meters) they are exposed, and especially during spring and fall numerous beach and water birds assemble here. The tide in the Chilkat River goes up to the village of Jendestake. At low tide the water near Pyramid Island in Chilkat Inlet is almost drinkable. The fjord never freezes. During the winter a barrier of irregularly stacked ice floes forms at the boundary line between tide and current. Above this barrier, an even blanket of ice and snow covers the Chilkat River which is about 2 miles (3.7 kilometers) wide here. Also farther upriver the bottom of the valley is almost entirely covered by the river. In fact, at the time of high water the entire lowland is flooded. At other times the river is divided into numerous arms and has to squeeze through a maze of low wooded islands, whereby the main current touches alternately each steep bank of the valley. All the rivers of the Chilkat area are relatively short, but extraordinarily full of water, because they are fed by numerous glaciers. On a cloudless summer day, the effect of the sun upon the snow and ice fields of the mountains can cause a rapid swelling by 1 to 2 meters. According to several measurements, the gradient of the rivers is very significant.

Sunday, December 25

We are still occupied with unpacking and getting settled. The weather is very unfavorable; it snows all day long, the snow is about 4 to 5 feet deep (120 to 150 centimeters); only narrow footpaths lead from one house to the next.

The establishment of a trading station here, too, caused the founding of an Indian settlement. About 200 persons live in nine houses. They moved here both from Chilkat and Chilkoot.

The only path free of snow is found along the beach at low tide. Numerous flocks of ducks live in the water. We already realize that the fauna as well as the flora will give us plenty to do even during the winter.

Chilkoot, December 25, 1881

Dear Mother and Sisters,

From December 15 to the eighteenth we stayed in Juneau, a gold miners' town only one year old. The first night we spent aboard ship, the next two in the warehouse of the North West Trading Company, where a comfortable bed of bear and sheep skins was made for us on the floor of the attic. Dick Willoughby, the general helper of the trading post and a personality well known throughout the entire area, took charge of our further transportation. The negotiations with the Indians did not lead to any result, so Dick advised us to accept the offer of a gold miner, Mr. Barrents, to take us and all our luggage to Chilkoot in a sailboat for $35. During the winter the mines about 5 to 6 miles outside Juneau are closed, so the people lead a more or less leisurely, quiet life. This is interrupted only once a month by the arrival of the steamer *Eureka* (say "yoo re ka", but say it in a low voice, so no ancient Greek can hear you).

The attic of the North West Trading Company was the assembly place of the better elements who came here to talk. Strange stories did we hear there, one more incredible than the next. Finally, further exaggerations were temporarily stopped by the indignant question, "Who is next?" The news that we wanted to go on to Chilkoot spread quickly. Soon we met several people who had been there last summer and from there over to the Yukon and downriver a few hundred miles to the vicinity of the now deserted trading post, Ft. Selkirk. From them we could learn some interesting details about this area never before visited by white people. It was typical for their point of view that they considered us to be another variety of the species gold miner. One miner had become very talkative through the consumption of the brandy that had been smuggled in on our ship. He advised us, since we were such "healthy looking fellows," to go over the mountains to the Yukon, to prospect the land all over, and when we find something, to send them a message, so they could make a good rush there. Among the miners we saw many typical, truly Bret-Harte kind of gold miners, people who had searched for, found, and lost gold in California, Montana, Nevada, even in Australia. On the whole, good order was maintained in the city, which, like all of Alaska, had no other government than the tax office. Every place protects and governs itself. In the evening after the arrival of our steamer, it was rather lively in town, a few brawls, but nothing of a serious nature, without the usual pistol shots, etc.

Our trip by boat to Chilkoot went relatively well. The little sketch of this trip will give you an idea of the course we took. The numbers one through five indicate camp sites, some of which were beautiful in spite of the rather great discomforts. Upon arrival at a good camp site, Jim, the tall silent Indian armed with an axe, got off the boat first. A large dead tree was felled, cut up into logs, and a mighty fire was started. Next we had to melt snow or get water to make tea or coffee, etc., to dry wet clothing and blankets, and prepare the camp site. Some of the snow was shoveled off, then a thick layer of fir boughs [...end missing]

Monday, December 26

The weather improves somewhat today, so we use this day for a hunting trip along the beach both north and south. We become aware of the large variety of birds. Ducks, jays, water starlings, and eagles are observed. On the bank we find some beautiful hornblende.

Thursday, December 29

During the night and throughout the day, the wind becomes stronger and more or less violent; at the same time, we have clear weather with frost. When returning from a hunting excursion before breakfast, I accidentally drop my gun trying to catch my hat which the wind was blowing into the ocean. The butt of the gun broke off.

Later we take a walk north to the four huts at the mouth of the Chilkoot River.[9] We enter one of them and find about twenty people, men, women, and children, sitting in a circle around the fire. One woman knits a fishnet, one man carves a snowshoe. A pair of gloves is offered for sale and we buy them. The view was very beautiful today, particularly on our return, while the setting sun shone upon the mountains.

Friday, December 30

We hike to the opposite bank. Today the snow is hard enough so that we can walk along the footpath without snowshoes. The entire trail goes through evergreen forest mixed with a few deciduous trees. The last stretch is all alder, called *kashish* by the Indians. At the coast a strong north wind makes walking difficult. There are numerous ice blocks on the beach, probably stemming from the Davidson Glacier. We observed the glacier itself during our arrival and now we have a good view of its lower part. After our return we take another short walk along the beach. In the evening we learn that the Indians use alder twigs to beat each other in the morning. They sit on the beach by the ocean with naked upper bodies. First one person beats another, then he hands the twigs to the other person and is beaten by him. They do this to make themselves strong and hardened.

Saturday, December 31

We intend to take a longer excursion along the beach southward, but the poor weather, stormy with drifting snow, prevents us from doing so. We go for a short walk along the trail, collect some lichen and evergreen twigs, and then return.

In the evening we attend a performance of Indian dances to celebrate New Year's Eve in the schoolhouse. Women and children are also participating in the dances. These consist of rhythmic movements of the entire body while the beat is given by a drum and feet, often increased by knocking a staff against a wooden board. This is accompanied by a not unpleasant tune in which the entire audience, especially the children, participates with liveliness. Several rattles are also used. These consist of two parts; the hollow interior is filled with small pebbles. The dancers' faces are painted with red and blue colors or hidden by painted wooden masks.

First a few Indian dances are performed. One after another, different masked persons—men, women, boys, and girls—enter through the door. Each one dances his own movement to the same beat until they all form a circle. These dance movements, becoming more and more vigorous, are continued for a long time. Some of the dancers wear the fur clothes of the Stick Indians and feathers in their hair and nostrils. Finally, they amuse their audience with mimicry of white people's dances. These dances are performed by black-faced dancers, perhaps out of consideration of the presence of white people. One has to admit that the Indian audience is entitled to find our dances ridiculous, even if it were no parody. In our dances they cannot discover any special aesthetic value.

Late in the evening numerous gunshots go off to celebrate the end of the old year.

At the moment a few Stick Indians are still here; those who were here a few days ago went back when new frost hardened the snow again. The Stick Indians belong to a different nomadic tribe living beyond the mountains in the interior. Their language is different, and only a few Tlingit can understand them. They like to decorate themselves with feathers, which they stick into their hair and through their pierced nasal septum. For this reason, Americans call them Stick Indians. The Tlingit call them *Gunanas.* Their physiognomies are quite attractive. The Stick Indians are on very favorable terms with the Tlingit, but they are not allowed to have direct contact with white people. This middleman's business is the monopoly of the Tlingit.

125

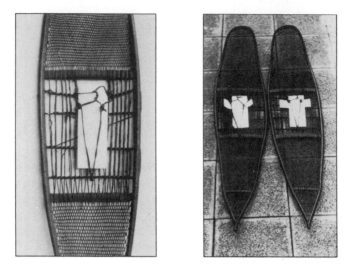

*The photograph on the right shows Aurel Krause's
snowshoes which he bought and used in Alaska. On the
left is a close-up view of the binding. These snowshoes are
in the possession of Gerhard Krause.
Photograph by Gerhard Krause.*

Sunday, January 1, 1882

Today the snowshoes which we had bought from the missionary's
brother for $2.75 finally arrived. We also bought some moccasins. Imme-
diately we try out the snowshoes. Now we can walk through the forest in
6 feet of snow!

*In a personal letter Arthur Krause writes the following about snow-
shoes in Alaska:*

The Indians report that they learned from the animals the
manufacture of snowshoes. Once, after a heavy snowfall, the
grouse was in a great dilemma about how to move forward. It
tried to make some snowshoes, but did not succeed and started
to cry and complain miserably. At that moment the ptarmigan
came running across the loose snow on its excellent snowshoes.
It asked the grouse what was the cause of its grief, and then

showed him how to start making snowshoes. That is how the grouse received its at least half-finished snowshoes. The sight of them gave the Indians the idea to manufacture similar ones for themselves.

In fact, such a snowshoe is a true piece of art, in which pleasing shape and light weight are combined with extraordinary stability. A frame of maple or birch wood is bent by fire and smoke into the appropriate shape. The front and end sections are covered by a net made of thin leather strips. The stronger net in the middle serves as foot binding. It is no wonder that it takes some time to learn how to behave with such 4- to 5-foot-long appendages. The difficulty starts right away when putting them on. A peculiar screwlike turn of the foot, which magically puts into motion joints and muscles, moves the foot, covered with a leather stocking, into the leather sling. Finally, when you have managed this, you try to walk on level snow and, to your amazement, it works splendidly, just like walking in giant felt slippers. But when you try to turn around, you probably step on your own heel and naturally fall on your nose. Now you are in real trouble. One leg is here, the other one there, the snowshoes are still attached to your feet. They are, however, twisted into the snow in such a way that you cannot pull them out. You try to support yourself on your arm, but you find no resistance and only work yourself deeper into the snow. You grab a branch, but it breaks like glass in this frost, and the jolt brings new amounts of snow on your neck. Your snowshoes offer the only firm spot. You must try to get hold of them, or at least one of them, to turn it into the correct position. Then you should try gradually to lift your whole body and soul. That is how you learn to walk on snowshoes. But before you learn how to run, jump, climb up slopes and slide down on them, you need more than one opportunity to practice getting up. Especially difficult is penetrating through dense underbrush. On the other hand, it is easy to walk over entire trees and bushes covered by snow. So, on the whole, roaming through the woods is easier in winter than in summer.

First only one pair of snowshoes are bought; therefore, Arthur stays on the footpath and Aurel traverses the woods. He writes in his journal:

Walking with snowshoes is not difficult, but when going uphill and downhill or turning, one has to watch out. I fell several times because I was not too careful. The forest is very dense. A great deal of partly thorny underbrush and fallen tree trunks hinders one's progress in summer, but now we can walk right over all these obstacles with our snowshoes. Only the tips of the larger bushes can be seen above the snow cover. The berries of *Cornus sanguinea* Linné were still found in the woods; their acid taste was not unpleasant. Birds apparently like them, too. Today snow fell again all day.

The second chief of the village shows us his papers, among them a letter of recommendation which tells that he owes tobacco to somebody, another one [stating] that he has a weakness for falling in love with white ladies.

In the evening we briefly visit the missionary to wish him a happy New Year. His wife is still sick in bed.

Abridged letter to the German Geographical Society in Bremen:

Chilkoot, Monday, January 2, 1882

The unfavorable weather until now, first steady southerly winds, then very strong northerly winds, has kept Mr. Barrents, the man who brought us here from Juneau City, from returning. Today, I am able to give him my travel report and describe our further experiences to this date. There is not too much to report yet. Daily we are making excursions in good or bad weather, mostly along the beach either north or south, because there we find a more or less wide space free from snow at low tide. The difference between low and high tide is about 20 feet (about 6 meters, but we have not yet taken exact measurements). The deeply fissured igneous rocks, rich in hornblende, slope steeply down to the ocean and make it very difficult to walk here. For a few days the trail leading from here to the Chilkat side was passable, since the snow was hardened by the frost.

The best opportunity for contact with the Indians is here in this house. The Indian hostess speaks the Thlingit or Klingit language fluently and also speaks enough English to be our teacher for the study of the Indian language.

Until now the English language has found extraordinarily little acceptance here. It would be much more difficult here than on the Bering Strait, if we had to look for an interpreter among the Native population.

Tuesday, January 3

Today I make an excursion with snowshoes along the beach, find almost nothing, and have a rather arduous day. Arthur, however, went along the trail with his gun, where he observed a woodpecker and other animals. We buy a second pair of snowshoes, larger and wider, for the same price as the first pair.

Thursday, January 5

Since the weather is beautiful and mild, a trip to Chilkoot is taken with missionary Willard. Arthur stays home because of a toothache. We take the missionary's canoe, which is rather small and narrow, but sufficient in calm weather. We decide to go to the glacier first. The sea is almost completely smooth. After a two-hour trip we reach the glacier's bay and find the ice difficult to break. It is impossible or very difficult to move on. The glacier still seems to be far away. We now go back with the tide, but get caught in ice which starts moving. Several times we are in danger of being crushed by ice or being surrounded by newly forming ice. With great difficulty we have to row through the ice or break it with the paddle. A few times Willard jumps overboard to push the ice floes aside, until we finally reach the open water. The back part of the bay is very shallow. Furthermore, it is enclosed by a sand bar visible only at low tide, apparently a moraine. The bay is very deep only at one place where the rocks climb vertically out of the water. Since it is turning dark when we reach the open water, we give up our trip to Chilkoot. Instead we go to Tanani, the small settlement across from here, and enter the same house we visited before. We serve some hard bread to the people and at the same time have our own meal. We have not had anything since breakfast, so, naturally, we are quite hungry. Seventeen persons, men, women, and children, squat around the hearth, built in the usual way with crosswise stacked large logs. There are no chairs or stools; only mats are scattered on the floor on which the Tlingit squats or lies stretched out resting his head on one arm.

He can spend hours in this, for us, uncomfortable position. However, for us they quickly find a seat. In the recognized place of honor across from the door they place a box used for storage of household utensils and cover it with cloth or a woolen blanket. The occupants of this house are busy preparing and eating their meal, a porridge, dried salmon, and berries. Afterwards one person continues working on snowshoes, another returns from hunting and brings some ducks. One man shows us his sore foot, perhaps to attract our generosity. The people are very quiet but not unfriendly. On the return trip we are rather tired, mainly caused by the hard work among the floating ice, but also by the cramped position in our boat.

Friday, January 6

While preparing for a hunting trip, we notice that the inside leather of one snowshoe has been removed. It could only have been done with a sharp knife. All speculations as to the offender and the place of the deed are unclear at first. Not until later do we understand the connections. The Tlingits are accustomed to receiving a reward for every little service. The night before, when we returned at low tide, we had asked an Indian, who idly stood on the beach, to assist us in pulling up the boat. Since it was rather late, we forgot to reward him for this insignificant work. People here are convinced that it was this Indian who cut the leather netting of our snowshoe with a knife because he had not received the expected reward. That evening he did not demand it, and otherwise we had not been sparing with the distribution of small gifts.

In the evening we visited with the missionary, looked at all the rooms, and learned some interesting facts. Some Indians keep slaves, but mostly these are given wages now. They usually are Flatheads, who became slaves through war and purchase. The missionary also had quite a number of Indian tools, also a stone hatchet, which he had found near his house.

Saturday, January 7

All day long it snows so heavily that we have to omit our usual hunting trip. The temperature is very mild, one degree above the freezing point.

Sunday, January 8

Early in the morning we take a hunting trip southward along the beach. Wet snow is falling. The duck I shoot is carried away by the wind. A little brown bird, similar to a troglodytide (wren), appears on the rock at the beach and flies back into the woods. Then I walk along the trail with Arthur. On the way back I shoot a duck which can be retrieved.

Our host reminds us of the holiness of Sunday. The missionary lectures that one should not hunt or fish on Sunday; even skating means the desecration of Sunday to him. In the evening we went to the missionary for a short while.

Monday, January 9

This morning we try to go into the woods. The walk is very difficult, so that we have trouble moving ahead. We fall several times, because the snowshoes become stuck in the hardened crust of the snow. We see two conifers which we had not noticed before, a *Pinus*, perhaps *contorta*, and an *Abies*. We return early, although the weather turns very beautiful in the afternoon. While we prepare some cartridges, the missionary's visit distracts us.

Tuesday, January 10

Not until rather late do we start on today's little hike. It is clear, but rather cold. We walk along the trail to the opposite bank and then southward.

Mouth of the Chilkat River. This view was sketched from Portage Point. Jan. 10, 1881 [1882].[10]

While Arthur takes a few bearings, he sees two wolflike animals approaching him. We meet an Indian who gives Arthur the names of the mountains. While I sketch, an eagle flies close over my head. Then the wolves come again within gunshot. I am not sure, however, whether these might be wolflike dogs, consequently I do not shoot. In the meantime, Arthur had gone ahead to take some more bearings.

Upon our return, we discuss with Mr. Willard the longer excursion we had planned for tomorrow to go to Klukwan[11] on the Chilkat River for several days. Then we skinned two ducks which we had received this morning, and finally prepared our equipment for tomorrow.

Wednesday, January 11

Early in the morning we set out with missionary Willard and two Indians. One of these, Kasko, serves as our guide. At dawn we walk quickly along the trail through the forest to the opposite side of the peninsula. Going along on the well-trodden path by the beach, we reach the lower Chilkat village, Jendestake. At this time of the year it is completely deserted, because during the winter its inhabitants move to the trading post here at Deshu, where they find a larger supply of wood. In the summer, during salmon season, they all go back to their old places, and then the little winter huts are deserted.

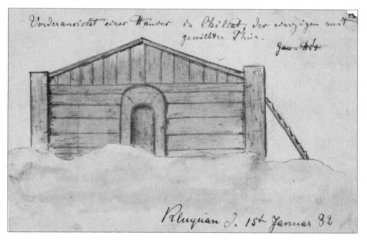

This shaman's house (gau-hit) *is the only one with an arched door.*
Klukwan, January 15, 1882.

The houses are all built of boards in the same style. These boards are cut from a tree with an axe. The houses have an almost square ground plan and a flat gabled roof. The 'doctor,' as the shaman is often called, is having a new house built for himself here. At the four corners, mighty posts have been set into the earth, so that they stand about 3 meters high.

From this presently deserted Chilkat village we continue our hike on the ice of the Chilkat River. Because of repeated floods, most of the snow is melted here, so we can put on our ice skates, which really astonishes our Indian companions. In the morning we were extremely cold because we were heading into an unpleasant cold wind. Now the wind has diminished; our movement on the ice warmed us up, so that we can enjoy the beautiful scenery. The river valley, about 1 to 3 kilometers wide, is interrupted by numerous smaller and larger islets among which the shallow river arms wind their way. Poplar is the main tree here on this alluvial soil, while the mountainous banks adjoining the valley are covered with evergreens.

Finally, toward evening, we reach Katwaltu [Katkwaltu],[12] a place consisting of eight houses with about 125 inhabitants. Upon Kasko's advice, we leave our snowshoes here. A two-hour laborious hike along the river still has to be covered. Here the river never completely freezes over. The small path leading through the poplars along the bank is not easy in daylight, but in darkness it is particularly difficult. Several times we have to squeeze through underbrush or slide down slopes. Our guide frequently has to use his hatchet to enlarge the path for himself and our luggage, which he carries on his back. The air is filled with the smell of decaying salmon lying in large numbers on the bank and in the river. We are glad when, finally, in complete darkness, we reach the houses of Klukwan.

One of our companions runs ahead and announces our arrival to old Tschartritsch, the most respected chief of the Chilkat Indians. In his house we receive his best hospitality. Opposite the door the seat of honor, boxes covered with white linen, is prepared for us. In the house we greet Tschartritsch and his wife, who is quite pretty in spite of her blackened face. She wears a 2-centimeters-long silver peg in the lower lip which protrudes through the skin above her chin. In addition to the chief and his wife, their son Jelchkuchu and the young Willy Dickinson are present. A kettle is put on the huge fire in the center of the living area where we cook our tea. Then we fry a few salmon trout. After supper a sleeping place is prepared for us with woolen blankets belonging to Tschartritsch.

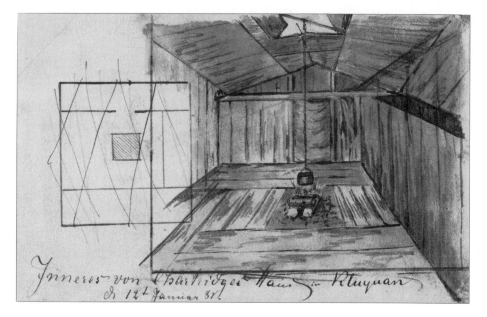

Interior of Tschartritsch's house in Klukwan. In the center of the room is a fire with big logs heating a kettle which is suspended from the ceiling next to the smoke opening in the roof. On the left is the sketch of a square floor plan. January 12, 1882.

Thursday, January 12, to Tuesday, the seventeenth, in Klukwan

In spite of our fatigue we slept poorly. The blankets were too short and it was a little too cold. We get up late and prepare our morning tea. And during our eight days in this house, we get to know the domestic life of the Chilkat Indians and the village of Klukwan. On several longer trips up river we also gain some information about this territory rarely ever visited by white people until now.

Tschartritsch lives in his house only with his own family, including two slaves. Most other houses are occupied by several families; often there are more than thirty people in larger houses. In addition to the house he lives in, Tschartritsch owns two large warehouses; one is on an island in the river. The slaves are acquired through war or purchase from other tribes. The relationship between master and slave is entirely satisfactory. We never heard or saw anything about mistreatment or oppression nor did we hear any complaints by the slaves, who enjoy a great deal of freedom.

When Tschartritsch let us have one of his slaves as a guide, this man was even allowed to keep a certain amount of the reward for himself.

In former times, sacrifices of slaves were customary at large feasts; however, in recent years nothing has been heard about them. This may be due to the small number of slaves as well as to the fact that the large, expensive feasts are celebrated only seldom. The American government is trying to prevent such sacrifices and in some cases ordered the freeing of slaves.

The domestic life in the Tschartritsch house offers not too much variety. At dawn, i.e., in winter between eight and nine o'clock, they get up. First the two slaves start the fire in the woodpile in the middle of the living area. Logs, sometimes as big as a foot in diameter, are stacked in pairs crosswise. Dressing does not take much time, since the Indians do not take off any clothes at night. They wash their faces and hands, and sweep the board floor. There are no definite hours set for meals. Dried or roasted salmon, roasted duck, a porridge made of flour, and berries in fish oil mainly comprise their food. Seldom do they indulge in the luxury of a cup of tea. The day's work is not strenuous, but they are not idle. Firewood is procured by slaves and lesser ranking members of the household. The main occupation of the men outside the house is hunting and fishing. Inside the house they spend their time making and repairing all kinds of tools and household utensils. During our stay in Klukwan the Indians are busy preparing a trading expedition to the territory of the Gunana,[13] to take three to six weeks. The men make snowshoes, the women moccasins. Weapons are repaired. Every man owns a box with tools; the woman's box contains sewing materials and jewelry. Strangely bent short knives are skillfully used for wood carving.

After the morning tea in Tschartritsch's house, we visit the house of Three-Finger Jack. He lost two fingers when a gun exploded in his hand. The missionary would like to use his house as a school. In the house we see several old objects, dance masks with copper (however, as we learn from Willy Dickinson, these are the work of Simpson Indians) and spoons carved of horn and wood. In front of the doors are big piles of wood. The women are busy making moccasins, the man works on snowshoes. Then we go on and Willy and the missionary go fishing for trout. While they are getting ready for fishing, we walk across the ice and along some good trails. The woods on this side consist mostly of deciduous trees, poplars and alders. Farther on we find very good ice for skating. Upon our return, we

135

watch the trout fishing. A small hole is made in the ice, into which a piece of meat, wrapped in a net, is lowered. When the trout arrive, they are transfixed with a spear. The hunter squats with his head bent over the hole, completely covered with a blanket, holding the lance in the water. When a fish approaches, the lance is carefully lowered and then the fish is pierced with a quick thrust.

After dinner, which consisted of duck, we attend the initiation of a new shaman. The old one belonging to the Raven clan had died recently and had been buried ceremoniously. The house is packed with the members of the clan. A circle of people, men and boys, is assembled around a big fire built of thick logs. The boys are closest to the fire. They are dressed in festive clothing, which is cleaner than usual, but does not show any tribal features. All have fresh fir twigs garlanded around their necks. We stand with Tschartritsch among the spectators near the door. In the background, opposite us and to our left, the women squat with their small children. At the right of the entrance, on a raised platform, stands the leader of the ceremony, who, with the help of several old Indians, gives the beat for the songs. On racks close to him hang the regalia of the shaman, the necklace with pendants of teeth, beaks, and other rattling objects, the headdress with ermine furs hanging down over the back, the dance apron woven of mountain goat wool, various masks, and other objects.

The loud songs are accompanied by the drum and the beating together of two wooden sticks. The drum was a brightly painted wooden box with one side covered with skin; the rhythm is beaten by foot. From time to time the songs are interrupted by shouted questions and answers which we do not understand. Then all the participants resume with wild gesticulations, shaking their clenched fists and stamping the floor with their feet, as they move toward the fire and back again. All these movements are carried out with extraordinary rhythm and great precision. They allow themselves only short pauses between the individual songs, of which altogether four are sung with great earnestness and devoted attention by the assembly.

During the third song two wooden chests of the dead shaman are lowered through the smoke hole into the room, and the masks, rattles, drums, etc., which they contain are individually unpacked. Each mask is held toward the fire for a short time, while the song continues without interruption.

The fourth song had a more lively tempo. During the wildest noises, suddenly a young Indian who had hidden among the spectators, plunges through the row of dancers almost through the fire toward the wooden drum. After some convulsive contortions he falls down next to it, appar-

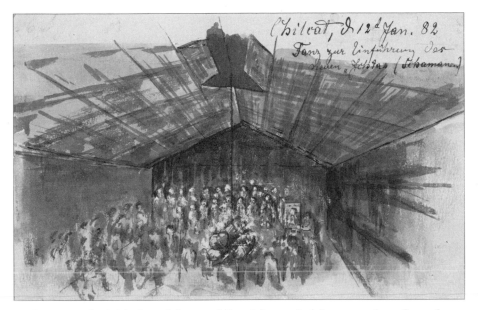

Dance at the initiation of the new ichta *(shaman). A large number of people are crowded inside a house, dancing around the fire to celebrate the initiation. The author observed this initiation in Klukwan.*
Chilkat, January 12, 1882.

ently unconscious, and someone standing nearby throws the shaman's necklace over his neck. This is the new shaman. For a while he remains motionless on the floor while the song continues and the disturbance seems to be ignored. When he recovers, he withdraws unnoticed into the row of spectators and soon thereafter the ceremony ends.

The shaman's regalia are now removed in the same way in which they had arrived, namely, through the smoke hole. At the end, white down feathers, which had come through the smoke hole earlier, were blown upward into the air. Then the spectators left the room, while the Raven clan, men, women, and children, remained for a four-day fast.

On the evening of the third day, the new shaman performs a dance around the fire wearing only a colorful dance blanket and holding a pointed knife. Unfortunately, we could not be present, because we did not return from a longer excursion until late.

The fourth and final evening started out with the same ceremonies of the first night. We notice, however, a great deal of relaxation and fatigue of the participants. Some of the younger boys seem to have left the group of fasting persons. Children are supposed to fast for two days only. Also the wife of Tschartritsch and her children, who follow the mother's clan, do not fast. Since she also belongs to the Raven clan, this exception is difficult to understand. Young Dickinson explains that the so-called nobility is excepted. The new shaman has to fast for eight days, but is permitted to take a light meal on the morning of the fifth day.

In the evening we talk with Tschartritsch; Willy is our interpreter. More to the missionary's satisfaction than ours, Tschartritsch maintains that this initiation was the last of its kind. His people want to live the new way. Until now these local Chilkat Indians had the least amount of contact with whites. Therefore, their original morals and customs are best preserved here. Their willingness to change leads to the conclusion that in a few years these people will lose their peculiar characteristics. Then these Indians, too, will accept the advantages and disadvantages of our civilization. This summer there is to be stationed in Klukwan a missionary, whose reformatory efforts certainly will be aimed at the quick abolishment of the old conditions.

The freedom of action which the Tlingit, little restricted by imposed conditions, could enjoy, are limited by numerous superstitious ideas and fears. Any deviation from the traditional customs, anything unusual, is called *chlaskass* and considered to be the general cause for every misfortune, for bad weather, illness, hunting and war accidents. During a walk near Klukwan we made the following observation: in the woods somewhat aside from the trail and leaning against a tree trunk, are three completely carved figures, in the middle a larger one with its right arm raised as though throwing a spear, and two smaller figures next to it. Apparently people took these carvings out there and seem to be afraid of them. Whoever approaches them is supposed to die. In fact, out of the large group of children who accompanies us, only one small girl dares step next to them. Around here most of the rock cranberry bushes are still fully covered with fruits, while everywhere else the berries have mostly been picked. We are told that in times of emergency the Chilkats burn a fire on the other side of the river across from the wooden carvings, supposedly to appease the figures' wrath.

After breakfast on January 13, Tschartritsch shows us his papers, which all speak very favorably of him. Among them are letters from Glass, Davidson, and others. He also shows us gifts he has received, a meerschaum pipe with cherry wood from the commander of a warship and a silver (or alloy of copper, zinc, and nickel) box from Paul Schulze.

From Tschartritsch we receive quite detailed information about the trade routes into the land of the Gunana. He illustrates his statements with chalk-drawn maps on the floor. Apparently two main routes exist; the most frequently traveled is an eight-day hike up the Chilkat River to a chain of lakes which is connected with the Yukon River. The other one goes up the Chilkoot side through a narrow inlet called Dejah,[14] the mouth of which can be seen from Deschu. From water to water, one also reaches a chain of lakes which flow into the Yukon. On this route the trip can be managed in three days; however, this route is less advantageous because of several rapids.

Upon arrival in the land of the Gunanas, the Chilkat Indians often have to roam the land for some time before they get the necessary number of skins from the nomadic Gunanas. Through breaking of twigs toward one direction, they indicate their presence as well as the direction they are going. A large store of dried salmon is taken along as supply for this long trip. This as well as barter goods are carried in tightly bundled packs on the back and are secured by wide leather straps across the forehead and chest. Amazing loads of 100 pounds and more can be carried by the people in this way on steep mountain paths and across large snowfields.

In winter almost the entire way is made on snowshoes, which have to be especially large to prevent the heavily loaded carrier, who carries a gun and axe in addition to his load, from sinking into the snow. Strangely enough, sleds are rarely used, although they might be very advantageous. The foxlike or wolflike dogs, so numerous in every village, could be trained to pull the sleds. Now the dogs only disturb the calm of the night with their ear-piercing howling.

Outfit for a hike to Chilkat.
A man is carrying a bundle on his back. It is held by straps across his forehead and chest.
Chilkoot, February 1, 1882.

After our conversation with Tschartritsch, we go on our way with our skates. During the night it had rained heavily, so the path is rather wet. We find only a short stretch of fair ice; we do not try too long, but go on. There we have a beautiful view of the mountains. We come to a place where the river valley becomes narrower. We have to return because of the soft ice. Once I even break through and fill my boots with water. Soon thereafter a strong north wind starts; however, it does not bother us during our return. At dusk we arrive in Klukwan. Tschartritsch is concerned about us and asks us not to stay out alone this late.

In the evening Arthur goes to Tschartritsch's house and observes the preparation of *hutschino*,[15] supposedly for the Stick Indians.

Saturday, January 14

After breakfast we again walk the same path and take our ice skates along. This time the path is hard and in several places we find smooth ice. On the bank are some water starlings. We go beyond yesterday's destination for an hour and a half. First we pass the little protruding mountain and then reach the foot of the large one. We see two fox traps, but without bait. Later we learn that the trap plate is only greased. Very few animals are found here. It takes us three and a half hours to get back. We arrive in complete darkness and toward the end it was difficult to find our way. Upon our arrival in the village we again hear the people sing in the shaman's house. The missionary was there. With him we had a discussion on the observation of Sunday.

Sunday, January 15

Next morning we are prevented from skating by heavy snowfall. We now visit first the warehouse of old Tschartritsch, where we see several painted boards, carved wooden bowls, etc. Then we go to several other houses and buy a few small items. Generally, however, the people are very reluctant to sell.

Monday, January 16

There is so much snow that we cannot make a larger excursion. We again visit a few houses, first the one of Three-Finger Jack, then to a man from Sitka, whose wife is weaving baskets. When we visit Sittie, he immediately

Wood carving (left). *The commentary tells that the wood carving on the left with a woman crouched on a bench is in one of Tschartritsch's warehouses (in the four corners). At the upper right of this image is a sled* (rittagit); *at the lower right a small picture of a shaman's grave house. Wooden picture* (right). *An upright picture of several stylized faces is in Tschartritsch's warehouse. On the right is a sketch of a ladder* (dset) *and one enlarged rung. Chilkat, January 12, 1882.*

prepares a seat of honor for us and gives us a staff as a present; however, he charges a rather high price for a pair of gloves.

Tschartritsch's house is kept the cleanest, but most other people are rather clean, too. There is always a big fire in the house of Tschartritsch; in the other houses it is much smaller. Everywhere people sit around the fire, some wear only a thin cotton shirt.

Every morning the Indians wash themselves. Once Arthur saw an Indian go to the river without clothes, take a complete bath, and roll himself in the snow afterwards!

In one house we see an improvised cradle. Often we see mothers still nursing their two- to three-year-old children.

141

Interior of a house. Three people sit around a fire. In a small alcove in the left background an improvised cradle is suspended from the ceiling. One woman near the fire is holding a string attached to the cradle.
Chilkat, January 15, 1882.

Tuesday, January 17

After a walk along the bank in the morning, we again visit a few houses and are invited into some of them.

In the evening we watch a dance held to celebrate the end of the fasting time for the Raven clan in the same house where the shaman's initiation took place. It is a dance of the Gunana. Even old Tschartritsch, as well as Three-Finger Jack, and Willy participate. All painted their faces. Using an old mirror, Tschartritsch prepares his face carefully, painting it with cinnabar and charcoal. The dance is very similar to the one we saw on New Year's Eve, but this time women and children do not dance. Again each dancer enters alone, Three-Finger Jack with a big spear, Willy with a gun, etc. The entire chorus sings the same melody, the drum beats the rhythm, and every dancer moves his entire body vigorously. The dance lasts only a short time; the participants are exhausted rather soon.

We return and make a few preparations for the next day.

Wednesday, January 18

This is the day of our return trip to the trading station at Deschu. We get up early and prepare a breakfast of pea soup.

We stayed longer in Klukwan than originally planned. After the mild frost weather of the first few days with the temperature dropping to -13°C only once, we later had weather above freezing with rain and then heavy snowfall. That is why our food supply had gone low and old Tschartritsch helped us out with some bread.

Then we get on our way with Kasko, Sittie, and a third Indian. The first part of our return trip is taken by canoe. It is rather small, built of poplar, the hull only about 3 centimeters thick. Six people have to find room in it, three whites, Kasko, Sittie, and a third Indian. We sit on the bottom of the canoe with our legs stretched out. Quickly we move down river. Several times we go aground in shallow, half-foot-deep water. The canoe circles in the strong current and drags over gravel. We fear it might break any moment. But through the Indians' skill and knowledge of the changing water, threatening accidents are avoided.

Beyond the second settlement we observe the large number of animals on the banks. We count twenty eagles sitting on trees at one point.[16] Furthermore, we observe many ducks, and now and then we enjoy the

View toward northeast. Chilkoot, January 18, 1882.

143

lively movements and the cheerful song of the delicate water starling, which reminds us of our crested lark.

After we have left the canoe we walk on ice, which is not easy because a thin layer of ice has formed over the old ice. Once I break through. At first there is heavy snowfall and a northerly wind. Later it becomes clearer. Finally, toward evening, just when we reach the lower Chilkat village, a strong southerly wind starts up and makes the last part of our hike very difficult. Soon after dark we return to the trading station where everything is well.

A woman has died during the last few days, and another woman who has been sick for some time dies this evening. The people want to cremate her; they claim the soil is too hard to dig a grave.

Thursday, January 19

The people at the trading post are in an uproar. The second chief and another Indian, each supported by numerous followers, are ready to fight each other. Mr. and Mrs. Dickinson try in vain to keep peace. The missionary does not succeed either. Mr. Dickinson is quite timid; his wife is more aggressive. The reason for the fight is that one man wants to leave for the trading trip to the Gunana earlier than the other.

Friday, January 20

Today peace has not yet been restored between the fighting parties.

We take a short walk to the opposite bank. When we come back, we meet Sitka Jack, our cook's father. Sitka Jack, a well-known Sitka Indian, arrived yesterday in a small canoe and plans to return within the next few days.

Last year he had visited Chilkoot. On his return trip he lost his large canoe, which was crushed by waves, while he was camping in a bay along Lynn Canal. He, his wife, and child were forced to spend the winter in that deserted area, suffering many hardships. A small canoe, traveling from Juneau City to here to get salmon, rescued him. This little story illustrates local traffic conditions. The rocks rise precipitously from the ocean, so the man felt it was impossible to walk the short distance which under normal conditions would take one day. It took the canoe eleven days from Juneau City, so we should be satisfied with our six-day trip.

The January steamer had not yet arrived in Juneau, so we do not receive any news from home. The last mail we received was dated September!

In the evening young Dickinson, Tschartritsch, and a few other Indians visit us.

Saturday, January 21

Tonight Chlunat, the second chief of the Grizzly Bear clan, invites us to his new house for a feast for the members of his clan. The meal consists of tea and baked goods. Then the guests go home, adorn themselves, and return for the dance performed by Chlunat. Chlunat's wife explains to us that it is a dance of the Indians of Fort Simpson, where she comes from. We have seen this dance several times. After the dance, short questions are asked or speeches are made by one of the dancers which are answered by someone standing outside. The hostess, who has provided us with the seat of honor, explains to us this dialogue. The dancer calls up guests by name and thanks the individual family members of friendly clans. After the dance performance everyone returns home. A small boy, about three years old, son of Chilkoot Jack, was fond of dancing and entertained his spectators. His mother had taken him to the Gunanas, where he had learned their dances. Our house is rather full now. Tschartritsch's son sleeps here. Also, several women and children are almost always in the house. Old Tschartritsch stays with the missionary.

Sunday, January 22

Today we go to the lower Chilkat village, Jendestake, without our gun in order not to provoke any annoyance, but we take our skates. The weather is clear again and the view magnificent, but on the other side of the peninsula we are greeted by a cold northwesterly wind. We find very smooth ice, but have to struggle against the wind, while we can go quickly for long distances with the wind without moving our feet. Arthur uses the sun to survey some map points, but the rocks in this area are extremely magnetic. This affects the magnetic needle of his compass significantly, making all measurements taken today and during the following day useless. At noon old Tschartritsch keeps us company.

In the evening there is another church service, the third one today.

Monday, January 23 to February 5

The thermometer fell to -23°C on January 23, the lowest temperature so far this month. In the morning our wash water and ink are frozen. In milder weather during the next few days large amounts of snow have fallen, so we cannot go on longer excursions until the trail is firm. Sitka Jack cannot start his return trip. The trading expedition to the Gunana in the interior, which had been prepared for a long time, has to be postponed because of the fresh snow. One of the slaves of Tschartritsch has arrived and reports that the people in Klukwan have thoroughly cleaned their bodies. They will not wash again until after their return. This slave had to camp half way down from Klukwan, because he had not taken snowshoes and could not go on in the deep snow. He had started out in most beautiful weather.

Our experiences, therefore, are mostly limited to daily hunting trips, which did not contribute too many items to the winter fauna. One day we again saw the so-called wolves at a carcass. They looked at us timidly and ran into the woods.

Interesting to us is our attendance at the funeral of a woman. Immediately after the woman's death, loud wailing songs arose from the house of mourning. The woman's body is dressed up and for four days displayed in seated position at the back wall of the decorated room. Daily the same wailing songs are repeated. This time we could not attend the cremation, since we had been given the wrong time. The following evening, however, we watch the ceremony in the new house of the second chief. The place of honor on a bench opposite the door has been reserved for us. First the guests are treated with berries, sugar and tobacco. The berries are served by the spoonful directly into the mouth or hand, likewise the sugar. The tobacco is passed around in large pipes carved with figures. The guests take turns smoking these. Then, blankets and various pieces of white and colored cloth, worth about $200, are distributed by the relatives of the dead woman. We and Mrs. Dickinson also brought along some calico.

An old man introduces each new gift with a few words. Several men stand near the door with poles in their hands which they strike on the floor to the rhythm of a monotonous melody. Also a few women with blackened faces and short poles in their hands get up several times and rock back and forth during the song with complex, almost twisting motions, not very pretty to look at. After the distribution, the shaman of the Raven clan expresses his thanks. He mentions all donors by name. Again one man goes outside and responds. Not until after 9:00 P.M. does the distribution end. The room was completely filled. Several adults and children watch this performance through the smoke hole in the roof. The smoky, overcrowded room makes us feel rather uncomfortable. The dead woman belonged to the Bear clan; therefore, members of the Raven clan, including the first chief Don-e-wak, the shaman, and the young Tschartritsch, receive the most generous gifts. The relatives of the woman have to cut their hair. During the songs a young boy presents himself wearing the woman's blanket.

Monday, February 6

All day long there is a blizzard. Arthur goes into the woods for a short while, but returns very soon. In the evening we talk with some of the people, write down a few lines of Native songs, and also show them the microscope. Jack brings a head louse, which all people present enjoy seeing magnified.

Wednesday, February 8

Clear, frosty weather, just like yesterday. Again we go into the woods, first along the trail and then to the opposite bank into the mountains. The snow is still very loose. Walking in the dense underbrush is very tiring and difficult, so that we fall several times. There are few animals. The young Dickinson has a fight with his parents and leaves the house to spend the night somewhere else.

Thursday, February 9

The same weather as yesterday. This time we go on the hill toward Tanani. During the ascent we encounter thick underbrush, and have trouble forcing our way through it. On top we get to a very beautiful forest, which was easy to pass through. The slope toward the ocean offers beautiful views, especially of the Davidson Glacier. We return on a better path and watch several birds.

The young Dickinson becomes reconciled with his parents. In the evening there is a dance at Chlunat's house, *hydato* dance. As far as we understand it, it is held to confirm the peace between young Dickinson and Chlunat. A few days ago they had gotten into a fight. During the dance, Mrs. Dickinson distributed seven woolen blankets, cloth, and tobacco. The Bear clan was assembled; we are considered to be members of it. There was another dance held, also to establish peace among two different clans.

We learn more details about the meteorite that supposedly fell near Chilkoot. A man had built a hut on the mountain and during the night he

147

saw the glow of a fire and heard a thundering noise. The next day he went to the place and found the rock, to which he and his people prayed. It was supposed to be all shiny like silver and flat on its lower side. Only one piece was found; it was bought and sent to Sitka.

In the evening there were beautiful northern lights. From an indistinct arc, beams of light were shooting toward the zenith. They seemed to change directions from east to west.

Friday, February 10

Today we want to go toward Chilkoot. We get along rather quickly on the same path we took downhill yesterday, and then followed the tracks of snowshoes down. The last part is a steep descent toward the coast. While falling, I break my snowshoes! Along the bank are numerous ducks. The continued hike along the beach becomes unpleasant because of the strong winds. We therefore return, but get caught in a deep ravine with almost vertical walls which are impossible to climb. We follow the ravine upward, looking in vain for a pass, and finally are forced to return to the beach. Now we hurry along the bank, because high tide is starting. Some places are not passable during high tide. We still can pass everywhere, but not without trouble. Climbing over wet rocks is especially difficult, whereas the foot can get a good hold on the frozen seaweed.

In the evening we visit the missionary for a short time.

Saturday, February 11

Several Indians came down from Klukwan. They report that today and yesterday ten people have left for the interior, among them Tschartritsch and his son.

Three Gunanas arrived. They want to have mostly tobacco, since they have run out of it.

Monday, February 13

Today again, like yesterday, it is stormy and cold, with constant snowfall. Sitka Jack tries to remove the heavy cover of snow from his canoe, but does not get very far with it. The shaman is supposed to make good weather, but is not satisfied with the payment by our Jack. Perhaps he thought the present weather could not change.

We hear about new disturbances. Kasko's nephew had an affair with one of his uncle's wives, and, therefore, Kasko plans to kill him. Dickinson tries to mediate. He invites Kasko and urges him to make peace.

Thursday, February 16

The wind has diminished, also the cold. The preparations for the departure of the canoe, therefore, are continued. The young Dickinson caught three magpies in traps and keeps them in the attic above our room. They are not shy, but stir up so much dust.

Friday, February 17 to Thursday, the twenty-third

Today the canoe eventually leaves, but it was rather late before everything was ready for the departure.

February continues to show a severe face. After the mild December and January days, we had not expected such prolonged cold this month with average temperatures of -15°C.

The second part of February, too, has more cold and snow than usual for local conditions. Consequently, we spend more time working indoors. One Sunday afternoon we listen to Mrs. Dickinson's lesson. She reads a passage of the Bible so often until the children know it by heart in English and Tlingit. First they have to repeat two words, then more and more words without considering the content. All children repeat together in chorus, but it is not very intelligible. Furthermore, the children learn a quotation for each letter of the alphabet. Only for the letter X has she been unable to find one.

In the evening Mrs. Dickinson often tells us about Tlingit customs and myths. Sometimes she interprets the stories of an old blind Indian who frequently visits the factory on winter evenings to entertain a group of Indians. The audience, men and women, listen attentively and often the storyteller is interrupted by loud laughing when he tells about the cunning pranks and the coarse jokes of Jelch.[17]

In order to dispel the bad weather the Indians burn huge fires on several days. One woman, whose child died last fall and was buried according to the missionary's wish, wants to dig up and cremate the body now. The Indians think that this noncremated child could be the cause of the bad weather. In vain they try to find this grave under the blanket of snow. The entire population is very excited. Even the upper village (Klukwan) demands that the child be cremated. There is another reason for the anxiety. Two girls had not been kept separate during puberty according to old tradition, and now the people threaten to enslave them. They also want to demand payment from the missionary and Mrs. Dickinson when somebody dies.

From Mr. Willard we hear a few more reasons the shaman blames for the bad weather. Once the children at Mr. Willard's house had made gooselike noises, therefore bringing all the bad weather. Also Mr. Willard had put on his snowshoes inside his house.

Even the two shamans, who usually do not wash, are said to have gone naked into the water to make good weather. Now the people have another reason for the bad weather. A woman came down, and they claim she threw away her child. They want to burn her in effigy. She came here into this house and showed her breasts to prove to the people that it was a lie.

In the evening we are often together with the Indians and ask for the names and colors of animals. Arthur takes a measurement on Kasko, I draw some shadow pictures. Sometimes Mrs. Dickinson tells us stories of the *Kushta* (land otter) people.

At right, eulachon, ssag. A drawing of the fish is surrounded by this written commentary: Color mostly bluish, lighter parts shiny silver, irregular, sometimes clearly marked spots on the upper part of the body. Natural size. [Author's original drawing approximately 8 inches long including tail fin, 1 inch wide without fins.] Coregonus szag from the Chilkoot River sample medium sized. Not so many run during February as in April. Then the fish are somewhat larger and fatter and used for the rendering of oil in wooden canoes with hot stones. In the Stikine River this fish runs at other times, according to Mrs. Dickinson. Called eulachon or small fish by the Americans. The fish appears in large numbers only in certain places along the coast, in the Nass River during March in two runs, then in the Stikine River less numerous, in the Chilkoot River during February and April and in the Yakutat River (Mr. Dickinson). Chilkoot, February 24, 1882.

Jack's boy, who must be about six years old, still suckles on his mother's breast. Today he danced again with his little sister who can barely walk. Kasko's nephew suddenly fell down dead when he returned from here to Chilkoot. The night before he was camping without making a fire.

On February 22, the small oil fish, called *ssag*, arrive in the Chilkat River. Especially in the lower Chilkat village, Jendestake, this fish is caught in large quantities. After this hard winter the Indians' food supplies are almost used up. Therefore, the population of the entire area rushes to the Chilkat side of the peninsula to arrive in time for the catch. The run of these fish lasts only a few days.

This fish accumulation attracts large numbers of gulls, eagles, and ravens. When we arrive there on the morning of the twenty-third, we startle first two, later five eagles.

Friday, February 24

The weather is worse than ever, and we limit ourselves to indoor work. We receive a few oil fish brought from Chilkoot. We identify them as belonging to the genus *Coregonus* or closely related to it. I sketch one of the oil fish, while Arthur preserves two in salicylic acid. Arthur observes the thermometer. Unfortunately, one breaks while he is trying to remove the mercury that had collected in the upper hollow.

Saturday, February 25

A mountain sheep is kept in the house; it is used to Mrs. Dickinson alone. It recognizes every stranger by his scent and greets him with indignant bleating. Tonight it was allowed into the room for a while. How droll to watch it turn aggressive upon meeting the two house cats!

The snow becomes so deep that our weather observatory is completely covered by snow. At first we dug a path to it with a shovel. On the twenty-eighth we have to install the instruments, which could not give accurate temperatures and measurements under the blanket of snow, in a wooden box and nail it to the outside of the house. At the beginning of March we record the coldest temperatures of this winter.

As soon as the weather allows, we take shorter excursions or measurements and bearings. Arthur found that the magnetic needle becomes completely useless here due to the effect of the rocks.

At 10:00 A.M. on March 4, we leave for Chilkoot with Kasko in his canoe. We sit fairly comfortably on a raised seat. The weather is warm, the sky only partly cloudy. In Tanani we stop for a moment; one of Kasko's wives lives here. From now on this terrain is unknown to us. It appears that a walk along the bank with its steep cliffs would be most uncomfortable at high tide. A moraine-like bar forms the end of the fjord to Chilkoot. The outlet of Chilkoot Lake has dug a small bed through it. Here everything is frozen over. We have to leave the canoe and walk about fifteen minutes to the few huts that make up the village of Chilkoot. We enter the hut of Kasko's father; it is empty. First Kasko removes 4 to 5 feet of snow from the roof. All the other huts are hidden under deep snow. We immediately make an excursion to the lake. The river is not frozen here and is very shallow. We find several water starlings, ravens, ducks, and gulls, also eagles. High above us a flock of ptarmigan flies south. We walk on the ice to a promontory where Arthur takes some compass measurements. Along the bank we discover numerous tracks of ptarmigan.

Upon our return we find Kasko busy preparing the meal. He had shot a small duck which we had not seen before.

During the night to Sunday, March 5, we did not sleep well because we had not sufficiently prepared for the cold. Soon after the frugal breakfast we are on our way. Following the same path as yesterday, we go along the eastern bank of the lake. We continue to the northern end of the lake where we see a flock of eight to twelve ptarmigan, one of which Arthur shoots. They scatter excitedly in several directions and then call. We go on to the northern end of the lake. The sky is cloudy, so Arthur can take compass bearings at only a few locations. The snow is soft; walking becomes increasingly difficult. The quacking of ducks attracts us to the opposite bank. There we startle a big flock of mallards. This time we get better prepared for the cold, but the weather is milder, so we sleep well.

At left: below the head of a duck is the author's description: a) Native name: daich-chr. Head: brown-black; the light areas of the bill are wax yellow. Iris: yellow. Body: grey, black, and white. Feet: yellow. Webs: black, hind toe with large paddle-like flap. b) On the upper left is the scoter (Oedemia). Bill from above, blackish along the rim; on the upper right a view from below, yellowish with blackish side rims, and on the lower left a side view.
Additional commentary says: Feet reddish, hind toe with strong paddle-like flap, webs: black, probably male, Native name: tutsch-gach.
Chilkoot, February 25, 1882.

153

Monday, March 6

We leave at 8:00 A.M. for our trip back. Heavy snow is falling and a foot of new, loose snow on the path slows us down. At low tide the canoe is pushed into the water and we are on our way. We meet a boat coming from Tanani and hear that two Gunanas had arrived from Deje. We ask about ssag. The reply indicates that none are left.

Again we land in Tanani for a minute while Kasko delivers salmon and berries to his wife. At noon we reach the station and find everything in order. Snow is falling all day.

The Klukwan Indians, with the exception of Tschartritsch and Three-Finger Jack, returned from their trading expedition with many furs. A canoe has arrived from Juneau, but without mail for us.

Tuesday, March 7

In beautiful weather I take a little hike along the beach toward the south. The incoming tide prevents my return trip and I have to try to take an inland route. Although it is only a short distance, it is very difficult to get around the point, because I do not have snowshoes. In the evening we watch northern lights consisting of several arcs. The outermost and brightest arc reaches way above zenith. Individual rays shoot up from the horizon. The Indians believe that the appearance of northern lights announces a man's death or a fight.

Wednesday, March 8

Today in the most beautiful weather we make an excursion to the beach north toward Tanani, mostly to take some bearings and to measure the elevation of mountains. After passing the steep, rocky bank, we observe two eagles.

Beyond Tanani, high tide stops our progress. For a few minutes we enter a house in Tanani where Kasko is with his wife. A pair of Stick Indian pants and gloves are offered for sale. One woman is busy making nets out of sinew. For our return trip we have to wait for low tide and do not arrive at the station till dusk.

Everywhere the canoes are taken out and some of them are being repaired.

In the evening we again see beautiful northern lights.

View of the valley of Ferebee Glacier.
The view is from Tanani. Zyskukadli Mountain is on the extreme left.
March 8, 1882.

These mountains are between Dejai Valley and Chkatzehin.
Chilkoot, March 8, 1882.

Thursday, March 9

Today the weather is beautiful again so we go along the beach south-ward. Without stop we go to the bare promontory, still visible from the station, and find out that there are two very similar promontories existing close to each other. We learn that the Indians call this point *Kätlkraxe* (also Ketlrachia),[18] which means dogs howling.

We see several canoes returning from duck hunting and searching for clams.

After taking some measurements, we return. At one place it becomes impossible to continue along the beach, so we accept an invitation to get a ride in a canoe. Back at the station we complete some work.

Friday, March 10

Around noon we walk over to Jendestake to take some measurements at two sites. The sea is smooth like a mirror and the view is gorgeous. From Mount Geissen[19] we watch an avalanche descend with a tremendous rumble. Upon our return we find two crabs and a cottus which Indians have brought us for our collection. In today's calm water they had been pierced by lance from a canoe, therefore they are somewhat damaged.

In the evening the school children and a number of adults are assembled here in the house. There are about twenty people in the small room. Mrs. Dickinson conducts a few songs, then they play a game, *hagu mac*. The object is for one person from one party to get a flag (here a handkerchief) from the opposite side without laughing. With much eagerness and shouting young and old participate in this game. Finally all the children perform the Gunana dance in which the adults join. Three real Stick Indians who had arrived from Deje happen to be present.

Saturday, March 11, to Monday, the thirteenth, are again cold, windy days. It is still difficult to walk without snowshoes. The Indians seem to protect a duck, the oldsquaw. One of the many causes given for the poor weather in February was that somebody killed an oldsquaw. The Native name *ja-a-uná* is a good rendition of the melodic call of this duck. The Stick Indians want to dance with us, if we wish it. They would like to become friends with us.

Thursday, March 16

George Tschartritsch, son of the chief, comes down from Klukwan. He reports that this year they did not go as far to the Gunana. It took them six days to get there and four days for the return trip. His father offers to let us travel to the interior with him. He tells about strange animals.

Since the Chilkat Indians went on only this one expedition this winter, Mr. Dickinson is worried because he receives so few furs. The middleman trading of the Chilkat Indians makes the fur business less profitable for the North West Trading Company than it might be in direct trade with the hunters. The prices paid the Indians are a little higher than the market value in San Francisco. Mr. Dickinson, however, cannot lower the prices, because the Chilkats do not mind a long, arduous canoe trip when they think they might gain a slight advantage. The company pays the Indians in coupons worth one, one-half, one-quarter, and one-eighth dollars recognizable by different colors and used like coins here. The most marketable articles are woolen blankets, calico, tobacco, flour, and sugar.

Friday, March 17

In cold, windy weather we hike to the ridge that leads to Mount Geissen. Without difficulty we climb up. The snow is rather hard. In especially steep places we take off either one or both snowshoes. Very few animals are seen, a few siskins, pine grosbeak, a ptarmigan; during the return, a hawk and an eagle, naturally also chickadees. Three larger ledges have to be surmounted to reach our last ridge, which is probably 150 meters below the summit. On the mountain the trees are still wrapped in hard snow, some so completely that not a trace of green can be seen. Up here the green hemlock is dominant. The strong wind increases in intensity where the tall forest ends. This and the low temperature of 15°C make us decide to return although we could reach the top without effort in about an hour. First we go back the same way, but then we descend straight down from a spruce which serves as our measuring object, a difficult descent, but it offers us the chance to see the cave of a porcupine in a rock. Large amounts of droppings are lying under the alder trees, and the trunks of some trees in the vicinity are eaten bare. The return takes only two hours, whereas the ascent took five, including several stops.

Sunday, March 19

It is colder and possibly stormier than on the previous days. Except for a short afternoon walk, we do not make any excursions.

In the evening we ask some Indians to give us the Indian names of places on our map, e.g. protruding rocks and sandy banks. Later Kal-zun joins us.

157

He is the Gunana brother-in-law of Mrs. Dickinson from Chlunat, the only one permitted to trade directly with whites. He wants to look through our microscope at the same object that we recently showed a Chilkat Indian, a head louse, which he had brought several days ago. Accompanying him are his little son and two younger boys; all look very friendly and show lively interest. Some experiments with magnets are really appreciated. With the gift of a knife and some small pencils we secure their benevolence in case we should visit their territory. In the evening, again northern lights.

Monday, March 20

The weather today is so unfavorable; it is stormy, cold, and cloudy, so we do not go out. We learn that the Indians now accuse us of causing the bad weather. First we dragged a dead porcupine through the snow instead of carrying it, then we washed the mountain sheep in salt water. Today they want to burn us in effigy.

Tuesday, March 2

The clear, although cold and windy, weather entices us to climb the highest peak[20] of the peninsula. We first get to the lower, nearer mountain easily and quickly, but on a fairly steep path. Then we have to go down to a small lake[21] in between the two mountains at about the same elevation as one of the settlements. From now on we have a good, not too steep, ascent through forest with more hemlocks at higher elevation. The highest part of the peak is bare with only a few knee-high trees. The wind is so strong that we have to find a sheltered place to use our measuring instruments. The view of the Deje Valley is very beautiful; we had never seen it so unobstructed. The temperature on the summit is about 17°C at 3:00 p.m. For our return trip at 3:15 P.M. we take the same route to the little lake and from there down the western slope. After two hours we arrive back at the station.

Three-Finger Jack and some other Indians have come down today. The former visits us in our room. The second visitor is Kaschkoe, the old blind man, who brings us a gift, a stone pestle which he claims is very old. "He-he-he-he" and many expressions not intelligible to us. We hear from Mrs. Dickinson that he claims to own many such old objects and hopes that he will get a good price from us. He has a hut in Dejah and expects our visit.

Kaschkoe had a dream. The god or goddess Kanuga,[22] the personified river that empties into the Dejah Valley, appeared to him and told him that

158

he had been here longer than the whites. Therefore, he should not be willing to yield.

Wednesday, March 22, to Sunday, April 2

A canoe arrives. It had left Juneau City eighteen days ago. The *Favorite* will soon arrive with mail!

There is another death in the village. The traditional ceremonies and distribution of gifts take place. Mrs. Dickinson does not want to attend the cremation. According to her, the Indians of Fort Simpson are now ashamed of their old superstitions and customs.

In the morning before breakfast we take a look at the preparations for the cremation of the body. I enter the house and watch the women busy preparing the cloth for wrapping the body; however, I could not distinguish details. Then we see the funeral pyre of large logs piled up right in front of the house. We cannot discover a trace of the body in it and assume that it will be carried out later. A number of men and women stood around the pyre at random. A few Indians stand in a line holding staffs in their hands. While singing a monotonous song, of which we understood only a few words, they beat the rhythm with their staffs on a board lying on the ground. Then, while the pyre is in bright flames, the small assembly disperses. We learn that the body had been placed in the middle of the pyre. After breakfast we go back once more and, after the fire is extinguished, observe the women searching for pieces of bone in the ashes. As we learned from

People stand around the pyre near tall conifers during a cremation. March 25, 1882.

Mrs. Dickinson, these bones are placed into a little box or bag and stored in the common grave house of the clan.

In the evening we learn from Mrs. Dickinson various names of settlements and clans of the coastal Indians.

The Chilkoot shaman is ill and complains that Mr. Willard does not visit him. The missionary had demanded that he cut his long hair, even offered to do it himself and give the shaman a new shirt. Old Tschartritsch is also very sick. Naturally, in both cases evil spirits are blamed.

The evening of March 30 we visit the missionary. He borrows our pliers to pull his wife's bad tooth.

On the beach we saw three snow buntings; migratory birds apparently have not yet arrived. In the woods we observe many corkscrew left-wound tree trunks. A combined effect of sun and prevailing winds might be the reason. The branches are also wound in the same direction as the main trunk. They are mostly white spruce. One of these trees has a circumference of 4.16 meters at a height of 3 meters. On April 1 an Indian caught a porcupine and delivered it alive to our house. Set free, it immediately tried to hide in a corner. It bristled every time it was touched. We had the meat for supper. It tasted somewhat like mutton, but was not very tasty, probably because it was cold. Perhaps it was not prepared well. The Indians even eat hawk.

On a hike one afternoon, Arthur shoots a cormorant, probably *Plagitus pallas*. Mrs. Dickinson tells us the following about cormorants: When the raven killed the bear, the cormorant wanted to tell his wives about it. The raven called him and under some pretext pulled out the cormorant's tongue so he could no longer speak clearly.

On Sunday, April 2, in the evening, we take a short walk with the Dickinsons along the beach. As we are passing some Indian huts, they point out to us a little snow hut. In it is a woman in childbed

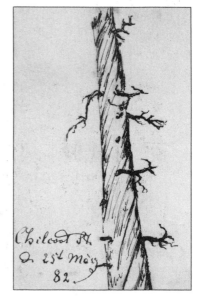

Twisted tree.
Chilkoot Strait March 25, 1882.

with her newborn child. We learn that a woman in labor has to leave the house and is taken to a hut of snow or twigs. During the delivery, female relatives assist her. The woman stays in that hut for five days and only drinks warm water during that time.

When the children cannot yet walk, they are tightly wrapped in moss and fur, now usually cloth, and tied to a board, which the woman carries around in her arms. Or, it is hung by ropes to the beams of the hut and represents a kind of cradle.

As soon as the children learn to walk, they used to be bathed in ocean or river water. The first bath must be done by the parents, but later the uncle replaces the mother, because he is supposed to be less lenient. Now these daily cold baths are no longer common. This perhaps was the reason for the high mortality of the children, but also for the hardened bodies of the survivors. Soon after birth the child is given the name of any maternal ancestor. With the ceremony in the memory of a dead relative, the Tlingit acquires the right to take a second name, that of a paternal ancestor. The Tlingits add a third name when a son is born. The father of the three-year-old Don-e-wak was called Don-e-wak-iisch and the mother Don-e-wak-tla.

Monday, April 3

Heavy snowfall. We are prevented from taking a longer excursion. A flying squirrel is brought to us by an Indian who had already stuffed it. It is preserved so poorly that it is useless for our collection.

In the afternoon Don-e-wak visits us and we measure his skull. He shows us a painful bump on his knee and asks for some medicine. We give him some harmless medication.

The departure of the canoe for Juneau again has to be postponed due to the bad weather. There is quite an emergency among the Indian population. Cold, strong winds and heavy snow have hindered hunting and fishing this winter. Even the supply of dried salmon and berries, the main food items, is used up. Due to the poor weather, fresh salmon cannot be transported from the storage houses in the villages to the winter huts.

Tuesday, April 4

In spite of the heavy snowfall, we take the missionary's canoe for a trip to Ketlrachia. On our return, the southerly wind increases and we rush back to shore. Just then Chlunat arrives in his canoe, which is equipped with a sail. He takes us in tow. Soon after our return, Arthur sees the approaching steamer. Immediately the school is closed and everything prepared for the arrival. Soon a boat comes ashore with letters. We receive good news from home. After reading our mail, we are taken to the steamer by Jack, who had arrived on the steamer. There we greet Vanderbilt and McClean and have dinner aboard. In the evening we return ashore with them. They spend the night here, because the wind is getting stronger.

Wednesday, April 5

Today we are so busy with packing that, in spite of the good weather, we do not get out for a short walk until evening. We hear the cry of an owl near the bank. Snow buntings fly in larger flocks than we have seen before.

From Kasko I receive a skinning knife as a farewell present; from Mrs. Dickinson a small table and ear pendants. I pay $20 to Mrs. Dickinson.

CHAPTER EIGHT

TRIP FROM CHILKOOT TO PORTLAND

Thursday, April 6, 1882

Shortly after midnight I leave Chilkoot on the *Favorite*, the small steamer of the North West Trading Company. The three and a half months' stay has familiarized me with the area and the population. Regretfully, I take leave from this place which promises new attractions during the approaching spring season. Everywhere the ground is covered with an average of 2 meters or more of snow, although some of it disappeared during the last few days. According to the Indians this winter was unusually cold and harsh. Even during the last part of March the temperature sank to 20°C, whereas a year ago on April 1 the ground was almost free of snow.

During the night I was not careful enough and therefore was quite cold. At sunrise I am up. We are cruising in a rather strong northerly wind at a speed of 7½ to 8 knots and already approach Berners Bay. Beautiful weather in Lynn Canal shows off the gorgeous scenery of this area. At the southern end the mighty Eagle Glacier catches the eye. Right after we pass Cross Sound, the majestic group of the Elias Mountains appears with its towering peaks of Mount Fairweather, 4,700 meters, Mount Crillon, and Mount Pérouse, 3,400 meters. At three o'clock we arrive in the village of Huna (Hoonah) on the north side of Chichagof Island on Cross Sound. In this Indian settlement a second trading post of the company was abandoned after a year; last fall a mission was established.

While the captain visits the missionary, I walk along the beach with McClean past the Indian village, consisting of fifteen houses. They are mostly built in the old style with square ground plan, flat slanting gabled roofs, oval door, and large square smoke opening. Some houses are somewhat modernized with steeper roof, window openings, and in one case even a kind of chimney. During the winter months there are about 600 to 800 people in the village, about fifty per house. During the summer they are scattered over various hunting grounds and the village stands deserted.

The Hunas are mostly fishermen; they own larger and better-built canoes than the Chilkats. The latter are more concerned with trade in the interior; the Hunas are occupied with fishing and boating. Also, here on Chichagof Island is found yellow cedar (*Chamaecyparis nootkaensis*) which supplies the best boat-building material. The village offers the usual sight; all houses are near the beach facing the ocean.

Only a few totems, among them one newly painted, are found here. Behind the houses we see little twig or snow huts for women in childbed, farther removed are grave houses, some for individuals, some for families. Only rich people can afford the luxury of an individual grave house. These are built while they are still living and decorated with flags, paintings, and wooden statues representing the family's emblems. Poorer people have to be content with family graves. Here, too, the bones are collected after cremation, wrapped in a blanket, put in a wooden box, and deposited in the common grave house. Only the shaman is not cremated; his body is wrapped in blankets and put in a small grave house standing on four posts. We enter a house where a man wants to show us some gold; it turns out to be only mica.

A few returning canoes bring halibut. The wide Hoonah Bay with its narrow shallow arms is ideal for hunting and fishing. Flocks of ducks and geese live in these waters and the abundance of salmon, herring, and other fish is said to be at times extraordinary. Right now is halibut season. We also see their decoratively carved fishing hooks.

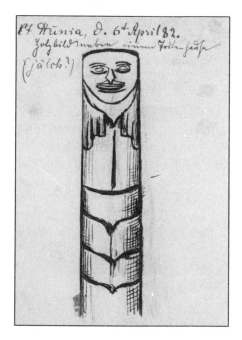

There is less snow here than in Chilkoot. The rock contains slate. A steep, rocky cliff at the edge of the water ends our walk.

Wooden picture (totem).
The totem is located next to
a grave house. The author's
note says jalch, *raven.*
Hoonah, April 6, 1882.

Upon our return we visit the missionary, Mr. Styles, who asks me to stay with him. His wife is going on this steamer to Sitka for a while, and he will follow her later. After some deliberation I accept his offer. The missionary is a young man who emigrated from New York to Alaska to find his luck in a business career. Later he became a gold miner and was the first one to build his house among the Indians in Juneau. He gave up employment in the mines, because he did not want to work on Sundays. Because of his knowledge of the Indians, he was proposed for the missionary position. This is a typical example of the ease with which different careers are accepted and changed. Apparently he has good relations with the Indians, and a few boys have progressed very nicely in the use of the English language. He also tries to introduce burials instead of the traditional cremation, but without success so far.

From April 7 to the twelfth I stay with the missionary in Hoonah. A bad cold unfortunately limits my activities.

At first the Hunas made life for the missionary very difficult; now they do not interfere and show respect. He does not put his house at their disposal, the way Willard does, where they can come and go as they please.

The Hunas are divided into four families, of which only one, the *Taktnitan* has the right to catch otters. The otters appear in July at Cape Spencer and are mostly shot by the Hunas. This kind of hunting is forbidden in the Aleutians; here it might soon lead to the disappearance of these animals.

The main settlement is called Gaudekan and has a population of 600 to 800. On the opposite side of Cross Sound, on the mainland, is a second settlement with five houses and about 400 inhabitants.

With the missionary I go on several short walks and watch children play with small boats, some of them with sails, and bows and arrows.

On April 9 again several boats leave, taking along all utensils, also bark mats for a tent. By the end of the month the missionary expects the departure of the entire population.

The Indians spread out to their hunting huts all the way to Yakutat Bay. As soon as the snow melts, the women plant potatoes which they leave unattended. We both visit several houses to find out if somebody can take us to Sitka. In most houses we are offered a seat, and letters of recommendation are presented. A wooden hat with carvings of a whale is shown as an especially valuable piece. On top of the hat is a basketlike cylinder which can be pulled out. This hat is not for sale and carefully wrapped in linen. I sketch a carved comb made of whalebone.

On the eleventh, the chief, his wife, and little girl, who is afraid of us, come to visit. All are dressed in their best clothes. The missionary is not very happy with the negotiations. Kin-tu-ka now does not want to take us to Sitka, although he had promised it before. During the conversation I sketch his portrait in my dairy. Another Indian now agrees to take us to Killisnoo.

Wednesday, April 12

On a morning walk I hear the steady call of grouse on the mountain slopes. One of the grouse is taken to the missionary. It is larger than the ones in Chilkoot and has a yellow bulge over the eyes. Since the Indians want to leave tomorrow, the missionary is packing his things. The weather is again beautiful today.

On my walk through the village I sketch one of the totems and an old carved drum. The people watch curiously without disturbing me and are delighted to see the finished picture.

Kin-tu-ka is the first chief of the Huna.

In the evening one of the two people who are going to take us in their canoe comes to visit. He is drunk from hutschino, but behaves fairly well mannered.

Thursday, April 13

Before four o'clock in the morning we get up, eat breakfast, and wait for the Indians. Around eight o'clock our canoe leaves at high tide. In the protected Hoonah Bay the sea is very calm. As soon as we enter Cross Sound we have a head wind, called *taku*, with rough seas. We are forced to look for a camping place on a small island. In such things one can trust the Indians. They know the coasts, the most dangerous spots, signs of good or bad weather, and they handle their canoes most competently.

The requirements for a good camping place are a sandy beach, a sheltered location, and most of all fresh water and good firewood. Our

The side view of a totem pole (ku-ti-ga) in Hoonah ,with the Native name of each figure, from top to bottom: ki-dschuk *(hawk),* ssach *(seal),* scha-ka-nari *(mythical person),* ketl *(dog). Hoonah, April 12, 1882.*

camping site was completely protected and had not much snow. Even in rainy weather a fire is made within a few minutes. There is, however, a different procedure, as one of our guides aptly remarked. White people build a large fire and stay at a distance, while Indians maintain a small fire and sit very close to it.

Several kingfishers live on the island. At low tide they search for sea urchins, clams, and especially chitons. Then they carry them to the rocks to eat them. Large mounds of shells are found there.

We cover the distance from Hoonah to Killisnoo (Känasnu), 60 nautical miles which includes crossing Chatham Strait, in three days.

On Friday, April 14, heavy snow is falling all morning, but we are getting on our way in calm seas. Soon we get a strong wind from Chilkoot. Several waves hit our boat and we are soaked through. We land and dry our clothes on a big fire and eat our noon meal. In the afternoon the weather improves. We continue our trip and enjoy the view of the Elias chain to the north.

Near Point Augusta we leave the coast and cross Chatham Strait in favorable wind. Near the coast of Admiralty Island the wind stops and we have to paddle. After sundown we again find a suitable place for camping. The coast is fairly free of snow and this place is also in every respect well suited for resting.

Saturday April 15

Now we are not too far from Chutsinu (Hudschinu),[23] the Indian village on Admiralty Island, and the nearby island of Killisnoo, our present destination, so the Indians are not in such a rush. Again the morning is very beautiful. Here for the first time I hear a bird whose monosyllabic call in different pitches sounds quite melodic. We notice deer tracks. On the rocky banks we find the same clams and snails as on the island at Cross Sound. During low tide buried bivalves squirt strong sprays of water into the air.

In a calm sea we paddle slowly while hunting for ducks. We get only one harlequin duck, which are numerous here. Large numbers of these ducks sit closely together on rocks. Along the coast we see beautiful white marble. Several whales are sighted.

Once we stop at an Indian summer hut and find only women. Several deer skins are hung up to dry. Our Indians buy a deer leg for four bullets.

Herring can also be seen hung up for drying outdoors. Now we pass Point Samuel and slowly approach Hudschinu, the Indian village of the

Chutsinu on Admiralty Island. It has six houses in a row next to each other and several single ones. About 2 miles from this village is the station of the North West Trading Company, Killisnoo, on a small island with the same name. The company's steamer had announced our arrival, so Mr. Spohn expected us and gave us a room which we occupied from Sunday, April 16, to Monday, the twenty-fourth.

The place where we land shows a picture of busy activity. No other place in Alaska except the gold miner city of Juneau is that busy. Here the North West Trading Company is establishing a fish oil factory, modeled after plants that are flourishing on the East Coast of the United States. Several years ago they became aware of the abundance of fish in these waters. Until now only an occasional stockfish or halibut fishing boat from San Francisco and a few salmon canneries had made use of this resource. Especially numerous schools of herring had been ignored. As done at the Manhattan plant in the East, the company expects to catch the herring in large, close-meshed nets, worth $1000 apiece, press them, and under the pressure of steam, render the oil and refine it. In addition, they plan to hunt whales with a small steam launch equipped with a cannon, loaded with explosive projectiles, which simultaneously acts as a harpoon.

Sunday, April 16

We rise rather early. After breakfast we walk around the island, which takes about three and one-half hours. Since the tide rises rather high, it is difficult to walk along the rocks at the end. The small herring are caught by eagles and gulls as well as small whales.

Monday, April 17

This morning is inclement. My cough is getting worse, so I prefer to stay here. Because of the rain, the huge herring net has to be carried into the station, a cumbersome task. Two more nets of this kind are expected.

Tuesday, April 18

7:00 A.M. maximum 3°C, minimum 1°C. Since the cough did not subside, I again stay home all day, although the weather turns out nice in the afternoon. Toward evening the steamboat arrives, but I do not receive any news.

169

In the evening religious conversations are held. Almy was raised as a Quaker and tells interesting details from his youth, also about the strict observance of Sunday.

Wednesday, April 19

In beautiful weather the missionary and I make an excursion to the Indian village Angoon, barely 2 miles away, which we had passed on our trip here. We take a small boat. I walk part way along the beach, while the missionary goes on alone in the boat. Giant, multipointed, colorfully speckled starfish can be seen on the ground between the cracks in the rocks.

The village of Angoon shows the increased influence of the whites. Several huts are built in the new style. I sketch the oldest one. The paintings on the wall are hardly visible. One of the graves has a Greek cross.

We enter several houses. One man just brought a large cuttlefish with 6-inch-long arms.

Above the door of the largest house we read this English inscription: "Kanatuk, first chief of the Chutsinus. Every white man especially every good Christian is asked to enter this house." The door is locked, but noises inside betray the presence of people. Our knocks at the door remain unanswered. A look through the small window opening reveals the cause of this strange behavior. The good Christian was busy distilling hutschino. Behind the village is a lagoon stretching deep into the interior. The village itself is really on a small peninsula.

Most of the Chutsinus have left their village and moved to their summer places. Many were employed in Killisnoo and Juneau. Mostly by cutting wood they earn $1 to $2 and more per day. The usual wage for Indians is $1 per day. Higher demand for labor brings higher wages in places like Juneau, Sitka, Wrangell, and here.

The summer huts of the Indians consist of a scaffold of sticks covered with mats of cedar bark and fir branches. Often they use cloth tents they have made themselves.

At noon Vanderbilt invites us to eat lunch with him on the steamer. This is the last meal aboard. Later the steamer was pulled ashore and converted for fishing. In the afternoon I go on a little hunting trip. Near the village many potato plants can be seen. The Natives here have learned to use them in the preparation of hutschino.

Thursday, April 20

The morning is beautiful, but later it becomes cloudy again. Last night the majority of the Indians was drunk. Apparently the stuff that we had seen being produced in the chief's house has been brought here. With the missionary I take a ride to the opposite shore and walk on the beach again.

Friday, April 21

Two finback whales are sighted. The small steamboat goes out to hunt them. We watch it for a long while. After we went back into the house tired of waiting, the Indians report that after a lengthy hunt one of the whales was hit and ran for two miles. A line broke. Indians climbed the back of the whale, while it still thrashed its tail, and killed it. After about ten minutes it sank. Now a buoy is attached to the line. If there are indications that sharks attack it, it will have to be raised. Otherwise the Indians will wait until the whale rises by itself, which usually happens after forty hours. Now we want to postpone our planned departure until the whale has been brought in.

Saturday, April 22

During the night heavy hail, in the morning hail stones the size of peas are on the ground. The little steamboat goes out to the whale.

In the afternoon the whale is pulled in. First they had raised it; sharks had already eaten large chunks. Tomorrow it is to be cut up.

During an afternoon walk I collect a few snails, also small ones, and warm up in the sun, because my cold is not yet gone. I sketched a live kind of helix.

Sunday, April 23

Today the whale is being cut up. During low tide it lies entirely on dry ground. Starting on the back, the blubber is cut into 4-inch strips, the tendons are loosened, and the whalebone chopped out. The skin is very smooth, with no sign of parasites. Only one piece of coral apparently got stuck between folds when it was dragged along the bottom. It is a female. The entire length is 63 feet (about 18.90 meters), greatest height $9^1/_2$ feet (about 2.85 meters). The eye is smaller than a walnut.

On the left is a side view, in the center a front view of a snail.
On the right is this description: shell yellowish green, feelers light grey,
body pale flesh-colored. Killisnoo, April 22, 1882.

Monday, April 24

The weather is probably even stormier than yesterday. In the morning
a shark is caught. It was attracted by the whale's smell. Large pieces of
whale meat and blubber are pulled out of his throat. The cutting of the
whale continues. In the uterus the Indians find a well-developed fetus about
4 feet (1.20 meters) long.

On Tuesday, April 25, the wind diminished. The morning is beautiful,
so we decide to leave for Sitka. After lengthy negotiations with the Indians,
a canoe crew is assembled, two Chutsinu Indians and one from Sitka. The
latter had been used by Vanderbilt and others as an interpreter. He speaks
English fairly well. But, of course, you cannot trust the boy. He refuses to
work because he was awake at night, but he gives us some interesting
explanations about the population.

After breakfast we leave. While crossing Chatham Strait, which is about
10 miles wide here, we have rather rough seas. In the northerly wind we can
use our sails and reach the other side after about two hours. Then we enter
the narrow Peril Strait, one of the loveliest passages of the archipelago. The
sea is calm, only a light wind, and we move ahead quickly. Before dusk we
find a camp site near Sand Island. All the banks are buried in deep snow.

Wednesday, April 26

We break up very early. At the narrowest place of Peril Strait there are
strong currents caused by the tides. Even steamers, which also pass through

this strait, are unable to struggle against the current and have to wait for the change of tides.

The weather is very beautiful. Even before arrival of the highest tide we pass the first riptide, at this time without danger, although the current and the eddies are also quite strong. The next riptide after about eight miles again presents no difficulties. We have good wind and reach Sitka before 6:00 P.M.

Here, too, there is still a foot of snow in the forest, but the little town itself and its immediate environment are free of snow.

My stay in Sitka lasts from April 26 to May 12. Sitka is now an entirely unimportant place. It has less than 300 white residents. The complete abandonment of the place may only be a matter of time, unless the nearby mines or the fisheries should prove more productive, or unless the government desired for Alaska should be placed here. Again the site of the place fills me with pleasure. It is magnificent, equal to a second Kristiania. A view of the scenery at sunrise and sunset from the now ruined old Russian castle reminds me of one of those artistic effects which cannot be analyzed or described but only enjoyed. It is the view of numerous densely wooded little islands in the bay, of the silhouette of the truncated pyramid of Mount Edgecumbe against the blue sky, remindful of Fujiyama, of the steeply rising mountains of the interior, among which the pointed cone of Mount Popof is especially attractive.

During the American rule hardly a single new house has been built in Sitka. In relatively good condition are the broad promenades built by the Russians. They lead along the coast, then through beautiful spruce forest to a lovely mountain brook, the Indian River. Sitka can truly be proud of these promenades.

The Indian village consists of fifty houses with about twelve hundred souls. Only a few modern house structures differ from the characteristic features of other Indian villages.

Today the Sitka Indian is considered to be most unreliable. Unrest was caused by the vacillating rule of the person representing the government. Each American warship captain was usually the only authority in the area. Each one pursued a different policy toward the Indians. The ease with which a large part of the white population was intimidated by empty threats also contributed to the unrest. It could have been prevented by a more stable rule.

The government tried to prevent slavery as well as witch hunting. Last winter when the two shamans again incited the people to a witch hunt, they were imprisoned in the guard house for several days, and finally, before their release, were robbed of their long hair. Like Samson, they jealously guard it all their life against desecration by scissors and comb, because they assume it is a part of their power. This hair was then displayed in the guard house as a trophy, but was stolen during a night while I was there. The thief could not be found.

Sitka is a place known for its large amount of rain; its annual rainfall exceeds that of Bergen, Norway. But clear, beautiful days are not rare, and during my almost three-week stay I enjoyed the most beautiful spring weather except for three rainy days. During the night the temperature often sank below freezing. On May 8 snow was falling, but this spring is considered to be extraordinarily late, and the vegetation is almost one month behind.

Very few gardens are seen in Sitka; grain and fruit are not raised at all. No doubt the climate would allow some agriculture, but the energetic and more intelligent part of the white population does not plan to stay here permanently and shuns the cost and effort of clearing and tilling. The others and the Indians do not show any initiative. Also, in spite of high prices for milk, butter, eggs, and meat with the exception of venison, very few domestic animals are raised. Only two cows, one bull, three horses, four pigs with piglets, two old goats with about four kids, and a few chickens are in town. Everywhere along the beach I see fish eggs being dried on strings hung up between poles. Some fish eggs are spread on rocks and cloths.

In the local store I purchase a few ethnological objects to add to my collection. Major Morris receives me very graciously and puts his large library at my disposal.

The Russian priest and George Castor Midanoff want to accompany us on a trip to the sulphur springs 15 miles south on the coast of Baranof Island. Our boat leaves May 2. First we go to the Redoubt, a distance of about 20 miles. This is an old Russian settlement fortified by palisades in a bay at the outlet of a 10-mile-long lake. There are five small blockhouses and a chapel, but only a single elderly Russian and a few Indians live in part of the rooms.

The Russians also had a grist mill here, which has long since been in ruins. Now only salmon are caught in the summer. A short hike along the bank of the lake leads to a ledge about 1.5 meters above the highest water

*Redoubt near Sitka. Inside an old Russian house, one man is lying,
another one sitting on a built-in bench along the back wall.*

level. From there we have a beautiful view of the lake to the right and left.
Its southern end is reportedly connected with the hot springs via a low
treeless plain.

The following morning we break camp in unfavorable weather and soon
we are forced to camp on a small island. Here we find an old grave of a
shaman, but the skull had been stolen. Several potato beds nearby are rather
neglected. Next to these are the remains of some Indian steam tents,
scaffolds built of poles. I learn that these are covered with blankets, heated
stones are carried into the tent, put into a pile, and water is poured on them.
We can see the piles of burned stones. Since the wind and rain do not
diminish, we finally set up camp for the night. Throughout the night we
maintain a mighty fire.

On the next morning the wind is still so unfavorable that we have to give
up the trip to the hot springs. We therefore return to Sitka. Our boat has
difficulty passing some cliffs, because the boat tacks poorly. After two
hours we reach the wharf in Sitka.

On Saturday, May 6, I again try to get to the hot springs, this time with
Aliskey Turnbuall and an Indian. The wind is strong, we have to paddle
and, when the wind gets very strong, look for a camp site to spend the night.

During the night the wind dies down. At six in the morning we leave, again we have to use the paddles. At ten o'clock we arrive at the hot springs. Here the Russians had built a hospital which was destroyed by Indians in 1852, but it was rebuilt and maintained also during the American rule until the troops were withdrawn. Then a white man, called Brown, took possession of the baths. He also produced hutschino on the side which he sold to the Indians. During the winter of 1878/79 he was robbed and killed by two Indians. The leader of the party friendly to the whites, however, handed the murderers over when they arrived in Sitka with their stolen goods. Since then the hot springs are neglected, only Indians using them occasionally. The springs emerge from granite rock. Since my thermometer broke on the rough boat trip, I cannot take the exact temperature. I can put my hand into the hottest spring for a short while; the other two are lukewarm. The three springs are separated by only a few paces. Two of the springs are enclosed. A crust of sulphur is deposited in the wooden drain that takes the water to the bathroom, a basin enclosed by boards. A larger open basin is called the Indian bath. Here an Indian took a bath while we were there. The taste of the water is not unpleasant, but the hottest spring has a strong taste of rotten eggs, indicating hydrogen sulfide.

Otherwise, this area does not offer anything peculiar. Also a typical flora cannot be seen, at least at this time.

After a short lunch we return to the boat and take a trip to Edgecumbe. The wind is getting so strong that once we even have to take down the sail. At that time the Indian pours a bucket of fresh water overboard. Is this some kind of sacrifice?

The sea is so stormy that we cannot land at the intended site. Instead we have to go to so-called Crab Bay, where we find a camping place. We are not entirely protected from the wind, snow, and rain. A big fire soon restores our good mood.

Monday, May 8

The weather has not improved, snow and rain prevent longer excursions. In the afternoon we leave. Our crossing to Sitka in a snowstorm and hailstorm is not easy. Not until 1:00 P.M. do we arrive there.

On May 10 the mail steamer, on which I intend to continue my trip south, arrives from Juneau. It brings the news that many miners arrived there with high expectations. Three quartz mills will start operating soon but, because of the snow, work has not yet begun. The enthusiasm and credulity of the miners is the same as in other gold districts. With greatest confidence, the yield of an entire mine is calculated on the basis of the doubtful analysis of a few single pieces. One expects $800, even $1000 per ton; later it might yield $10 or $15 per ton!

The May 11 is devoted to some purchases. During a walk through the Indian village I enter Sitka Jack's house and buy three small fur bags and an unfinished braided blanket. I sketch a richly decorated club for killing halibut. The weather is beautiful.

On Friday, the twelfth, I leave Sitka on the steamer at 9:00 P.M. in beautiful weather.

Saturday, May 13

Early in the morning we have a beautiful view. We have passed the southern tip of Baranof Island and are now opposite Coronation Island.

Dr. Choang tells several Tlingit myths. In general they agree with those we had heard. The story for the dead is supposed to have eight different stanzas. The happy arrival of the soul in the land of ghosts depends on the correct way to sing this song. First the soul has to pass the place where the ghosts of the crows live, then the place where the ghosts of the linden trees live, then the place of the bushes and that of the dogs. Then the soul reaches a lake. On the opposite side he sees many houses. Smoke rises from their midst and loud noises there drown his calls. He falls asleep. When he wakes up the next morning he yawns and with it makes the now quiet ghosts on the opposite bank aware of him. They bring the soul across the lake in their canoes. The soul is not allowed to sit near the fire at first, but only after his body is cremated.

On the other hand, if the soul had no friends among the dead, he would not be taken across. This is why so many souls can be found on the shore waiting in vain for the crossing. But even the fortunate souls who got to the other side did not lead an enviable life. They receive only as much food and drink as is donated by their friends on earth. That is why no Tlingit neglects to remember his dead friends during his meal and, calling their names, throws a little food into the fire.

For a long time we move ahead very slowly because of foggy weather. Later on the fog leaves and in beautiful weather we enter the harbor of Klawock at the west edge of Prince of Wales Island. It is a deep bay, often narrowed by promontories and islands, with a settlement at its end. Here is a salmon cannery; the salmon are conserved in tin cans. There is also a sawmill which produces crates. On several short excursions I find that the vegetation is far behind. Only a cardamine is in bloom. Quite a few cedars grow here.

The Indian houses are scattered and generally look quite poor. Through contact with white people the Indians, particularly the women, have lost their Native character. Hutschino production flourishes here and it is tolerated by whites.

Sunday, May 14

Again today, the most beautiful weather. At nine in the morning we leave Klawock and pass through the strait with beautiful views between Kuji [Kuiu] Island and Kupreanof Island in the north and Prince of Wales Island in the south. We land in Wrangell on Wrangell Island at 9:00 P.M. It is one of the three main places in southern Alaska. Compared to the other towns Wrangell has the advantage that, in addition to the mail steamer, ships from British Columbia arrive twice a month to unload goods for the mining district of Cassiar. The goods are taken from here by river boat up the Stikine a distance of about 200 miles, then on pack animals to the mines.

Wrangell has three imposing buildings, a Presbyterian church, a Catholic church, and a mission school for Indian girls. At no place in Alaska is the mission administered as energetically as here. According to reports, the efforts were successful even in the beginning in spite of difficulties and opposition. The missionaries' task was impeded by the fact that Wrangell is the winter headquarters of many miners, as well as the establishment of a competing Catholic mission. But shamans have already given up their work, burials take place instead of cremations, and school and church attendance are quite common. Still, in 1878 two Indian women accused of witchcraft were subjected to cruel tortures. Only one of them could be saved from agonizing death. The local missionary also makes an effort to learn the language of the Natives.

The Chinook jargon has developed as a trading language with the Natives. Indian, English, and French words are mixed together, often with complete loss of their original meanings. Traders and Natives learn and speak it with surprising ease. With its lack of any kind of inflection, it makes ambiguity unavoidable. It is, therefore, almost impossible to express in this jargon any thoughts beyond the ordinary conditions of daily life.

I visit Mrs. Young and read her husband's publications in the *Evangelist*. I receive a few garnets from her.

Then I visit the postmaster, Dr. Corlies, who will be responsible for Arthur's packages.

Monday, May 15

Again beautiful weather. Our next anchorage is Kasan Bay at the east coast of Prince of Wales Island. A salmon cannery had been established here by the Austrian Baranowitsch, whose widow, a Haida Indian, sold it after his death to the same San Francisco company that owns the Klawock cannery. The place itself is one of the few in Alaska that offers a friendly picture of human activity in the midst of beautiful scenery. The residence, as well as the other buildings, is kept in good condition and clean. The

A view of Baranowitsch's fishery, established in 1865, shows a small house in the left background with fenced gardens. In the foreground is a beach with two boats. On the right is a long fishery building built on poles and extending across the beach to the edge of the water.
Kasan Bay, May 15, 1882.

woman, her children, and the other Indians there are also dressed neatly. An old Indian with a tattooed cheek attracts my attention through his resemblance to Don-e-wak, but this Indian's features are more pleasant. A fenced garden, although not cultivated now, shows signs of former care.

It is remarkable that the Americans who settled in Alaska show so little concern for the beautification of their present place of residence. This neglect can only be explained by the lack of attachment to the soil and the constant thought of an early return to the States.

Here, too, some places are still covered by snow, but the vegetation is far advanced. Currant bushes are green and in flower. The village Kasan, with its Haida population, is located about 10 miles from the bay. We cannot see it from here and are told it is no longer important.

Tuesday, May 16

In the steady, beautiful and calm weather our trip continues not through the narrow straits near the mainland, but through the wide Hecate Strait, after crossing Dixon Entrance, the border between Alaska and British Columbia. This time we do not see Fort Simpson and Matlacatla [Metlakatla] which we had passed last winter. Everyone agrees that in the latter place a success, which is rare in the missions of the present, has been achieved through the devoted dedication and activity of a single man. In 1857, Mr. Duncan began his activity at Fort Simpson among the Tsimshian Indians under great difficulties. In order to save his congregation from the harmful influence of unscrupulous liquor dealers and in order to accomplish a complete break with the past, he settled his followers in Matlacatla, south of Fort Simpson. Here, under his leadership, a friendly town was soon established where various industries and an important trade were carried on by the Indians. A few years ago even a gasworks, financed by benevolent Englishmen, was established in Matlacatla. Recently, however, Mr. Duncan, who is not ordained, was removed from his position by the archbishop. But the Indians refused to have another pastor, and apparently due to their opposition the measure was revoked.

We meet several larger canoes, some of them engaged in fur seal hunting. The Queen Charlotte Islands on our right are the most isolated group of the entire archipelago. In the north they are separated by the broad Dixon Entrance from Prince of Wales Island and in the east by the equally wide Hecate Sound from the islands near the coast. They are occupied exclusively by Haida Indians. The Haidas as well as the Tsimshians completely resemble their northern neighbors, the Tlingits, in habits and traditions, but because of their entirely different language and their characteristic physical peculiarities, they are considered to be independent people. Fewer original traditions are maintained here. Shamanism has almost entirely disappeared, the dead are buried, European clothing and use of European goods are common. The Haida is a handsome, stately tribe. In former times women and daughters were sold in the mines, so that the men gained the means to live a life of leisure. Now this awful custom is less frequent, although it has not entirely ceased.

Wednesday, May 17

Cloudy and rainy weather. In the afternoon we reach the coast of Vancouver and cruise along near it. Only the higher mountains are still covered by some snow; deciduous trees show some fresh green.

Thursday, May 18

Beautiful weather and favorable wind. At eleven o'clock we reach Departure Bay, where we land on the east coast of Vancouver near Nanaimo. We take on coal for the steamer's own consumption and as freight for San Francisco.

On the entire West Coast of North America there is very little coal worth mining and often coal still has to be imported from England, so these mines are very important. During the ten years of the mines' existence, 33,000 tons of coal have been shipped. Now the two mines supply about 800 tons daily. When we arrive eight ships, among them four steamers, were lined up for loading. One of these steamers had brought twelve hundred Chinese to Victoria and will take coal back to China. The coal is from the Cretaceous Period and unsuitable for the production of gas, since it does not turn into coke; however, it is excellent for steamships and domestic use, so the demand is increasing steadily. Chinese are employed almost exclusively in the mines.

Friday, May 19

After breakfast I visit the coal mines. Before climbing into the empty coal wagon, I see a hummingbird hovering near flowering fruit trees. After a 1^1/$_2$-hour trip I get to the coal mines. Supplied with an oil lamp, I climb alone down into the tunnel. The inclination is about 5 degrees. Then it goes by horse-drawn train and finally by cable car to the place where the coal is dug. This room is low, filled with coal dust, and divided by a rubber blanket. The coal is about 5 to 10 feet (about 1.5 to 3 meters) thick; several weaker bands are above it. The veins of coal are often interrupted by stairs, since the profiles are said to be very irregular. At the moment there were no fossils available at the office.

I return through the woods botanizing. Cuts along the path show good rich farmland. In the evening I go aboard a local steamer to Victoria.

Saturday, May 20

We leave at 7:00 A.M. The route leads between many islands and often through narrow passages with strong currents. The scenery reminds me of Swedish lakes. Only a few settlements can be seen, although the soil seems to be very rich, especially for raising animals.

At 2:00 P.M. we arrive in Victoria. The town is a small place with only eight thousand inhabitants. The calm here is a pleasant contrast to the noisy activities of American cities. It has a pretty location in a wide, fertile plain, but the harbor is too small for a larger traffic. Small, neat houses with pretty gardens surround the city.

Without doubt, the completion of the Canadian Pacific Railroad will be the beginning of a new era for Victoria as well as all of British Columbia. As all larger American railroads, the Canadian is built mainly with the help of Chinese workers who are satisfied with a wage of one dollar per day, while the minimum wage for white workers is two dollars. According to newspaper reports, twenty-four thousand Chinese are expected. In Victoria, as in San Francisco and Portland, one can see Chinese in various positions as servants in private homes and hotels, as workers in all branches or as tradespeople. So far British Columbia does not think of denying them immigration. Workers are so scarce that one has to be glad to have found the Chinese as replacement.

Sunday, May 21

A fairly warm day. Captain George picks me up for a walk, takes me to his house, and shows me photographs, some of which he gives me. For dinner I am invited by a Mr. Brown-Lohenberg, who regularly gives Sunday dinners. I sit next to his brother, an old gentleman, and talk mostly German with him. He comes from Prenzlau. It is a very good dinner, with pleasant conversation. His wife is from Berlin, but I have little chance to talk with her. Several men are employees of the Hudson's Bay Company, others are officers in a voluntary militia, artillery and infantry stationed in Victoria. Around 11:00 P.M. we take our leave and at twelve o'clock we go to the steamer, which leaves twice a week for Tacoma in the interior of Puget Sound.

Monday, May 22

At 5:00 A.M. the ship leaves the harbor of Victoria. Since it is a beautiful morning, I also get up that early. The isolated mountain massif of Mount Baker (3,280 meters) and the beautiful group of the Washington mountains are the main attraction for some time. Soon, however, one can see the white pyramid of the 4,394-meter-high Mount Rainier rising from the horizon. The trip goes past the San Juan Islands, which almost caused the outbreak of war between England and the United States in 1859. Through arbitration by the German emperor in 1872, the United States was given the islands and thus they became the masters of the Straight of Juan de Fuca.

Around 9:00 A.M. we arrive at Port Townsend, a growing city at the mouth of Puget Sound. Here we touch American ground. Then the trip continues through the calm waters of the Sound. Its densely wooded banks become alive now and then with friendly settlements. The most important place along the Sound is Seattle, where we arrive at 5:00 P.M. It is important mostly through its coal mines, which supply a large part of the demand of San Francisco. The commercial importance of Puget Sound will lead to the development of a large city; Seattle and the younger Tacoma seem to contain the germ for such growth. Tacoma already is connected with the Columbia River via a railroad, to be continued to Portland. Portland is the end point of the Northern Pacific Railroad, to be opened next year. A part of the stream of immigrants to Oregon and Washington Territory will doubtless be directed by this railroad.

Tuesday, May 23

The trip is continued on this railroad. At 5:00 A.M. I am up, but the train does not leave New Tacoma until 7:00 A.M. At first we go up the valley of

183

the Willamette. We pass through flat, mostly fertile, but sometimes rocky land. The forests are open, numerous cedars, often extended grass areas. Only very little land is cultivated. At noon we reach Kalama, the present end of the railroad. From here a river steamer takes us to Portland. The water in the Columbia and the Willamette is rather high. We keep close to the bank in order to get ahead in the strong current. At three o'clock we arrive in Portland. There I meet Mr. Schulze, who asks me to stay for a few days. I have lunch with him. In the evening I go to Mrs. Köhler, the sister of Spohn. Hot day.

Wednesday, May 24

In the morning I visit Schulze in his office. He gives me photographs. We lunch together and he invites me for dinner, too. Mrs. Köhler is also there.

All crimes committed in Alaska are prosecuted in Portland. This winter a Yakutat Indian who had robbed and killed two gold miners was sentenced to death. As a special favor he asked for a speedy execution. Since witnesses and interpreters have to come from Sitka and other places farther away, the costs of such trials are enormous. The present lawlessness in Alaska is indeed an abnormality. The unsuccessful efforts so far to establish a government can only be explained by the conflict of personal interests. The bill before Congress now demands only the creation of three new posts, attorney general, judge, and clerk, together with a budget of $20,000.

Friends of this bill assume that lawful conditions would encourage expanded industrial and commercial enterprises. In the near future, however, Alaska would hardly be the destination of significant numbers of immigrants. So far, the more attractive areas of California, Oregon, Washington, and British Columbia have only one hundredth the population of similar European countries. The gold rush alone will bring only a temporary influx of people to the rougher, less accessible Alaska, which will hardly advance the steady development of the country.

Only by raising the civilization of the Native population, which feels attached to the soil, could the land be cultivated now. Immigrant Americans lack this attachment. Such attempts at civilization can be successful only under the strong arm of a consistent government. The efforts of the missionary societies, in spite of temporary successes of individual personalities, will fail due to lack of coordination, one-sided religious viewpoints, and insufficient budgets.

Thursday, May 25

Around noon I watch a Chinese funeral. First, pairs of Chinese with flags and standards, a few also on horseback, then a band, but not Chinese, then the hearse, the body in a black coffin, then more Chinese in pairs. The first Chinese were dressed in white clothes, partly with red sashes, the following Chinese wear brown clothes. The end is formed by twelve carriages, in some of which are women.

Friday, May 26, to Saturday, the twenty-seventh

These two days are used for a longer excursion. Participating in addition to Schulze were Dr. Stübler and Mr. Nitmo, whom I met in Schulze's office and who also is a writer for *Harper's Magazine*. Schulze takes along his Negro and a basket with wine. The train ride goes south up river through the wide Willamette valley. Main points of interest are the falls of Oregon City,[24] one of the oldest cities, then Salem with the capitol, and Eugene City with the state university. Steamships also go up to this point. Now we leave the valley and the most beautiful part of the train ride begins. It leads through hilly, scenic mountains with gentle slopes, covered with grass, bushes, or open cedar forests. In addition to a kind of dark fir and cedars, there are many oaks. Maple also looks pretty in its fresh foliage. The settlements are generally quite clean, also the fields. Wheat is grown almost exclusively. In Roseburg we stay overnight, part of the group in carriages, the others in a hotel.

The return trip on the following day is taken the same way. Today the weather is beautiful again, only later it becomes warm and dusty. Dinner is taken at the same station as yesterday. The hostess, a Viennese, serves us excellent roast chicken. At 5:00 P.M. we are back in Portland.

After a bath and stowing my luggage on the steamer, I once more visit Schulze in the evening and then go aboard the steamer, which will leave tomorrow for San Francisco.

On May 28 I leave Portland on the steamer *Oregon*. Captain Pohlmann, a German, introduces me to my cabin mate, a German beer brewer.

After two days, on the morning of the thirtieth, I arrive in San Francisco, where I stay at the Occidental Hotel.

The next day I ask at the German consulate for the address of Captain Jacobsen and visit him. He is very satisfied with the success of his collections, but it had cost him a great deal of money. He is now planning to sail up the Yukon and spend another summer there. He makes the impression of a very efficient man. He has not gone beyond British Columbia.

The days go by quickly with many visits, often to Pastor [Mülsteph] and his friends, also a short visit to the mushroom researcher, Dr. Harknatzni.

Friday, June 2

I again visit Jacobsen. During our conversations it becomes evident again that he solves his tasks with understanding and success. In the afternoon I visit the consul for dinner, where I meet the Italian consul and his wife. The conversation is quite good.

In the evening I go to Beber and with him pay a short visit to a family where I meet Professor Herbst. Then we drink beer until 1:00 A.M.

Saturday, June 3

In the morning, luggage transportation, etc., also writing a short article about Alaska for the Academy. At twelve o'clock, departure of the steamer; Beber, the pastor, and the young Kruse are present.

We get under way slowly because we have an old ship in tow. There are only a few passengers. I have a spacious cabin all by myself. The weather is cloudy. Not much of the coast can be seen.

The return trip takes Aurel via Mazatlan and San Salvador to Panama. From there he took the 76-kilometer-long Panama railroad opened in 1855 to Colon, where the tropical vegetation to the right and left of the train especially impressed him. From there the steamer Colon *took him to New York.*

After a visit to his oldest brother Albert in Buffalo and an excursion with him to Niagara Falls, Aurel left New York on July 14, 1882, aboard the Donau *for Bremen, where he concluded his journal with the following entry:*

Thursday, July 27

Early in the morning, arrival at Bremen. A small steamer takes us ashore. Since I do not see anyone at the train station, I first try to visit Albrecht, who was not home, then Dr. Wolkenhauer, who has to lend me 25 marks because I do not have enough money for the ticket to Berlin. Aboard ship I also had to borrow 20 marks to tip the stewards. With Dr. Wolkenhauer I visit another board member, Mr. Malchers, and then leave by train for Berlin at 1:00 P.M., where I arrive at 8:45 P.M.

CHAPTER NINE

SPRING EXCURSIONS FROM CHILKOOT

Letter written by Arthur to the Geographical Society in Bremen, slightly abridged:

Chilkoot, May 4, 1882

Since my brother's departure from here on April 5 there was only one chance to send a short postcard. The little steamer of the local trading company this summer unfortunately will not arrive here once a month, as in previous summers, but probably only once in the fall. Sometimes the connection with the outside world is very limited and handled only by individual Indian canoes going to Juneau. This letter is being taken by an Indian from Klukwan who wants to bypass the local trading station and take the furs he has bought from the Stick Indians to Juneau, where he wants to sell them for a higher price than he would get here. Then he will be quite satisfied, when after a ten- to fourteen-day difficult trip he can return to his Native village with goods worth a few dollars more. The value of time is unknown to him. Perhaps the thought of trading a larger quantity of molasses there for the production of hutschino made him take the long trip. He himself is a great friend of this customary liquor substitute. He also knows that for a few bottles of it he can get all the precious furs from the Gunanas beyond the mountains, for which he otherwise would have to pay a full one man's load of powder, lead, blankets, and cloth.

For almost two weeks we have had beautiful clear weather, but the sun had little effect on the colossal amount of snow. Only the rain yesterday and today helped to reduce it somewhat. Every night until yesterday the temperature sank below the freezing point, while the day's maximum during the last days of April was 6° to 10°C.

On the tenth, I made a longer excursion to the uninhabited Takhin Valley and especially to the Bertha Glacier. At 9:00 A.M. I started out in rather clear and cold weather accompanied by the Indian boy, Jim. He carried my blanket and a second gun. A much used path took us in less than half an hour through the woods to the western side of the peninsula and then to the northeastern bank of the Chilkat River. After another forty-five minutes we reached the village Jendestake directly under the steep slopes of Geissen Mountain.

The houses buried under the snow have stood empty all winter; the population has settled near the factory (Deshu) and comes here now and then only to get the dry salmon stored here. A little below Jendestake a sand bar stretches across the river, offering a path from one bank to the other at low tide. Upriver from this bar an ice barricade has formed through the effect of tide and current. Beyond this barricade a uniform ice and snow blanket covers the river, which is a half a German mile wide here. In bright sunshine the eyes are severely strained by the glare of this great snow cover. The Indians who come toward us envy the white man who has found a much more effective protection with his sun glasses than the complete blackening of their faces.

In Jendestake we leave the trail, which, although less used, leads from here to Klukwan, and in order to reach the opposite bank, we walk in almost a westerly direction. The snow conditions were favorable for walking on snowshoes and within an hour we reached the low deposited land near the mouth of the Katzekahin (also Chatzekahin, Ch'kasekahin) and the Takhin. We used our snowshoes until our return and took them off only while we were resting at night. After we passed a narrow belt of elms and willows, where numerous ptarmigans stayed, we went in a westerly direction through a quite dense forest of evergreens and deciduous trees. We crossed the rapidly flowing Katzekahin on a snow bridge. On the other bank we rested a short while to take some measurements. From here the path went through a dense stand of poplars, where we had trouble getting along because the sun had softened the snow and because of all the underbrush. Therefore, we had to stop when we finally reached the entrance to the Takhin Valley. The Indian prepared a soft camp of hemlock twigs under a big spruce, started a fire, and cooked the grouse, shot before in a pine stand. Meanwhile I was attracted by the mating call of the dusky grouse, heard for the first time today, called *nukt* by the Natives because of its call, and then I went higher up into the mountains. Numerous tracks of snowhares and porcupines, a few of wolves, marten, and mountain goats, indicate that there are more animals in this unpopulated valley than in any other place previously visited by us. Now, toward evening, there is complete silence in the woods. From an open location there was a magnificent view of the valley below and the steeply rising rocky crest on the other side, behind which the sun had just disappeared.

After convincing myself that the glacier was really far more distant than I first had assumed, I descended slowly to the Takhin River, followed it, and reached the camp site at dusk. There I found Jim busy repairing his snowshoes and drying his footwear.

When using the local snowshoes, it is impossible to wear our boots. Moccasins made of reindeer or deer skin are so permeable to water that one has completely wet feet after a short while in fairly mild weather, i.e., only a few degrees below freezing. The sealskin boots worn in the land of the Chukchis would be just right here.

After dinner and after drying all clothes, we got our blankets and slept so well that we did not wake up until 5:00 A.M. at a temperature of 5.5°C. Meanwhile, the fire had melted a 5-foot-deep (1.50 meter) hole into the snow and had gone out. We immediately started out, first in order to reach a small log hut I had discovered the previous day on the bank of the Takhin. Here we left the blankets and walked in a westerly direction upward through an open spruce forest with imposing tall trees in the second part of the valley. Mighty high trunks with a diameter of 1 meter are common here. I measured the circumference of two giant spruce trees at 5.35 meters and 4.92 meters and that of an exceptionally tall hemlock at 4.34 meters at about 7 feet (2.10 meters) above the ground. In this beautiful clear weather the walk through this forest with no underbrush obstructing the path could be compared to a walk through an old park. The higher rising sun, however, softened the snow more and more and made this walk extremely fatiguing. Numerous bird calls were heard. The master singer of all is the pine grosbeak *(Pinicola enucleator)*; faithfully accompanying him are the red and the white-winged crossbills (*Loxia curvirostra* and *L. leucoptera*). From the bank of the Takhin, rapidly flowing through its rocky bed, the song of the cheerful water starlings is heard.

Numerous flocks of red finches, siskin, and the small, extremely tame boreal chickadee, flying by in the company of creepers and goldcrests, the screaming of the blue jay (*Cyanocitta*), the dignified representatives of our häher [a colorful German raptor], the dissonant cawing of the raven, the sonorous call of the osprey high up in the air, the pecking sound of numerous woodpeckers (we saw a total of five kinds of woodpeckers this winter), all of these remind me of our German forests. There are also numerous squirrels not much different from ours in shape and habits. Finally, the adventurous figure of a tree porcupine on top of a tall spruce makes me aware of the fact that I am in a forest of North America. One shot scares the animal out of his hiding place, a second shot brings it down dead near our feet. It is a huge specimen of its kind. Jim, too, declares he had never seen such a big one before. A large amount of droppings and big patches of fresh torn spruce bark from which the inner phloem (also savored by Indians as food) had been gnawed, indicated that the animal had taken his meals up there regularly. Several paths deeply trodden into the snow led to several other trees of the same kind and to the subterranean cave under the roots of a spruce, which he had just left a few weeks ago after hibernating. Phloem and needles of spruce seem to be his main nourishment. In other places I found that he also eats the bark of willows and during the summer numerous berries are a welcome change. The meat of the porcupine is edible any time of the year, but it tastes best in the fall. The Indians of the interior use the quills for pretty decorations of their leather goods. Not until evening did I learn about a first-rate delicacy hidden in its inside.

After hanging up our game on a low tree branch, we slowly followed the river on its right side. The warm rays of the sun had brought out numerous insects.[25] At the same time the snow had turned so soft that it stuck to our snowshoes in large balls and made it extremely difficult to walk. Around 10:00 A.M. we stopped for a forty-five-minute rest, took some measurements, and had breakfast. At this place the rapidly flowing Takhin was about 20 feet wide and 2 feet deep and touched the wooded high banks. Around noon we reached the place on the Takhin River where the outflow of the glacier enters. We walked upward along this outflow and after half an hour we finally stood in front of the mighty ice wall, the end of Bertha Glacier, here bending down to the spruce forest. Our location directly under the steeply towering and partly fissured ice wall did not offer a good overview. The vast cover of snow also hid all details. It almost seemed as if outflows from several glacier gates were pouring into one main valley. They were all frozen now and passable without danger. In some places we could step very close to the ice. In its crevices there was a dark green, impure color and now and then I noticed large pieces of rock in them. In the east the glacier valley is bordered by a mountain ridge with extraordinarily steep slopes toward east and west. Farther toward the west there are also high mountain ranges.

On our return trip when we reached the place where we had hunted the porcupine, I wanted to tie it on the spruce branch and easily pull it like a sled to our camp site. But Jim refused: "It would be *ch' lakass* (taboo) and make great wind." He preferred to carry the heavy animal on his back to the fortunately not too distant hut where we had planned to spend the following night. When we got there, he quickly finished the usual preparations for the night. Then he sat next to me and attentively watched me skinning the animal. At first I thought he had the praiseworthy intention of taking over this unpleasant task next time. It is not easy to skin a porcupine in this freezing temperature with completely wet feet. But he only did not want to miss the delicacy which he had hinted at before. When I gave him the carcass, he cut open the intestine and in the half-digested mash of inner bark of spruce he fished for the enormous number of a kind of short, broad tapeworm and gulped them down with signs of well-being at such speed, that I could barely save a handful for our collection.

An owl quartet *(Bubo virginianus)* which was heard in the evening enticed me to an excursion. But soon it got entirely dark, and because of unfavorable snow conditions I was forced to give up any further hunt.

The night was clear and cold, but, tired from the strenuous walk, I slept so well that I did not awake until the sun was high in the sky. The temperature at 6:30 A.M. was 9.1°C, while the minimum of this night at the station (Portage Bay or Deshu) was -5.6°C. In the afternoon it had snowed there, whereas here on the Takhin we had continuous, clear weather.

On our return to Portage Bay I noticed several signs of the approaching spring. Flocks of snow buntings searched for scattered seeds under the alder bushes. Only a few of them had spent the winter here. On the beach there was a large number of sandpipers seldom seen here during the winter. In the bushes I also saw for the first time a little sparrowlike bird. Not until the end of April did it appear in larger numbers and then it mainly contributed to enlivening the quiet forest. The catkins of the willows and poplars (called *kúteki,* i.e., young dogs, by the Indians) shed their winter cover. In some places free of snow along the bank I saw women searching for the now-growing edible root sprouts of a plant called *klechún.*

The following week brought snow again and strong winds. Finally on the nineteenth the weather permitted me to take a longer excursion by canoe to Dejah. It was a small thing of a canoe in which Kasko, the guide we had used several times, wanted to take me across. It is a dugout canoe or so-called cockleshell. Last winter he carved it himself from a tall, straight spruce. With the help of an axe and fire he felled the huge tree and then carved out the canoe with a kind of hatchet. When stepping into this swaying means of transportation, be careful to maintain the "golden middle" and hurry to place your center of gravity as low as possible. This means you sit with horizontally stretched-out legs on the bottom of the boat exactly where your careful boat guide has marked the location of the seat with a few fir twigs. On the other hand, try to sit as comfortably as possible under such circumstances, because for the next few hours you, as an unexperienced passenger, may not think of leaving your seat. With the gun and ammunition to my right, the short paddle to my left, compass and watch, notebook and pencil handy, I can safely say yes to the boatman's question, "all light," who as a typical Tlingit exchanges r and l. And off we go at great speed to Tanani, where Kasko's home is. Shouting with joy, his little son runs toward him. He knows that his dear father has brought a present of hard bread, which he expects just as the white man's child would ask for sugar bread.

Our Kasko is a real heathen: owner of two wives, a good one and a bad one, and proprietor of the thickest skull in the entire Chilkat territory, strong like a giant, phlegmatic bordering on laziness, but during hunting and fishing, among the first, and possessed of unshakable placidity. In his younger years he must have been more hot tempered. It is said that in Klukwan once, irritated by malicious mockery, he killed or wounded seven of his enemies. Although his uncle, the old chief Tschartritsch, settled his nephew's capital crime with so and so many blankets, he deemed it prudent to leave his Native village. He knows that firewater opens up old wounds, and Native instincts do not demand compensation but rather an eye for an eye and a tooth for a tooth.

After a short stay in Tanani, we paddled across Chilkoot Inlet, leading to Chilkoot, to the northern point of Dejah fjord. Since there was a favorable wind from the south, we entered a little bay to set a rather primitive sail. From now on we went with a gradually increasing wind at a speed of 5 to 6 knots in a diagonal direction across the Dejah fjord, then along its eastern bank until, after passing two bays on our right, we came to the northernmost, narrowest part of the fjord. The water was so choppy that sometimes the bow of our canoe was submerged under water. On the whole, however, the little boat held up better than I had suspected. Any anxiety at the sight of white-capped waves disappeared completely with one look at the constantly smiling face of our guide.

The coasts on both sides of the Dejah fjord are syenite rocks of light color, rising steeply upward and just as precipitously falling into the water. Even a small canoe would have trouble finding a refuge along these coasts. Just as we passed the precipitous slate cliffs in the highest waves, my guide tells me that several years ago a big canoe crashed here and sank with everyone aboard. The slopes are only sparsely covered with spruce, pine, in some places with hemlock and birches. Mostly the bare rock is visible, often showing traces of glacial grooves.

The fauna in the fjord is not different from that near the factory. The real spring flocks of water birds have not yet arrived; however, the great black *Oidemia* (scoter), two kinds of *Clangula,* the graceful oldsquaw and the colorful *Anas histrionica* (harlequin duck) are frequently seen. Less frequent are some songbirds like guillemot and the little grebes. The elegant flight of the sea gull is in peculiar contrast to the timid, unskillful flutter of the local cormorant *(Phalacrocorax pelagicus)*, whose feathers are prettier than most other cormorants and who represents in dignified manner, in shape, and in motion the "turpe habitu, indole ignavum et stolidum etc. *Phalacrocoracis* genus" (Pallas). The Indians tell that in former times it had a tongue and could speak like other birds. Once, however, the raven, fearing that his talkative friend might gossip about one of his many misdeeds, pulled out the cormorant's tongue, and since then it can only mumble indistinctly. A number of dolphins, whose backs rise above the waves in regular intervals, and the round head of a seal emerging at a safe distance, indicate to us that the "small fish" (eulachon, a kind of smelt) has arrived to swim up the Dejah fjord.

At its outermost end the bay is extremely shallow, but since we arrived during high tide, we could go out into the eastern shallow arm with our flat-bottomed boat until we could pull the canoe ashore at a place where several others were lying. After we had been sitting uncomfortably for four and a half hours, the fifteen-minute short walk [that followed] was truly refreshing. We reached the so-called house, a little hut of about 5 paces square, almost attached to the rock. It was full of people, so we preferred, as most others did, to camp outside. On a small island where low alders and willows grew, in the at present mostly dry river bed, a so-called fly was erected out of a few poles and a sail for protection against the wind. In front of it a fire was lit, and after my blanket and my few belongings were placed into the preferred location, I was as comfortably established as one could wish to be for a few days in weather that was not too bad. Kasko set up lodgings with wife and child next to me. His favorite wife and their three-year-old daughter, who was still eagerly nursing, were awaiting him here. Soon he was busy with preparations for fishing, while I started on a hike upriver to get to know the area. During the trip I had noticed that the slopes of the Dejah fjord were entirely free of snow in some places and here there was knee-deep snow only in protected places in the woods and in ravines where the sun could not penetrate. The actual river bed and the large open marsh and meadow terrain were completely free from snow.

In Deshu (Portage Bay), even in open places, the snow was still 5 feet (1½ meters) deep.

This evening I went a distance upriver, then took a tiring, slow walk through the woods, which were rather impassable through snow and underbrush, and went to the western side of the valley. I erroneously had assumed that I would find the main stream there. Not until the beginning of darkness did I return to the camp site.

At 4:00 the following morning, the twentieth, we were disturbed by the noise of people rushing by. Kasko quickly reached for his net and hurried after them. The ssag had arrived. I walked fifteen minutes upriver and met about fifteen people— men, women, and boys—eagerly occupied with catching the small fish not much larger than a hand span. They came swimming upriver, unfortunately in not very large numbers. The Indians' tools were hand nets (made by the women out of animal sinews during the winter) and long, thin poles with a simple hook at their ends, the use of which required great skill. The fish baskets laid out last night also yielded only an insignificant catch, so everybody was upset. Several times the word ch'lakass was heard. The presence of the *gutzkakon*, the stranger from far away, was definitely at fault for the low catch. Without doubt, his shooting of raven, oldsquaws, and other sacred animals had caused the severe winter and heavy snowfall. In regard to the latter, there exists another version. Mr. Dickinson's anemometer is the real scapegoat. Kanagu, the stone woman who lives in the first of the above-mentioned bays, and who does not like to see white men with all their new inventions and their different religion, said that she wants to try to knock over the thing and is sending one snowstorm after another. Fortunately, the anemometer is located at a location so well protected from the wind that it is still merrily turning, at least in fairly strong wind.

The freshly caught fish, pierced by a peculiarly carved piece of wood and roasted on the fire, proved to be a kind of delicacy. After this quick breakfast I started out on a longer hike toward the north.

Earlier the second chief of our village, Chlunat, had left with another Indian who carried the luggage. He wants to go over the mountains into the land of the Stick Indians to trade blankets, cloth, tobacco, powder, lead, etc., for precious furs which he will sell to the white trader at great profit. Heavily loaded with about 100 pounds of merchandise in addition to their own provisions, consisting of smoked salmon, fish oil and flour, snowshoes, gun, and axe, they slowly trudge along their way. And yet, they will arrive at the bank of the big lake from which the Yukon flows in two to three days' time. When they passed Kanagu's stone house yesterday, as good believers in the old faith, they prayed for good weather and a happy trip and threw away some small items as sacrifices. During the last camp fire they conscientiously remembered their dead friends and for each one threw a piece of dried salmon into the fire.

On a wooded island in the bed of the river, I found a log cabin and a few sawn-up logs, traces of the presence of those four gold miners who went over to the Yukon last year and went down the Yukon to the vicinity of Fort Selkirk. The snowless path in the bed of the river or on the frozen river itself covered with a little snow was very easy to follow, but it offered so little that I returned within a few hours, after I had gained a sufficient overview of the end of the valley. Here the valley narrows to about 800 paces. The sparsely wooded, steep slopes reach a height of 900 to 1,200 meters. Across the end of the valley in a northeasterly direction is a mountain range which has large glaciers in two depressions. Another, even mightier glacier is on the western mountain chain. I assume there are smaller ones in the ravines, but with the even snow cover on those high elevations one cannot recognize them with certainty. In the middle of summer, when the snow in the high mountains melts, this path through the greatly swollen river is said to be very difficult. Then it leads over crisscross, piled-up trunks, through thick underbrush of berry bushes (currant, gooseberries, blackberries, *Cornus sanguinea* Linné, etc.) and a very prickly aralia that do not help to make this walk easier. Snowhares and squirrels were the only mammals I saw. In the woods I found several times large wolf and fox traps built of strong logs. The next morning a wolf track very close to our camp site was noticed. The wolf traps and similarly built bear traps are deadfalls of the simplest construction. Strong trees weighted down with a log or stones are held in a slanted position by a support which is connected to the bait. A small horseshoe-shaped shelter forces the animal to approach the bait in such a way that the weight of the falling beam will break its back. Now iron traps are used more frequently than these deadfalls. Two minks, called "slaves of otters" by the Natives, were caught while I was there. Bears are frequently seen when the berries are ripe. There were very few birds here. It was different on the meadow terrain in the south, which I visited after my return in the late afternoon. There were numerous flocks of birds which had just arrived from the south. Snow buntings, longspur, and larks were eagerly hunted by hawks, a sparrow hawk, and a middle-sized owl, while a pretty, swift, blue-white songbird *(Vireo silvia?)* did not shy away from attacking his hunter. During the summer the flora of this meadow must be manifold, as far as I could judge from the remains of last year's plants. Here, too, the Indians searched eagerly for the roots of an umbellifera (carrot or parsley family). When cooked it supplies them with a very good-tasting, nourishing food.

The twenty-first was used for hunting and taking some measurements, but unfortunately the latter were very limited because of the unfavorable weather. Toward evening we had light snow. During the following night the wind switched to north and covered us with a light snow blanket. It hardly disturbed me and I did not even notice that Kasko got up and tied the fly to the other side. On the twenty-second, in clear, calm weather, we mostly paddled or sailed in moderate wind back to the factory and arrived there safely soon after noon.

On the twenty-ninth I went on an excursion by canoe with the missionary's family and Mrs. Dickinson to Nachk'(u) Bay, on the east side of the peninsula about 8 miles south, where the herring had arrived to spawn. The water on the southern bank was quite milky from the deposited spawn and at low tide all over the seaweed was covered with fish eggs, eagerly collected by old and young. Poles about 3-meters-long were used to catch the fish; at their lower end they were equipped with a row of sharp-pointed nails. They are dipped into the water like a paddle, and the speared fish, sometimes one on each nail, are dropped into the canoe with a short shake.

Several eagles, flocks of sea gulls and swallows, as well as raven, crows, and the conspicuous kingfisher (*Ceryle alcion*) participated in the fishing. Numerous small songbirds, swallows, pipers, and the pretty redbreasted thrush enlivened the snow-free banks and the wooded slopes, where here and there some fresh green sprouted. What a contrast to Deshu, still almost entirely buried under snow! Joy and happiness prevailed in the Indian camp; the days of need were over now. Herring and halibut were caught in large numbers, also some porcupine, marmots, seal and dolphins were hunted.

During the first week of May we still had a few quite inclement days with snow and rain. Not until May 3 did the thermometer not go below the freezing point; but even today, on the eleventh, a snow cover of 60 to 90 centimeters makes forest and field impassable. The number of daily arrivals of new birds is extremely large, and I have trouble in securing a skin or at least in identifying the kinds, which is not easy with the lack of necessary literature.

Unfortunately, the canoes which arrived today from Juneau did not bring any news from home. In the American newspapers, Europe hardly seems to exist, Germany not at all, and the little they have to say is not even pleasant.

Translation of the postcard from Arthur to Aurel Krause. It was probably written on April 18, 1882:

Dear Aurel,

A canoe, which came up from Wrangell to trade, will take this postcard to Captain Vanderbilt and to you. On the whole, I have been doing quite well, except for shooting ducks, which I cannot quite manage, neither from the beach or from the canoe. Yet I still see one or another kind not yet collected by us. Today, in Vollert's(?) canoe, I got four ducks with fourteen shots, none of them useful to me. After having finished the birds on the first of the month, I went into the lower run of the Kantekoo(?), but got only one of the usual grouse. Old Tschartritsch and his wife came down for a few days. He urgently invited me to come up again. Saturday I went with Jimmy, a fourteen-year-old boy who carried my gun and barometer, to Mt. Geissen, but forgot the matches. Since it started to snow, I soon returned with only one entirely shot-up grouse of the other kind. April 10, eleventh, and twelfth were spent on an excursion to Bertha Glacier. The boy carried blankets and some cooking utensils, so that, when the snow became soft at noon, we had trouble proceeding and had to camp rather early at the southern point. In the woods the call of the other grouse rang out, but the hunt for it was in vain. Until dark I roamed alone through the woods and found really fresh tracks of a mountain goat and its droppings as well as the tracks of a porcupine. A grouse, shot earlier, was made into a delicious dinner. I slept extremely well and did not wake until 5:00 A.M. at the refreshing temperature of 5°C. We started out immediately and left our blankets at a little log cabin I had discovered the night before. Then with light luggage to the glacier. Along the way I shot a porcupine of enormous size which the Indians later confirmed. Then we went on in the increasingly soft snow [that was] more and more tiresome, so that after resting for an hour for breakfast and some measurements, we did not reach the ice waters of the glacier until noon. Difficult overview because of the snow. We spent the night in the cabin. For dinner, porcupine. The boy consumed tapeworms, a delicacy for him, occurring in large numbers. In the morning -10°C. A new kind of woodpecker with red upper body was shot. On the fifteenth I shot two newcomers, the large kingfisher and a little sparrow with black upper body. Tomorrow I am going by canoe with Kasko to Dajeah. Weather and snow conditions are quite unfavorable.

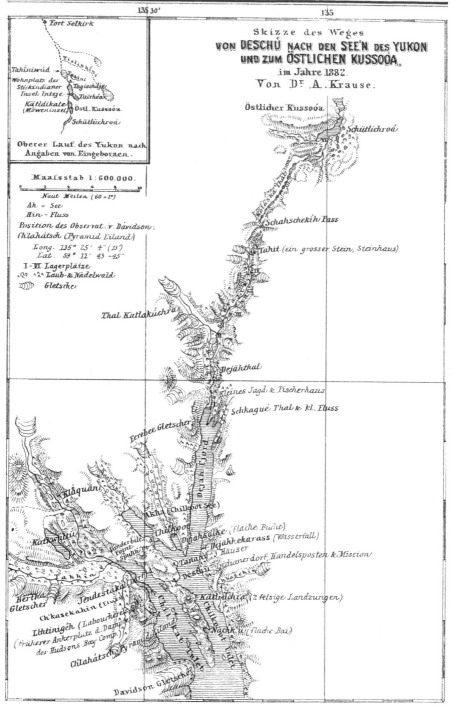

135 30'   135

Skizze des Weges
VON DESCHÚ NACH DEN SEE'N DES YUKON
UND ZUM ÖSTLICHEN KUSSOÓA,
im Jahre 1882.
Von Dr. A. Krause.

Oberer Lauf des Yukon nach
Angaben von Eingebornen.

Maaſsstab 1:600.000.

Naut Meilen (60 = 1°)
Ah = See
Hin - Fluss
Position des Observat. v. Davidson:
Chlahátsch (Pyramid Eiland)
    Long. 135° 25' 4" (13')
    Lat. 59° 11' 43 -45"
I - VI Lagerplätze
Laub-& Nadelwald
Gletscher

Path from Deshu to the Yukon Lakes and the Eastern Kussoóa.

202

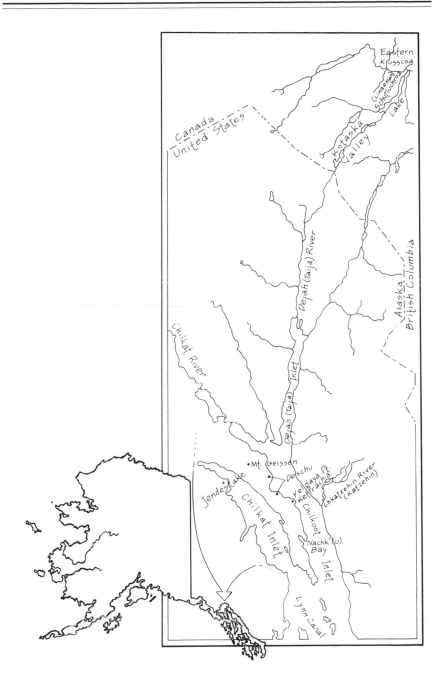

NOTHING BUT THE ADDRESS CAN BE PLACED ON THIS SIDE.

Herrn Dr. Aurel. Krause

per. Adr. Cpt. Vanderbilt N.W.T.C.

Sitka.

Postcard to Aurel Krause from Arthur Krause.

CHAPTER TEN

TWO EXCURSIONS LASTING SEVERAL DAYS
NORTH ACROSS THE WATERSHED INTO
THE YUKON TERRITORY

Letters written by Arthur Krause to the Geographical Society in Bremen, slightly abridged:

On the afternoon of May 23, I left Portage Bay by canoe to go over the Deja Pass to the Yukon Lakes. My companions were two fifteen-year-old Indian boys who had proven helpful in former excursions and again this time. Around 8:00 P.M. we reached the mouth of the Dejah River after a quick favorable trip. It was low tide now, therefore, we had to get out of the canoe and pull it up the shallow bed of the stream quite some distance, until we reached the first grassy areas where we could pitch our tent. Not until midnight were we able to sleep (Point I of the map).[26]

The following morning my boys pulled the canoe up river for about 5 miles against the strong current, while I wandered through the maze of larger and smaller islands hunting and collecting specimens. Once in a while I had to wait for the canoe to cross the deeper river arms. The lower slopes were completely free of snow now, the bottom of the valley was almost without snow. During my last stay here (April 19 and 20) the rocks appeared grey and bare; now they were hidden by the young foliage of birches and green alder.

On one island where I had camped on a previous trip, I met several Indian families busy rendering fish oil from ssag.

During my hike upstream I unexpectedly met one of the gold miners on a little island. He waited for the return of his carriers to send the last pieces of luggage across and then follow himself. He told me that his companions had safely arrived over there, but that there was still plenty of snow on the other side and now in soft condition, so passage is very difficult.

About 1 ½ miles farther upriver I crossed the river for the last time. The canoe was pulled on the left bank and after a longer rest we started on our hike. We walked alternately on the rocky river bed and the left bank. The thick underbrush and the many trunks lying in every direction hindered us considerably. We advanced with great trouble only step by step, and not until evening did we camp at the place where the waters of the Katlakuchra and the Ssidrajik[27] join (II on the map). The fact that the snow has receded makes several glaciers of the Dejah Valley more prominent than before. I saw the largest one about one and a half miles north of our camp last night on the right side elevations. According to the Natives it seems to be connected by giant fields of perpetual snow with the Ferebee Glacier. Exactly opposite our noon resting place there was another mighty, wildly fissured ice mass high up in a narrow ravine. In the next ravine there was a narrow glacier, almost without snow, which extended down like a long pointed tongue to about 100 to 200 meters above the bottom of the valley. In its deep crevasses it displayed a magnificent blue. On the convex side there were several distinct side moraines.

About noon on May 25, after a slow, again difficult hike in the morning, we reached the slope of the barrier which closes the northern end of the Dejah Valley. Here we stop for several hours, while I take some measurements and get a glimpse of the Katlakuchra Valley branching off to the left. The valley is widened here and shows areas of bare gravel and sand, sparsely covered by grey mosses and lichen.

After crossing or, better, wading through the swift current of the Ssidrajik River, we walked along its left bank, often high above its bed. We set up camp (III on the map) about 330 to 495 feet above the bottom of the valley. Here the river falls in several cataracts through narrow rock crevices. A small party of Indian carriers, who had caught up with us a little earlier, camped near us. While hunting and collecting plants, I climbed over moss-covered rocks and fallen trunks on the slopes for quite a while. I came to the conclusion that our trail so far, bad as it was, after all was better than no trail at all.

On Friday, the twenty-sixth, we break camp rather late and after a troublesome walk over large and small stretches of soft

snow we finally descend into the valley. Here the above-
mentioned miner caught up with me. I walked in his company
for another mile up the valley, where, fairly early for this day,
we stopped (IV). He and the carriers, who arrived a little later,
wanted to go over the pass to their next camp site during the
night, while the snow was hard. Indeed, they broke up at 2:00
A.M., while I explored the slopes on the left bank, climbing
above the tree line, and finding many samples of European
alpine flora, among them *Azalea procumbens* in full bloom.
Laden with a collection of numerous plants and many small
insects, birds, and a large grouse, the *nukt* whose call is frequently heard here, I return to our camp at 7:00 A.M. where I find
both boys still sound asleep. Our path leads across the rocky
valley through dense green alder bushes in a steep ascent to the
tree line. Camp (V) was set up in the last knee-high timber. This
scrub is mostly mountain hemlock, which I first saw below
Tahit. Beyond the pass it is first found as knee-high timber and
then near the lakes as a stately tree in large stands. Above our
camp to the right we could see two mighty glaciers. The one
farther north comes steeply down and attracted our attention
with its repeated roar. A lengthy excursion up the left slopes in
late afternoon again yields an interesting collection of not-yet-
flowering alpine plants. In a pleasant way my carriers remind
me of a peculiarity of the northern flora. Upon my return from
a short excursion, they handed me in a clean paper bag some
cranberries which they had picked in the meantime on the snow-
free ground. Last fall's red berries were conserved by sudden
frost and the thick snow cover and they did not rot during the few
warm but dry days since the snow melted; however, they
underwent a kind of fermentation which makes them extremely
tasty. Today and during the following days, we often bent down
to put one of the full clusters of berries into our mouths. Also the
mealy fruit of the bearberry and crowberries was in almost fresh
condition. Now ptarmigan are seen frequently. During the
present mating season the males act out bitter fights. During our
descent my attention was attracted by a loud creaking, like the
sound of ptarmigans flying up and down, to two white birds who
settled down near me. When one of them, wounded by a shot,
jerkingly rolled down the slope, the other one flew to him and

ruthlessly attacked his now defenseless opponent and both rolled down the slope several hundred feet. Not until ten minutes later, when I arrived, did it fly away, leaving his opponent in almost plucked condition.

From four o'clock we had steady rain; in the evening the temperature at our camp site was only 4.5°C. A large camp fire in front of our tent made us quite comfortable. On Sunday, the twenty-eighth, we got up at 2:30 A.M., but breakfast and careful packing took so much time that we did not leave until 4:30 A.M. From here on, our trail was continuously covered by snow, so I, too, had to put on my moccasins and snowshoes. In the melting snow we could climb the less steep slopes with our snowshoes in a zigzag course, but during steeper ascents they had to be taken off, and we advanced with great difficulty step by step. Often sinking up to our waist in snow, we slowly climbed up to the pass,[28] which we did not reach until 8:00 A.M. At first the weather was not unfavorable, although a thick fog hid every view. As we approached the pass, it started to rain, turning to snow at the top. A strong wind blew at this exposed elevation. The temperature was 0.6°C. Under these conditions it unfortunately was impossible to determine the elevation of the pass with my measuring instruments. Soon after crossing the pass, one descends about 30 to 50 meters into the valley which opens toward the southwest. The trail soon climbs toward a flat ridge from where one has the first view of the Yukon Valley. Today it was a bleak view of a snow desert, its blinding white color somewhat softened by the heavy snowfall and rain and occasionally interrupted by black rock cliffs. Near and on the pass I picked up numerous spiders and insects on the snow, some of them in almost frozen condition. Apparently they were swept by the wind from the surrounding snow-free slopes. Other animals, particularly glacier fleas and beetles, were so active that one could assume that these snow areas are their native habitat, where they find sufficient food on animal and plant remains which are swept down here. About 200 meters below the pass, on a cliff face free from snow, I discovered a single flowering plant, a pretty alpine ranunculus with numerous yellow flowers.

A steep descent took us to the bank of the first small lake,[29] the source of the Yukon. From here we walked about 1½ kilometers across an almost level snowfield then through a chain of canyons and across several lakes which could safely be crossed on the ice. The entrance and outflow of the first larger lake[30] showed spots with open water or icy mash through which we waded up to our knees. At the northern end of this lake we found the first substantial trees. We stopped here for a few hours to dry our clothes at a fire and strengthen ourselves with an opulent meal for the continued hike. A climb from here to the northern elevations did not yield anything remarkable. There seems to be a pass leading from here to the valley of the Schüttlichroa in a northerly direction. At about 6:00 P.M. we broke up and walked in an easterly direction, first across the next larger lake,[31] then for 2 miles up a steep bank to a larger tributary flowing into the main valley which we follow downriver. This part of the hike reminds me vividly of a similar one in Norway in the summer of 1880. Here, too, it goes alternately over snowfields, bare rocks, and tundra with moss and lichen. Dwarf birches, creeping willows, elder, and green alder are the scarce representatives of the tree world. The ground cover mostly consists of crowberries *(Empetrum nigrum),* then numerous members of the Ericaceae family, further a stately polydrusa, *Andromeda polifolia, Andromeda tetragona, Andromeda hypnoides, Azalea procumbens, Vaccinium vitis idaea, Arctostaphylos alpina, Ledum latifolium,* and a second small-leaf kind. Among them *Linnaea borealis* is creeping, *Dryas octopetala* is spreading, and *Lycopodium selago* and *Lycopodium alpinum* are sprouting here and there. Among the mosses the grey *Rhycomitrium langinosum* covers slabs of rocks on large areas, various kinds of polytrichum and pogonatum form a turf in dry areas while sphagnum types thrive in bogs. A splachnum proliferating on reindeer dung, which just now grows its densely placed red gametophytes, seems to be the same kind we saw in Norway as well as in Chukchi Land under the same conditions. Also among lichen, the abundant kinds of cladonies, cetraries, and peltigeres seem to be identical with those of the above countries. I, of course, cannot predict to what extent a further development of the flora during the summer will limit or confirm the picture of its typical traits which I tried to portray based on plant remains that lasted through the winter. Animal life is far behind here. I saw and killed a so-called ground squirrel, *Spermophilus* sp., just as it hurried in big leaps toward its subterranean cave. Among birds I only saw snow buntings, mountain larks, and golden-crowned sparrows, *Zonotrichia coronata*, which I first observed on May 9 while they passed through Portage Bay. The Indians call it *deschutahi,* meaning chief of Deschu (Portage Bay), and it is well known to every visitor to the land of the Gunanas (Stick Indians).

After crossing the above-mentioned tributary, we hike along the east side of the valley in a northerly direction through open forest, sometimes across snow, over bare rocks, or through extended bogs. A successful hunt for the small grouse, frequently found here, as well as a small owl unknown to me, brought some diversion into the monotony of the walk, but also caused some delay. Not until 10:00 P.M. do we arrive in the camp of the miners on the banks of the Schutluchroa.[32] Some of them had gone to sleep, but others, informed of my arrival by my last shot, got up to greet me and offered me a hearty evening meal in front of a bright fire, which I gratefully accepted, since I was soaked through, tired, and hungry. A sound, long sleep on a bed of fragrant balsam fir branches let me soon forget the arduous exertions of this day. The lake was still completely covered by ice; therefore, I could not continue my trip to the nearest settlement of the Gunanas in one of the canoes of the Chilkat Indians lying on the beach. Walking along the beach would have taken considerable time for which provisions and ammunition would have been insufficient. I therefore decided to spend a few days for the necessary observations and then return. Unfortunately, I was hindered in my efforts to determine the longitude and latitude of the lake by unfavorable weather conditions. More reliable is the elevation of only 702 meters above sea level, gained as a result of several observations with my special instruments.

The forest on the banks of the Schutluchroa consists mostly of lodgepole pine *(Pinus contorta)* and balsam fir *(Abies balsamea)*. The latter contains so much resin in blisters under its bark that, by piercing and pressing these, one can fill a whole bottle within a short time. Rarer is Sitka spruce *(Picea sitchensis)* which by far does not attain the height it reaches along the coast. Low elder is found here and there. Among deciduous trees here, only green alder, dwarf birch, and shrublike willows are to be mentioned.

The entire undulating, more or less forested high plateau east and south of the lake is said to be full of smaller lakes. I visited three of these on a further excursion. Their water flows into the Schutluchroa. They are beautifully located in the midst of forest and show a richer fauna and flora on and in their waters. There for the first time I hear the croaking of frogs. In dry places the grassy plain is a field of lupines. Everywhere mice have built up piles of finger-thick pieces of root bitten into $1^1/2$- to 2 inch-length. The Indians also eat these bitter-tasting roots (kantak); however, when eaten in larger quantities they reportedly cause a kind of intoxication. The rocks along the banks of the Schutluchroa are igneous, light-colored, consisting of quartz, feldspar, and a little hornblende. It is greatly modified by varying amounts of each part and by the addition of a dark mica and is similar to the rocks found in the entire upper Lynn Canal area.

Meanwhile the miners were progressing vigorously with the construction of two flatboats. They hoped to leave within a few days, as the ice melted. With the low elevation of the lake, it is safe to assume that the Yukon presents very few hindrances for the passage. Only between Schutluchroa and Kussooa[33] is a one-mile portage necessary, and farther north, a second one. According to reports by the Indians, the other source of the Yukon on the Chilkat side, which flows into a larger lake also called Kussooa, is entirely free of rapids.

Although the Chilkoot Indians welcome the arrival of miners as a good chance to earn some money, they nevertheless are worried that these might compete in their trade with the Gunana. Chief Don-e-wak therefore sent a letter to the miners, declaring that he and his people alone are entitled to this trade. Should any of the miners need a piece of leather to mend his clothes, he should not pay more than ten cents in tobacco for a piece of tanned reindeer skin. They asked me, too, upon my return whether I had met the Gunana and they were relieved to hear that I brought back from excursions only weeds and a few bird skins but no black fox or beaver. With increasing concern the local Indians hear of reports that white traders are coming higher and higher up the Yukon River. The destruction of Fort Selkirk at the confluence of the Pelly River and Yukon by the Chilkats in 1851 can definitely be attributed to the same trading jealousy.

On June 1, we start the return trip. Steady rain and even more unfavorable conditions of the terrain make the crossing of the pass more difficult than the first time. In the Kotaska Valley[34] we had to climb high up on the southern slopes, since it was no longer advisable to cross the ice of the lakes. Furthermore, we still met the same snow desert in the upper Kotaska Valley, yet here on a bare rocky cliff the beautiful red blossoms of *Saxifraga oppositifolia* gave joy to the tired eye. Just as we crossed the pass, we experienced the worst weather. Elevation and other measurements again were impossible. From May 26 to the twenty-seventh, without rest we descended to our camp site (IV on the map), which we reached at 8:00 P.M. Half-soaked through in continuing rain, we wrapped ourselves in our blankets and slept well till late next morning. Wind and sun soon dried our clothes.

In the afternoon of June 3 we reached our canoe and quickly went downriver to the Indian camping place. In the morning of June 5, we safely returned to Deschu. During the last night we were fortunate enough to return, because we could take advantage of a short break in the steady southern wind, which lasted for several weeks.

On June 17 a second, larger excursion to the western Kussooa was undertaken. It, too, is reported in a travel letter to the Geographical Society in Bremen:

Chilkoot, July 6, 1882

I left the factory at Portage Bay on June 17 shortly before noon, walked to the other side of the peninsula and got into the canoe that was waiting for me. A strong southern wind brought us quickly up the wide but shallow Chilkat River. Between the islands below Katwaltu [Katkwaltu] the current was so strong that we advanced only slowly and at dusk were forced to camp. Not until noon of the eighteenth did we reach Klukwan, where I received friendly hospitality in the house of old Tschartritsch. For several weeks a missionary teacher has been staying in the village. She is a half Indian (called Tillie Paul), educated at the Wrangell Mission. She seems to teach the children English and religion with great success. She and her husband temporarily found lodging in Tschartritsch's house. Her presence was not only pleasant for my meals, but also most advantageous in the following negotiations about the continuation of my excursion. I indeed was right not to wait for old Tschartritsch. He first wanted to go once more to the Portage Bay factory to make a few purchases. In two days he wanted to be back to go to the interior with me. Now there was still too much snow on the mountains, etc. I was unwilling to wait and was actually very glad to leave Klukwan the next morning with Jelchtelch, whom I had hired earlier, and one of Tschartritsch's sons. Unfortunately the older son had become ill, so I had to take the younger one who later proved to be not strong enough for the exertions.

A canoe brought our luggage up the Chilkat and the Klehini, while I walked with the older Indian, sometimes on the gravel of the river bed, sometimes through the shrubs on the left bank. Often we had to wait for the canoe to cross the deeper arms of the rushing river. It was late in the evening when we reached the place a little above the mouth of the Jokeach[35] where the Indians usually leave their canoes and continue their trip on foot.

On the next morning, June 20, we went only a short distance upriver, then we climbed the 900- to 1,200- meter-high mountains beyond the tree line and from here on we stayed at this elevation and followed the river in a west-northwest direction.

The woods through which we climbed were mostly deciduous (poplar, willow, maple, birch) and a few evergreens (hemlock and white spruce). At an elevation of about 700 meters we followed a zone of abundant green alder bushes and above these only low willows and elders and single crippled mountain hemlock, which, strangely enough, I had not observed farther

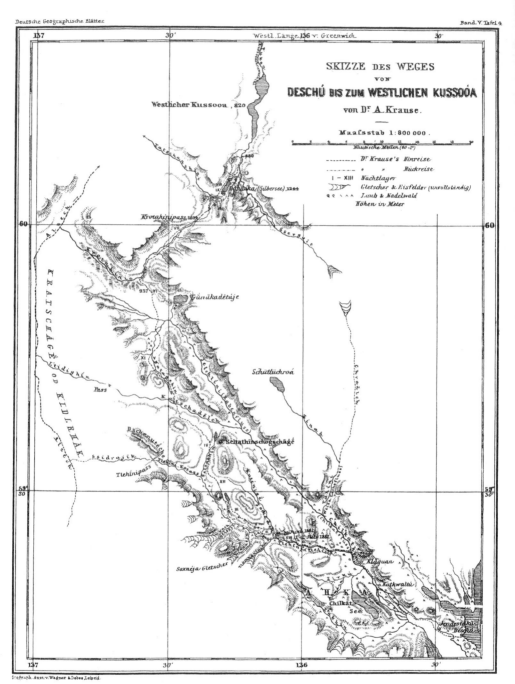

Path from Deshu to the western Kussoóa.

below. The higher we climbed, the more advanced was the flora. What we had seen below in bud was resplendent in full flower here. This is due to the intensified effect of light at the higher elevation with fewer trees. On the high tundra itself we only find the typical nordic flora. Specific American plants only grow lower down, so only the pretty nodding blossoms of *Dodecatheon* look strange in this environment of alpine anemone, ranunculaceae, types of saxifrage and rosemary, *Dryas octopetala, Azalea procumbens, Primula minima,* and others.

Although we had left the actual trail, walking here was not difficult at all, only once in a while we had to cross a snowfield or wade through a rushing brook. In the beautiful, clear weather we continually had a gorgeous view of the green Klehini Valley (*hin* means river) and of the numerous glaciers on the opposite slopes. From several points (e.g. still from II) we can see the well-known peaks near Lynn Canal and at one point we even see over the low part of Chilkat Peninsula near Nachk(u) the water of Chilkoot Inlet. The reason for our slow advance during the first two days was my constant botanizing and occasional hunting for marmot, ground squirrel, or ptarmigan. Not until the afternoon of the twenty-second did we reach the Sseltathin River[36] and on the evening of the same day camped near its source, a small lake (camp IV). Only low hills separate this from the Katschadelch. The path does not climb here but goes up quite high on the right bank of the Katschadelch, then after about 5 nautical miles drops again down to the river. Here we had to wade through the water up to our hips. This was the first larger river bath in ice cold water; from now on it was to become a daily habit. The elevation of the river bed is about 1,012 meters. On the other side one climbs up through rolling tundra and soon one meets two small, narrow lakes from where the Natagehin[37] flows north. Hardly noticeable is the watershed between the Natagehin and the Krotahini (or between Chilkat River and Alsek), which we passed the following day.

Around noon on June 25, we reach the Krotahini at a place where it rushes with plenty of water from a narrow canyon of softer limestone and clay into the wide plain. From here it flows slowly toward the Alsek, forming several swamps and lakes.

The valleys of the lower Krotahini, the Jelchhini[38] or Raven River (this is what the Natagehin is called after its turn to the southwest), and the Chilkat River form an almost straight line. After climbing the first heights on the left bank of the Krotahini, my guide excitedly pointed toward the far southeast at the rocky cliffs of his beloved native village Klukwan. Just a little while ago he was complaining bitterly how impassable they are in contrast to the flat tundra we were traversing. The upper Krotahini Valley is bleak; the pass (5,326 feet) falls off quickly toward both sides and is a wild heap of fallen pieces of syenite. From here, or even better from a knoll below, one has a good overview of the Tatschantshini Valley. Farther north we arrive at the Danaaku or Silver Lake (4,105 feet), whose waters flow in a series of cataracts into the Ssergoit, the western source of the Yukon. From here it flows into the Kussooa (small lake). From the summit of a small hill near Danaaku Lake I can see the southern end of Kussooa.

Because of the illness of my young companion—apparently it is the same disease (scarlet fever?) which broke out among many children in Klukwan at that time—I was forced to stop. For Jelchtelch this was an excuse to stop this trip which had become boring for him. He claimed I had seen the Kusawa, upon which the eye of a gutzgakon (stranger from far away) had never before looked, and that I should be satisfied with that. In vain I tried to convince him that a two- or three-day stay at the near Kussooa was more beneficial for the sick boy than a hasty retreat through the most arduous part of the trip. Only with difficulty could I persuade him to wait until the following day or return only as far as the southern end of Danaaka. I determined to go ahead alone.

Indeed, I got up alone the following morning, went along the left bank of the lake and then descended steeply but slowly through the dense scrub of dwarf birches, willows, and green alders down to the Ssergoit. I followed its course for about 2 nautical miles upriver (elevation 880 meters). There I ascended over loose rock on the western banks to the level of Danaaka. Quickly walking across rocky or moss-covered rolling tundra, I returned toward evening. At the place where the Danaaka outflow and the Ssergoit, probably the outflow of a mighty glacier, join, I again met the first evergreen trees. On the banks of the Ssergoit I found an abundant flora far advanced. For the first time I discovered a faded pulsatilla. The bushy potentilla was in full bloom here. A few days later on my return to the coast I found it still in the bud stage.

The higher animal life is well represented here. Several times I watched foxes, wolves, and reindeer; fresh bear tracks were found very often. Everywhere I could hear the chirping of ground squirrels or the drawn-out piercing whistle of the marmot. On the higher knolls, mountain goats and mountain sheep are not uncommon, while beavers live among the willows on the banks of rivers and streams. Ptarmigans are found often, but I saw only two females. They are sitting on their eggs now and fly up only when one almost steps on them.

On my return to our camp site (VIII), I found it deserted, but I discovered a "letter" from Jelchtelch, two small sticks put vertically into the ground and two willow twigs next to them pointing south. This was to tell me that he and the boy had gone to the upper end of the lake where I actually found them after half an hour (IX). The sick boy's improved condition made it possible to start the return trip immediately. My guide's longing for his wife and children and Klukwan's fresh salmon accelerated his pace, so that we arrived in Klukwan on July 2 and at Portage Bay that same afternoon.

During these excursions and several smaller trips from the station, Arthur mostly concentrated on the natural science collections. The herbarium which he collected during the course of the summer contains about 500 kinds of vascular plants. Through the steady contact with the Indians, he became increasingly familiar with their lifestyle, customs, and their language. His written notes (unfortunately they no longer exist) and his oral explanations helped to contribute to the observations made during the brothers' joint winter stay.

On September 6 Arthur left the station to return home. After a three-day canoe trip he reached Juneau. From here he took the mail steamer to Taku Bay with its mighty glacier, then via Wrangell and Klawock to Kasan Bay. From Port Townsend he went through Puget Sound to Portland and from here he followed the route of the North Pacific Railroad, at that time still under construction.

On October 21 Arthur left New York on the Oder, *which took him to Bremen, arriving on November 2, from where he returned to Berlin.*

Immediately after their arrival, both brothers resumed their duties as teachers. In their free time they shared the work of the evaluation of the scientific results, as far as this was not done by museums and institutions. They gave lectures and wrote treatises for scientific journals. A postcard to Arthur from Professor Urban of the Botanical Garden in Berlin says that a bed had been started to plant the seeds they had brought back from the Chukchi Peninsula. Today in the Herbarium of the Geobotanical Institute at Georg-August University in Göttingen some pressed plants collected by the Krause brothers from the Chukchi Peninsula still exist.

APPENDIX

Copy of a letter by Professor von Martens of Berlin University, given to Aurel Krause to submit to Dr. Gustav Nachtigal, President of the Geographical Society in Berlin (the original is in the State Archives in Bremen):

Berlin, March 5, 1881

Dear Sir,

In connection with the proposed Bremen expedition to the Chukchi Peninsula, I believe that with my best conscience I can highly recommend the bearer of this letter, Dr. A. Krause. I have known him and his brother for eight years and have always admired their energy and resourcefulness during our joint excursions and their versatile knowledge in specific natural sciences. Both men repeatedly have used their vacations for longer journeys, some of them on foot. Two years ago they traveled to the Alps and Northern Italy, last year to Norway to the Arctic Circle. From these trips they brought back precious collections of zoological, botanical, and paleontological objects, some of which were highly desired by the zoological museum here. I am just about to publish a related treatise about the molluscs they collected in Norway. I therefore believe that these gentlemen are very well qualified in respect to their physical health, their perseverance during hardships, as well as to their scientific knowledge and experience in collecting natural science specimens. Therefore, allow me to highly recommend them to you.

Respectfully yours,
Prof. E. von Martens

Letter from Mr. Dickinson with whom the brothers had stayed:

Pyramid Harbor Chilcat

November 26, 1883

Drs. Krauses

Dear Friends! I received your wellcome letter of March 21st. I was very glad to hear from you and to know you and your Brother arrived safe and are well, in which it leaves us at present.

I never can forget, what a pleasant time we had during your stay with us. I suppose it was quite a treat to you both, to be landed once more amongst your friends, we missed your pleasant company so very much I tell you time hung very heavily on our hands after you left.

Between Indian rows and Siwash Wa. was the Old thing— Your Indian friends are thankful for the likenesses you so kindly sent them and they all wished to be remembered. (Old Shrotritch) Chief is as great a beger as ever and several others, who are too numerous to mention.

The N.W.T. Com. has put up a large Building and Wharf with several other sundry Buildings. The cannery is 100 x 60 feet and wharf 200 x 16, with a T on the end of it. Steamer comes to it and can lay at low water without geting aground there is 30 feet of water at low water mark. The[y] did not do very much this season it was more a prospecting season, than anything else. They put up about 4000 cases and 350 Barrels salted salmon. They had a great number of white Labor employed also Indians. You know the Indian we call the murderer, that Curry cut in Urangly. He came and pulled Mr. Spuhns Ear one Day, consequently Mr. Spuhn put him out of the store. So he swore he would have revenge that night. And about 12 O'clock next day the U.S.S.S. Adams came in commanders Name Capt. Merryman. As soon as he had seen her coming, he sent and Apologised for his bad conduct. But it was no use. Mr. Spuhn and I reputed him and Capt. Merryman made him weaken, he told him the next time he touched a white man he would hang him to the Yard arm. So that was good consolation for the Brute.

There has been several rows in Harrisburg between Indians and whites. One man by the name of John Cambell went a hunting on admiralty Island. So he was Minus and supposed to be killed by Indians.

An other case is some Sitka Indians broke into a liquor saloon and stole whiskey and the saloon keeper came out and wanted his whiskey back so 3 Indians pitched on to him, with clubs and smashed his skull fragments he lived but 3 hours But never spoke his name was Ritchard Rainy. So the Miners arrested the 3 Indians and put them in jail. A man by the name of Dennis to guard them, he made a sad Mistake for he took the Handcuffs off from one Indian and while Dennis was cooking his Breakfast, he laid his pistol down on the table and the unhandcuffed Indian took up Dennises pistol and shot Dennis only wounding him. So the Indians ran off to the ranch and cut their irons off. So the miners went after them. One man by the name of Gibbins went a head and looked into the house where those Indians were, and One of the Indians shot him with Dennises Pistol and another run and choped him with an axe which finished him. The Miners tried the 2 Indians and found them guilty and the 3 Indian run away and shot himself. The Miners took the remaining 2 Indians and hung them in Harrisburg, there was no Man of War there at that time. So Dennis Died about 20 Days ago from his wounds— that makes 3 white men and 3 Indians killed.

The coldest we had it here this month was 2 Below Zero. Today min. tem. 26+ 6 inches snow on the ground. Mr. and Mrs. Paul have left the[y] have gone to Fortsimpson, have a young son also.

About One week after you left I sent your Box which I found in the wood shed to Harrisburg and telling them to forward it on to you if you had left before its arrival. So I find by your letter it has been laying there ever since. I told Mr. Spuhn about it he says he will forward it this winter, if I had of got my way, you would of had it long since.

Mr. and Mrs. Willard are quite well the[y] wish to be remembered to you, Willard has a young son pretty near as large as fiirst one.

Lutnt Swatka, Docter and I 6 soldiers and 1 sitizen carpenter started last May up the Dia for the Uncon country to survey it and c. [etc.] I have heard that he has arrived at Sanfrancisco. But I have heard nothing up to date.

I went on a Visit to Portland this summer with the June Boat and came back on the July steamer it was like geting my freedom after Been transported for 20 years, the only fault I had, my Visit was not of long duration.

Mr. Adams winters with me this winter. The old store is shut up and has been all summer. Capt. Merryman of Gun Boat Adams gave Mr. Donawak and 2nd Chief an overalling for collecting toll from white men going up the Dia and 2nd Chief for Breaking open packs, we have an opposition cannery on the other side of the river from here owned by Kinny of Astoria, the[y] run the fish up as high as 15¢ each. Oh what fools. The Indians had a good thing better than the whites.

I would like and would feel happy if you would allways communicate with me and anything you would like to know allways ask me and I will allways answer your letters, if you would like to have my Temratures from the time you left to any stated time or any other information. I will be very glad to aid you in whatever you require. I would like to have a coppy of one of your charts, if you could let me have one conveniently and let me know the cost.

My Wife allways thinks of you and your Brother, she says your kindness she will allways remember and she wishes to be remembered to you Both. I think the[y] Have struck good Mines in a river that runs through the rocky Mountain range and emptys into the Ucon, perhaps next mail, I will know more definitely about and I shall write and let you know about it or any other news that will be of service to you Both.

So I must conclude wishing you gentlemen every prosperity

I remain
Yours respectfully
G. Dickinson
Pyramid Harbor
Chilcat, Alaska

Excerpt from the Weser-Zeitung *of Bremen dated Saturday, October 17, 1885 Nor 13943. The article was probably written by a member of the Geographical Society under the headline "The Tlingit Indians in Alaska" :*

In the spring of 1881 the Bremen Geographical Society sent its members, the Krause brothers, two natural science explorers from Berlin, on a scientific journey to the coastal areas of the Bering Sea. The journey lasted one and one-half years; the summer of 1881 was devoted to the Chukchi Peninsula, the following winter and spring 1882 the gentlemen spent in southeastern Alaska among the Tlingit Indians. With rich scientific and ethnological collections they returned in the fall of 1882. While these collections were evaluated by experts, Dr. Aurel Krause undertook the task of writing an ethnological monograph based on the studies and observations he and his brother made among the Tlingit Indians, including careful evaluation of material presented in former related travel reports and writings. This monograph is now available in a book recently published by H. Constenoble in Jena, *The Tlingit Indians, Results of a Trip to the Northwest Coast of America and the Bering Strait, carried out under the auspices of the Bremen Geographical Society in the years 1881 and 1882 by the Drs. Arthur and Aurel Krause, written by Aurel Krause.* This book of over 400 pages includes an ethnological map, 4 plates, and 32 illustrations. In a foreword the author points out that, because of the contact with the quickly approaching white civilization everywhere, Native populations are presently subjected to rapid changes and degeneration or even complete annihilation. It therefore is high time to preserve for ethnology the knowledge about the still existing remnants of these Native people. The author modestly describes his work "as a small contribution to the history of the American people." We, however, must say that we have here an extraordinarily diligent and thorough work striving for clarity everywhere. With its command of the subject area as well as its calm and objective treatment it will reflect credit on

German science, especially in the trans-Atlantic republic with its vast territory to which Alaska has belonged for quite some time. The extent to which the works and research of the Drs. Krause are already being recognized over there is evident in a copy we received of an address by the well-known American expert, Professor Dall, to the anthropological section of the Science Congress at Ann Arbor in August of this year. In it he mentions the "admirable work" accomplished by the two German scientists in southern Alaska and directly emphasizes that "the contributions by the Krause brothers to the cultural and ethnological history of southern Alaska are the most important ones since 1875."

An overview of the contents of the individual chapters of the book follows and then in conclusion these words:

This condensed news should suffice to show that Krause's work offers something of interest to every educated person, especially to us here in Bremen, who followed the course of the journey at that time, listened to the oral reports, and viewed the beautiful collections brought together with so much effort. Finally, we want to praise the good appearance of the book and the selection and the excellent production of the illustrations; even an ethnographic map for the reader's orientation is included.

These journals also have their own history. In 1920, after the death of her parents, Aurel Krause's eldest daughter Ella, a geography and mathematics teacher at the high school in Brandenburg an der Havel, started systematically to put the parental estate in order. Among her father's many small notebooks she found some recognizable by their dates and sketches as the journals of the expedition to the Chukchi Peninsula and to the Tlingit Indians. She could not, however, decipher the text, for it was written in the oldest stenography by Stolze, developed by him in 1841. In all of Brandenburg nobody could read this old shorthand. Yet with the assistance of the Organization for Stenography clubs, in 1926 she finally succeeded in locating an elderly lady in Berlin-Zehlendorf who could transcribe the text. Then Ella Krause worked for several decades to put together the course of the expedition using journals, old letters, and reports and completed it with the addition of Aurel's sketches.

In this selection, the pictures and longer paragraphs from the book The Tlingit Indians *were deleted. They were replaced with additional entries and sketches from Aurel's not yet published journals.*

Heidelberg, August 1983
The Editors

ENDNOTES

NOTES TO THE EDITOR'S NOTE

1. For a brief description of ethnographic collecting on the Northwest Coast that emphasizes collections in North America see E. S. Lohse and Frances Sundt "History of Research: Museum Collections" in Handbook of North American Indians. vol. 7. Northwest Coast. Smithsonian Institution, 1990, pp. 88-97. For a wider view that includes private collectors see Douglas Cole, *Captured Heritage: The Scramble for Northwest Coast Artifacts*. Seattle: University of Washington Press, 1985.

2. The translated expedition narrative was first published in the United States as *The voyage of the Vega round Asia and Europe; with historical review of previous journeys along the north coast of the Old World.* New York: Macmillian & Co., 1882. The scientific results, including observations made in Chukotia were published as *Vega-expeditionens vetenskapliga iakttagelser bearbetade af deltagare i resan och andra forskare.* Stockholm: F. & G. Beijer, 1882-87, 5 vols. A contemporary German edition was issued in Leipzig by F. A. Brockhaus as well.

NOTES TO THE FOREWORD

1. Adrian Jacobsen, a Norwegian, became wellknown through his ethnological research and collections. Aurel Krause visited him several times in San Francisco in 1881-82. A troupe of nine Bella Coolas from British Columbia were hired by Adrian and his brother Fillip and traveled through Germany in 1886. They performed dances and songs in an ethnic show.

2. Franz Boas was working in Berlin in 1886 on his thesis about his twelve-month geographical research on Baffin Island for admission as academic lecturer at the university. Encouraged and supported by Aurel Krause, he made his first ethnological studies, mostly language studies, with the Bella Coolas during their Berlin visit. These studies were the beginning of further ethnological work with other Indian tribes of the northwest coast of North America.

NOTES TO PART I

1. Curator at the Royal Museum for Natural Science in Berlin.

2. Both Dr. Lindemann and Dr. Wolkenhauer were members of the executive board of the Geographical Society in Bremen.

3. At that time these piers were the tallest structures in New York. The builder of this first East River Bridge (Brooklyn Bridge), the German immigrant Johann Augustus Röbling (John Roebling), died during the construction. His son Washington completed the structure on May 24, 1883.

4. Today Oslo, Norway.

5. Born in Germany, in 1871-73 he was in charge of scientific exploration on the North American polar expedition under Charles Francis Hall.

6. Tunnel made of wooden structures to keep snow off the track during the winter so trains can pass.

7. Near East Cape.

8. Principal of Luisenstädtische Oberrealschule (high school) in Berlin.

9. Easternmost island of the Aleutians.

10. According to Horace, *carmen* [poems] II.3.1f: Remember to keep calm in difficult situations!

11. Captain's name for an arc of fog.

12. In addition to the journals, this chapter is based on the report the brothers wrote aboard the *Golden Fleece* on their return to San Francisco (*Deutsche Geographische Blätter*, Vol. V, p. 1-35, Bremen 1882).

13. *Kaukau* is not a Chukchi word, but imported jargon used by whalers from Honolulu. It is synonymous with the word "food."

14. To collect plants and animals from the ocean with dredge nets.

15. Today Mys Dezhneva.

16. No journals exist from September 10 to October 5. Therefore, excerpts from the travel reports to the Geographical Society in Bremen are used (*Deutsche Geographische Blätter*, Vol. V, p. 111-141, Bremen 1882).

17. Ellipses are to show the entry point for a section of text added after the original German publication.

18. In early February 1882, five crates with these collections arrived in Bremen.

First they were checked and cataloged by Dr. Spängel, then turned over to experts for evaluation. A sixth crate with ethnological objects did not arrive until later (*Deutsche Geographische Blätter*, Vol. V, p. 70, Bremen 1882).

19. Frederick Schwatka, polar explorer, led the expedition to search for the remains of the Franklin expedition in 1878/80 and explored the Yukon River in Alaska in 1883. The brothers visited with him in San Francisco several times.

NOTES TO PART II

1. Chilkats, on the Chilkat River in the west, Chilkoots, east from there in and around Chilkoot.

2. Eagle River Glacier and Herbert Glacier.

3. The trading station belonging to Chilkoot is in Deshu, today Haines.

4. The Tsimshians live on the west coast of British Columbia.

5. From Arthur Krause, Das Chilcatgebiet von Alaska, *Zeitschrift der Gesellschaft für Erdkunde zu Berlin*, Vol. XVIII, p. 344-368, 1883, and from Aurel Krause, Reisebriefe, *Deutsche Geographische Blätter*, Vol. V, p. 202-203, abridged, Bremen 1882. Different spellings alternate in the original, Chilcoot and Chilkoot, as well as Tschilkat, Chilkat, and Chilcat.

6. Today Chilkat Peninsula or Haines Peninsula.

7. Indian footpath.

8. End of the trail.

9. Today Lutak Inlet; Taan-Aani (Tanani).

10. The author dated this sketch "Jan. 10, '81" in error. The year in brackets is the German editor's correction.

11. Also Kloquan, Klokwan, Kluquan, Klukquan, Klaquan. For all other names many different spellings are used.

12. Katkwaltu was destroyed by a slide in the 1890s.

13. Konana, Kunana, or Gunana (Athabaskan). The Americans mostly called them Stick Indians because of their custom of piercing a quill through the septum of their noses.

14. Today Dyea Inlet.

15. Hutschino, a drink brewed from molasses, named after the strongest and most militant clan of the Tlingits, the Chutsinus. They were the first to produce this drink which is hardly palatable for Europeans.

16. Today Eagle Council Grounds.

17. The mythology of the Tlingit revolves around the adventures and deeds of Jelch, the raven, about whom a large number of legends are told by these people. These are the bases for ethics and customs of the Tlingit (Aurel Krause, *The Tlingit Indians,* 1956, p. 174).

18. Today Kelgaya Point.

19. Gei-sun (today Mount Ripinski).

20. Today Riley Summit.

21. Today Lily Lake.

22. A mythical woman who is supposed to have turned to stone and unleashes winds when angry; the rock is in the Taiya Valley.

23. Today Angoon, also called Hudchinu, Hudschinu, Chutsinu, Hudschiano.

24. About 20 miles south of Portland.

25. Diptera (flies with two pairs of wings), hymenoptera (insects with membranous wings, including wasps, bees, and ants), and microlepidoptera (small butterflies, moths).

26. Near the mouth of the Dejah River.

27. Ssidrajik, name of the northern continuation of the Dejah River.

28. Chilkoot Pass.

29. Today Crater Lake.

30. Today Long Lake.

31. Today Deep Lake.

32. Today Lindemann Lake.

33. Today Bennett Lake.

34. Between Crater Lake and Long Lake.

35. Today Chilkat Canoe Camp.

36. Today Seltat River.

37. Today Nadahini.

38. Today Kelsall River.